STOPPING
DIABETES
IN ITS TRACKS

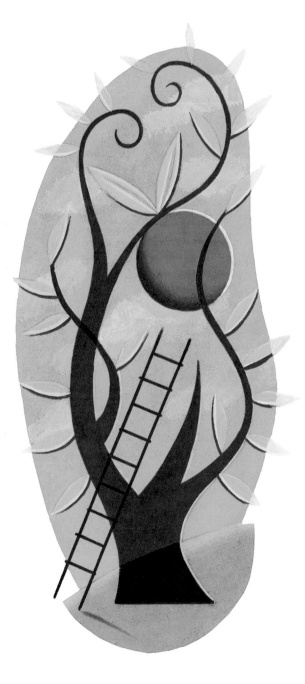

STOPPING
DIABETES
IN ITS TRACKS

THE DEFINITIVE TAKE-CHARGE GUIDE

Richard Laliberte

The Reader's Digest Association, Inc., Pleasantville, New York/Montreal

Reader's Digest Project Staff

Senior Editor
Marianne Wait

Senior Designer
Judith Carmel

Recipe Editor
Nancy Shuker

Production Technology Manager
Douglas A. Croll

Manufacturing Manager
John L. Cassidy

Contributors

Writer
Richard Laliberte

Designer
Andrew Ploski

Copy Editor
Gina Grant

Indexer
Nanette Bendyna

Medical Consultant

Carol J. Levy, M.D., C.D.E.
Assistant Professor of Medicine
New York-Presbyterian Hospital
Weill Medical College
Division of Endocrinology

Reader's Digest Health Publishing

Editor-in-Chief
Neil Wertheimer

Editorial Director
Christopher Cavanaugh

Marketing Director
James H. Malloy

Vice President and General Manager
Keira Kuhs

The Reader's Digest Association, Inc.

Editor-in-Chief
Eric W. Schrier

President, North American Books and Home Entertainment
Thomas D. Gardner

Library of Congress Cataloging-in-Publication Data

Laliberte, Richard.
    Stopping diabetes in its tracks : the definitive take-charge guide/Richard laliberte.
        p. cm.
    Includes index.
    ISBN 0-7621-0439-2 (hardcover)
    ISBN 0-7621-8441-4 (paperback)

    1. Diabetes--Popular works. I. Title.

RC660.4 .L355 2002
616.4'62--dc21

                                                    2002031758

Address any comments about *Stopping Diabetes in Its Tracks* to:
Reader's Digest
Editor-in-Chief, Reader's Digest Health Publishing
Reader's Digest Road, Pleasantville, NY 10570

To order copies of *Stopping Diabetes in Its Tracks*, call 1-800-846-2100

Visit our website at rd.com

Printed in the United States of America
    5 7 9 10 8 6 4   (hardcover)
    3 5 7 9 10 8 6 4 2 (paperback)

Note to Readers
The information in this book should not be substituted for, or used to alter, medical therapy without your doctor's advice. For a specific health problem, consult your physician for guidance.

US 4359 H/G

Diabetes is a bit like an uninvited house guest: You didn't want it in the first place, and it won't go away. Worse still, it demands daily attention. But, while you can't send diabetes home, you can minimize the impact it has on your health and your quality of life.

Unlike most diseases, diabetes is patient-centered—meaning that you, not your doctor, are calling the shots (and perhaps even *giving* yourself shots) every day. Your doctor and your dietitian will help you formulate a game plan for keeping your blood sugar in line, but it's up to you to make smart food choices, monitor your glucose levels, and figure out an exercise regimen you'll really stick with. That's the bad news (because yes, it will take a bit of effort on your part); it's also very good news because it means you're in control. And *Stopping Diabetes in Its Tracks* will show you how to take the reins.

Each chapter is packed with information that will help you manage your condition, whether you have type 1 diabetes, type 2 diabetes, or impaired glucose tolerance (sometimes called pre-diabetes). If you're at risk for developing diabetes but aren't sure you have it, you'll learn how to find out—a critical first step that millions of people haven't taken. If you have the disease, you'll discover a host of practical strategies for everything from meal planning to weight loss to battling diabetes burnout. You'll also find a comprehensive guide to the latest drug and insulin options and learn how to fine-tune your regimen for the best possible blood-sugar control.

Living with a chronic condition can be downright frustrating at times. That's why we've included inspiring profiles of people just like you who successfully faced the various challenges of diabetes and are living better, happier lives as a result. Finally, because food is a large part of the blood-sugar solution, we've put together a collection of nearly 50 truly satisfying recipes that will make eating to manage diabetes a joy.

The overall message is one of hope. Doctors have made huge strides in their ability to predict, diagnose, and treat diabetes with a wide variety of therapeutic options. And now we know just how powerful diet and exercise can be in keeping the condition, and related complications, in check. Best of all, if you take to heart the lifestyle advice that will help you control your blood sugar, chances are you'll feel better than you've ever felt before.

CONTENTS

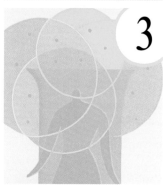

1

Take Charge Today

If you have diabetes and aren't taking measures to stop it in its tracks, there's no time to waste. Diabetes is a serious disease, but it's well within your power to control both high blood sugar and the complications it can cause. If you're at risk for diabetes or are uncertain you have it, get the tests you need. Then get your game on! Steps like eating right, losing weight, and taking medication or insulin if necessary will make you feel better physically and mentally—now and over the long haul.

You can look at diabetes in two ways. One is the big picture, which, frankly, is not very pretty: Diabetes is the fifth-deadliest disease in the United States, and it's becoming increasingly more common. The other is the small-scale picture, the scale of one—you. Here, the news is much brighter: More than ever before, diabetes is a disease you can control and even conquer. And the tools available to help you are getting better all the time.

On the large scale, you can't ignore the fact that if you have diabetes, you've got plenty of company. Across the country (and throughout the world), rates of diabetes have grown to epidemic proportions. During the past 10 years, the percentage of Americans with diabetes has jumped by 40 percent, and the number of people battling the disease now stands between 16 million and 17 million. Just as alarming, rates among children, who in the past rarely developed the most prevalent form of diabetes (type 2), are climbing as well.

The silver lining in this cloud of gloom and doom is the fact that few serious diseases allow you to fight back as much as diabetes does. If you take the right steps to keep the condition under your control, you can live a full and active life. In fact, some people who successfully turn their diabetes around say that because of action they took, they now feel healthier overall than they have in years.

Your Take-Charge Tool Kit

If there's an upside to the diabetes epidemic, it's this: Chronic diseases that threaten growing numbers of people also capture the interest of researchers (not to mention the companies and federal health agencies that fund them). As a result, the past decade has seen significant advances in the way doctors understand, prevent, and treat diabetes. Look at how new findings have improved three key components of diabetes treatment:

Blood-sugar control. Complications of diabetes, such as cardiovascular problems, poor vision, kidney disease, and nerve damage, were once thought to be inevitable no matter how hard you tried to manage erratic swings in blood sugar—the core problem of diabetes. But that thinking is no longer acceptable. Several major studies from around the world have shown that if you bring blood sugar into a normal range with drugs, insulin, diet, exercise, or some combination of these, you can cut your risk of complications by anywhere from one third to three quarters. If you're diagnosed before you develop complications, it's possible to sidestep diabetes-related health problems completely, sometimes with lifestyle changes alone. Meanwhile, technology for monitoring your own blood sugar continues to improve and is now remarkably convenient and relatively pain-free.

Lifestyle. Diet and exercise are powerful tools for lowering blood sugar—so powerful, in fact, that they free many people with diabetes from medication and insulin. And using these "power" tools is easier than ever before. Recent research into how foods affect blood sugar has shown that your diet need not be as restrictive as experts once believed. It can include virtually any food you like, as long as you watch your calorie intake. On the exercise side, it turns out that your workouts don't have to be as vigorous as once thought. Even short bouts of activity throughout the day add up to significant benefits to your health.

Drugs. Earlier generations of diabetes medications have been bolstered by a growing roster of newer drugs that tackle the disease in a variety of ways. In many cases, you can combine these drugs to take advantage of their different modes of operation. The fact that there are also several varieties of insulin (which regulates the body's use of blood sugar) gives you more flexibility in finding a regimen that matches your lifestyle.

Do You Have Diabetes?

If you don't know the answer to this question but feel you have cause to wonder, that's probably reason enough to see a doctor. In its early stages, when it's easiest to control, diabetes can be sneaky and silent, slowly causing damage throughout your body without obvious symptoms. But if you're alert to subtle signs, you can catch the disease at the outset and get a jump on beating it back.

It's human nature not to look for problems if they haven't already found you—which explains why between one third and one half of people with diabetes don't know they have it.

DID YOU KNOW

Researchers have been toying with the idea that starting insulin therapy before diabetes even starts can help prevent it in people at risk of developing type 1 diabetes, though it's unclear whether this would actually work. In mid-2002, a disappointing study published in the *New England Journal of Medicine* found that pre-disease injections made no difference. Researchers still hold out hope that someday an insulin pill, which would work in a different way, may prevent the disease.

According to the American College of Endocrinology, half of all people who finally go to their doctor to be tested have already developed some degree of complications.

How can you recognize when diabetes is at your door? There are three fundamental ways.

Figure your risk factors. The first thing to look at is whether any element of your background makes you more likely than the general population to develop diabetes. Among the most important factors to evaluate are:

▶ **Family history.** If anyone in your immediate family—a parent, sibling, or grandparent—has had diabetes, you have a higher chance of developing the disease yourself. The extent of the risk depends on the type of diabetes and how closely related you are to the person who has it (the risk is highest among identical twins).

▶ **Ethnic group.** The most common type of diabetes (called type 2) is most prevalent in African Americans, Hispanic Americans, Native Americans, and Asian Americans. The other major form (type 1) is most prevalent in Caucasians, especially those with backgrounds in northern European regions, such as Scandinavia.

▶ **Weight.** Being overweight significantly raises your risk of developing type 2 diabetes. That makes it one of the most important risk factors because it's one you can control.

▶ **Age.** Type 1 usually occurs in children or teens (it's rarely diagnosed after age 30). Type 2 generally develops after age 40, although it's becoming more common in younger people.

Keep a sharp eye for symptoms. While the signs of diabetes can be subtle at first, they're not impossible to pick up on. The longer diabetes progresses, the more likely symptoms are to become obvious and troublesome. The hallmarks of diabetes are:

▶ Excessive thirst
▶ Increased appetite
▶ Frequent urination
▶ Fatigue
▶ Blurred vision
▶ Frequent infections
▶ Tingling in your hands and feet
▶ Sexual dysfunction

Get tested. Tests for diabetes are easy; they involve nothing more painful than a finger prick to draw a drop of your blood (although some tests require that you prepare by fasting ahead of time). It's best to see a doctor for a full evaluation if you want to nail down your diagnosis: Blood screenings at health fairs or malls provide less accurate results than those your doctor can give you. If your results fall short of a diagnosis but your background suggests you're at risk, schedule a return visit at least every year to make sure nothing's changed.

Dealing with the Diagnosis

Hearing that you have a chronic disease is never easy. One day it seems you have a clean bill of health (though you may suspect that something is wrong), and the next you have a problem for the rest of your life. But don't despair. You've probably had diabetes for some time, and now that you know it, you've taken a major step toward being healthier, not sicker.

Still, it can be tough to be optimistic initially. You might feel as if your body has betrayed you or that it's out of control. Some people assume that the worst they've heard about diabetes (accurate or not) lies just around the corner, and they jump to panicky conclusions like "I'll go blind!" or "I can never eat dessert again!" Others are nonchalant, figuring that they've managed to get by up to now with diabetes, so "worrying about it won't get me anywhere."

You're probably somewhere in the middle of the spectrum between panic and denial. You may even be relieved to finally know why you've been feeling so lousy. All of these emotions are normal. In fact, you can anticipate moving through several emotional stages after being diagnosed. Typically, an I-can't-believe-it phase gives way to feelings of anger and the realization that there's a long road ahead, which can sometimes lead to depression. To deal with the dismay a diagnosis can produce:

➲ **View your emotions as progress.** The next time you snap at a family member or find yourself in a fog and staring out the window, play the moment out as a mental movie—an emotional scene in an unfolding story that continues to move progressively toward something better. When you accept your feelings as a natural, important part of an ongoing process, it's an indication you're actually working through them and going ahead with the rest of your life.

➲ **Talk to someone.** Sharing emotions with a loved one, joining a support group, or attending a class about diabetes in which you can meet others with the disease can help put your feelings in perspective and make you feel less alone.

➲ **Think short-term.** You may feel overwhelmed by all the changes you have to make in your life, the new self-care skills you have to learn, and the sheer volume of medical information you need to absorb. Rest assured that eventually it will all seem second nature. For now, focus on immediate goals ("Today I'll meet my dietitian") that will move you further down the road.

➲ **Forge ahead.** The key is not to let your diabetes diagnosis paralyze you. The sooner you take action, the sooner you'll feel you've gotten your life back under control—and the sooner you'll start to feel better.

What You Can Expect

When you're diagnosed with diabetes, your doctor will need to cover a lot of ground in a short time. In fact, he'll want to know virtually everything about you: eating patterns, weight history, blood pressure, medications you're taking, whether you smoke or drink, how satisfying you find sex, how many kids you've had, any family history of heart disease, and any treatment you've received for other problems, including endocrine and eating disorders. If you're a woman, you'll even be asked about your children's development. Your doctor isn't prying. All of this information has a bearing on your condition and the management program you'll eventually follow.

Your doctor will also want to do a thorough physical exam, including a cardiac workup that may involve an electrocardiogram (which records the heart's electrical activity) and a careful look at your mouth, feet, eyes, abdomen, skin, and thyroid gland. You'll have a battery of tests, including a blood-lipid test for cholesterol (among other things) and at least two different blood-sugar tests—one that shows what your blood sugar is right now and the other, what it has averaged for the past two to three months.

It may seem like a lot to begin with, but this initial assessment is arguably the most important phase of your overall care. Other parts of this phase may include questions that determine how much you know about your disease and how motivated you are to do something about it. Eventually, you'll move on to the next phases, in which you're in charge from one day to the next and your doctor is a resource for follow-up assessments and treatment of any complications.

Will You Need Insulin?

Insulin generally means needles, and dealing with this one element of care is the single biggest fear for many people with diabetes to overcome. Whether you'll actually have to confront the business end of a syringe depends first on which type of diabetes you have. All people with type 1 diabetes need insulin (and often find injections to be less daunting than they imagined), but not everybody with type 2 does.

If you have type 2 diabetes, your requirement for insulin will depend on a number of factors, including:

▶ **How much insulin your body makes on its own.** If you have type 1 diabetes, your body doesn't make any insulin; if you have type 2, your body's insulin-making ability is only partially impaired, and the extent of the impairment is different from one person to the next.

▶ **How well your body uses the insulin it has.** If your cells have trouble using the insulin that's naturally available, you may need supplemental doses.

INTERESTING STATISTICS

■ Number of diabetics in the U.S. . . .**16–17 million**

■ Approximate percentage of the population this represents **6**

■ People ages 40 to 74 with prediabetes (impaired glucose tolerance) . . . . **16 million**

■ Estimated percentage of people with prediabetes who develop full-blown type 2 diabetes each year **11**

■ Estimated number of people who have diabetes but don't know it . . . . . **5.9 million**

■ Increased risk of heart disease and stroke in people with diabetes . . . .**2–4 times**

■ Rank of diabetes as a cause of new cases of blindness **1**

■ Rank of diabetes as a cause of kidney failure **1**

■ Rank of diabetes as a cause of "nontraumatic" lower-limb amputations **1**

■ Percentage by which these risks can be lowered with diet and exercise alone in people with prediabetes **58**

■ Percentage by which these risks can be lowered with new medications alone in people with prediabetes **31**

■ Percentage by which good blood-sugar control in people with type 2 diabetes reduces risk of heart failure **56**

■ Percentage by which good blood-sugar control in people with type 1 diabetes reduces risk of eye damage, kidney disease, nerve damage, and cardio-vascular disease, respectively **76, 50, 60, 35**

▶ **Your blood-sugar levels.** How high above normal your blood-sugar levels tend to be will help guide your doctor in deciding whether insulin is necessary.

▶ **How effective other forms of treatment have been.** As a rule with type 2 diabetes, insulin is the last resort when lifestyle measures and oral medications fail to bring your blood sugar under control.

Where Do You Stand?

Your doctor looks at a lot of variables when deciding how to treat your diabetes, but he'll pay special attention to one in particular: your blood-sugar readings. If your blood sugar is sky-high in your initial assessment, you may go straight to drug and insulin therapy until your numbers are brought down. If you have type 2 diabetes, once your blood sugar has stabilized and you begin making lifestyle changes, you may be able to go off insulin and other medications.

One of the numbers your doctor will zero in on is your fasting blood-glucose level, a key test of blood sugar. While other tests also need to be considered and each case must be managed individually, you can roughly anticipate your options depending on what your fasting blood-glucose levels are (numbers are expressed as milligrams per deciliter). As a general guideline:

▶ If fasting blood glucose is between 110 mg/dl and 125 mg/dl, you have prediabetes (also known as impaired glucose tolerance), a condition in which elevated blood-sugar levels significantly raise the risk of developing diabetes. You'll be advised to start eating a healthier diet and to get more exercise, but you're unlikely to get a prescription for drugs or insulin.

▶ If fasting blood glucose is 126 mg/dl to around 140 or 150 mg/dl, you have full-blown diabetes, but you'll probably still

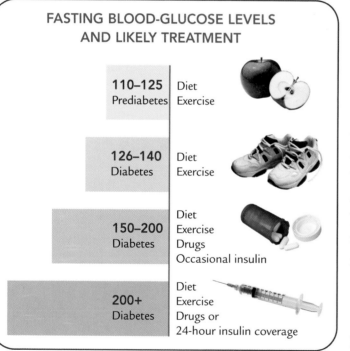

FASTING BLOOD-GLUCOSE LEVELS AND LIKELY TREATMENT

110–125 Prediabetes — Diet Exercise

126–140 Diabetes — Diet Exercise

150–200 Diabetes — Diet Exercise Drugs Occasional insulin

200+ Diabetes — Diet Exercise Drugs or 24-hour insulin coverage

be able to control your blood sugar with diet and exercise, depending on your condition and results from other tests.

▶ Once fasting blood glucose exceeds 150 mg/dl and ranges to 200 mg/dl, it's likely you'll need drugs in addition to diet and exercise. You may also need occasional doses of insulin for better control at certain times of the day (after meals, for example) when blood sugar tends to be higher.

▶ When fasting blood glucose goes above 200, you may need drugs or 24-hour insulin coverage—possibly both—along with lifestyle changes.

What's the Game Plan?

There's no getting around it: Once you have diabetes, you've got it for life, and no operation, therapy, or drug can cure it (at least, not yet). The good news is that controlling it can almost be like a cure in that lowering high blood sugar can stop diabetes in its tracks and reduce your risk of developing the health problems that go along with it.

Bringing diabetes under control is an important task—and there's no one better qualified to do it than you. Taking charge of diabetes doesn't have to be a full-time job, but you have to be mindful of it throughout your entire day, whether you're eating, doing yard work, or getting ready for bed. You'll have a team of other people to help you, but the doctors, nurses, and specialists aren't your primary caregivers—you are. And your success ultimately depends on managing a treatment plan that puts you squarely in charge. These are the key steps you need to take to get your diabetes under control.

Start Damage Control Immediately

Think about what happens when you spill honey: It gets on your fingers, sticks to everything you touch, and generally gums up your entire kitchen counter. Now imagine a honey spill taking place inside your bloodstream—which is essentially what high blood sugar is. What happens? Cells, proteins, and fats get stickier, slowing circulation, holding back tissue repair, and encouraging material to adhere to your artery walls and cause clots. In short, excess blood sugar gums up your entire body.

You don't leave honey on your countertop. Likewise, you should clean up blood sugar as quickly and thoroughly as possible because the "stickiness" only gets worse. Doing so can make you feel better right off the bat. And even if you have no symptoms of diabetes, taking this action will start to reduce your risk of such problems as these:

▶ Damage to delicate blood vessels at the back of the eye (the retina), which can lead to vision problems

▶ Ruined capillaries in the kidneys that filter waste from your body via the bloodstream

▶ Impaired nerve function due to less nourishment from damaged blood vessels

▶ Damage to artery walls that makes them more likely to snag blood clots and plaque that can cause heart attack, stroke, and high blood pressure

These complications wreak all kinds of havoc, including impaired healing, infections, lack of sensation that can lead to injury (especially in the feet), loss of vision, swollen ankles, fatigue, sexual dysfunction—the list can be long. Fortunately, the following steps will help you clean up the excess blood sugar and halt this parade of problems.

TAKE-CHARGE TIPS

While there may seem to be a lot of details to deal with in the first days of a diagnosis, the steps you should take boil down to a handful of key objectives:

➲ Learn how to test your own blood sugar using lancet devices, test strips, and a blood-glucose meter.

➲ Use the results to determine your average blood-sugar levels and how they tend to fluctuate throughout the day.

➲ Learn more from your doctor or a diabetes educator about how to stabilize your blood sugar with diet and exercise.

➲ Read everything you can about diabetes—a step you're already taking.

➲ Schedule an eye exam for a month after your diagnosis. Because high blood sugar can temporarily cause blurry vision, a complete visual exam to screen for more permanent damage will be more useful after a few weeks, when you've brought blood sugar under better control.

Know the Problems and the Solutions

That's the operative rule in business, sports, and politics, and it's just as important when you're fighting for your quality of life— if not for your life itself. The power to tame diabetes is within your grasp, but to use it, you need some know-how. Without a doubt, that means grappling with a lot of information—about your particular type of diabetes, medications, insulin varieties, blood-sugar tests, meal planning, and exercise, to name a few. But the details are not insurmountable, and you've got plenty of people to give you a hand—including specialists whose sole purpose is to impart knowledge and clear up your confusion.

Keep Tabs on Blood Sugar

Diabetes is a silent disease because you can't feel your blood sugar unless it becomes extremely high or low— two situations that you definitely want to avoid. How can you tell what's going on with the blood inside your body? Only one way: Get a bit of blood outside your body and do a little analysis. This isn't something you need to run to your doctor for (though certain tests should be performed on clinical turf). Handy, easy-to-use, and relatively pain-less lancets, test strips, and blood-glucose meters let you check your own blood sugar anywhere, anytime. Some people take blood-sugar readings four or more times a day, depending on their needs.

The blood-sugar readings that you—not your doctor— gather every day are a fulcrum by which you gain leverage over your disease. They provide data that will be a critical component of your care by allowing you to see how your blood sugar varies throughout the day and how much it swings in response to food, exercise, stress, or anything else that may affect it. They will help guide everything from which drugs you take and when you administer insulin (if you need them) to what you eat for breakfast.

Lose Body Baggage

Nothing signals more clearly that you're at risk for type 2 dia-betes than being overweight (which accounts for 9 of 10 cases of the disease). Excess baggage—especially in the gut—makes you more likely to develop insulin resistance, a condition in which cells don't use glucose (a form of sugar from food) as well as they should. The result: Glucose accumulates in the blood. Wearing a spare tire also increases the body's demand for insulin, which the pancreas (the maker of insulin) may have trouble meeting—again resulting in high blood sugar. Of course, there are other dangers in being overweight—high blood pressure, high cholesterol, and heart disease among them. One recent Boston University study found that obese people with type 2 diabetes had an alarming 99 to 100 percent chance of developing heart disease by age 85.

Losing weight may be the single most important thing you can do to control type 2 diabetes. There's no need for anything extreme; a slow and steady drop in weight keeps pounds off better than crash diets you're unlikely to stick to. And rest assured: You don't have to slim down to supermodel size to make a difference. Dropping as little as 10 pounds can give you a significant edge over diabetes if you keep the weight off.

Deconstruct Your Diet

On the food front, it may surprise you to learn that the main issue is not the amount of sugar or other carbohydrates you eat but how many calories you get from all types of food. A dietitian can show you how to eat ample amounts of appetizing edibles (including all of your favorites, within limits of course) yet still keep calories down so you lose weight. If you have type 1 diabetes, you'll need to balance your carbohydrate intake with your insulin injections to keep blood sugar from soaring too high or dropping too low. Whatever your diabetes type, you should put five food strategies into action right away:

1 Work up a meal plan that holds the reins on your blood sugar with tools like carbohydrate counting and food exchanges (see Chapter 4 for details on these methods).

2 Aim to get more—not fewer—carbohydrates in your diet; they supply the greatest amount of energy with the lowest number of calories.

3 Fill up on fiber. It slows digestion and therefore controls the rise of blood sugar after a meal, keeps your appetite under control by making you feel full, and scours damaging fats from your blood.

4 Cut back on saturated fat from foods like burgers and doughnuts, but allow yourself healthier monounsaturated fats in foods like peanuts and olive oil.

5 Eat a variety of fresh fruits and vegetables, such as apricots, spinach, and tomatoes to make sure you get enough nutrients like vitamin C and magnesium, in which people with diabetes are sometimes deficient.

Get Physical

Exercise gobbles up glucose, and this immediately brings your blood sugar down. If you do it regularly, it also enables your cells to better use glucose, even when you're not active. That can make you less dependent on insulin or medication. On top of that, exercise helps you lose weight, lowers your cholesterol and blood pressure, and makes your heart and lungs more powerful—all of which cut your risk of complications from diabetes.

Hate to exercise? Don't worry. Your workout plan doesn't have to be any more involved than making sure you pump up your heart rate and breathe a little harder several times a week, preferably for 20 minutes or more at a time. Classic aerobic exercises like walking, running, and biking are ideal, but ordinary chores, such as washing your car, mowing the lawn, and cleaning your house, do the trick too.

Beat Back Related Risks

Eating a healthy diet, getting more exercise, and losing weight are the most important things you can do to prevent complications from diabetes—but they're not the only steps you can take.

⊃ **Ask about aspirin.** Studies show that taking low-dose aspirin every day can cut your risk of a heart attack by as much as 60 percent. Check with your doctor to see if aspirin therapy might be right for you.

⊃ **Quit smoking.** Besides making a mess of your lungs and increasing your risk of cancer, smoking narrows arteries, which

WHEN DIABETES STRIKES YOUR CHILD

Treating diabetes in a child can be more challenging than dealing with the disease yourself. Depending on their age and temperament, children vary in their ability—or desire—to understand what's happening to them, take care of themselves, and follow your instructions. But you can put your child on the road to responsible self-care with either type 1 (the most common type in children) or type 2 diabetes if you bear these principles in mind:

TODDLERS AND PRESCHOOLERS

Learn to recognize how hypoglycemia and hyperglycemia affect your child's behavior, since she simply doesn't have the words to tell you how she feels herself. Expect some battles over insulin injections and blood-sugar tests around toilet-training time, as your child starts to assert herself more, but stick to your guns to get them done. Don't worry too much if blood sugar ranges between 150 mg/dl and 200 mg/dl (higher than what's recommended for adults): Children need more blood sugar for normal development. Forget trying to control when your child eats. Instead, accept irregular eating patterns and compensate by using shorter-acting insulin when your child does have a bite.

ELEMENTARY SCHOOL KIDS

As your child develops physically and mentally, he'll be better able to understand why his treatment is necessary and become more willing to cooperate with its demands. Educate him about how caring for his condition now will protect his health in the future, but don't scare him with the gory details of complications. Tighter blood-sugar control now becomes more important, especially at night, when there's a higher risk of hypoglycemia. Make sure

he has a bedtime snack and doesn't skip meals. Encourage him to participate in school and social activities to build friendships, promote self-esteem, and make him feel less different from other kids. Around age eight, your child can probably start taking on some of the responsibility for injections and blood tests himself—maybe with the daytime help of teachers or classmates, who benefit from the opportunity to learn about diabetes from your child.

PRETEENS AND ADOLESCENTS

Control—over a number of things—now starts falling into your child's hands. Studies find that tight blood-sugar monitoring as early as age 13 can prevent complications in adulthood, so encourage her to take charge—but don't expect the thought of future consequences to motivate her too much. Now's not the time to completely let go of the reins: Worries about what other kids think might cause her to skip steps in her care. Make an issue of it, expect an argument—but be confident that using you as an excuse ("My parents make me do it") can help her do the right thing. Gradually give your child more responsibility as she's able to handle it. By the time she's choosing which college to attend or looking for work, responsibility should pass to her.

raises your risk of heart attack and stroke and cuts circulation to your legs, making it harder for wounds to heal (especially on the feet). It also raises blood pressure and ratchets up your risk of kidney and nerve damage.

⭢ **Take the pressure off.** High blood pressure contributes to cardiovascular disease and kidney damage. If you eat plenty of fruits and vegetables, you're already bringing blood pressure down. You can bring it down further by eating less sodium (rampant in packaged foods) and more potassium from such foods as potatoes, yogurt, avocados, and bananas. Think about cutting back on caffeine, too: One cup of coffee can raise blood pressure for about two hours.

Get on a Schedule

It won't be long before dealing with diabetes seems like old hat. Once you've gotten used to the changes in your diet and exercise habits and learned to handle medications, day-to-day life may start to seem routine again. But you'll need to check back with your doctor regularly to make sure everything is going according to plan. Figure on getting a complete physical every year, including an eye exam, a cholesterol test, and a urine test to detect signs of kidney damage. In between visits, get a test called hemoglobin A1c, which shows your long-term average blood sugar, every three to six months.

Where to Get Support

You're in charge of managing your game plan from day to day (and hour to hour) because you're the one who's always there—to lace up your walking shoes, pour a bowl of bran cereal, take your medication, or prick your finger. But you're hardly in this alone. In fact, one of your most important jobs as the manager—and boss—of your care is to line up a team of professionals to help you.

Your first stop is your primary-care physician, who probably diagnosed your diabetes. Your family doctor is a general practitioner (GP), not a diabetes specialist, but just because you

have a specific disease doesn't mean you'll be bidding your regular doctor good-bye. In fact, GPs handle more than 90 percent of diabetes cases nationwide. That's partly because the insurance industry funnels most care through GPs. But generalists are also well suited to handle a variety of health problems—valuable when dealing with a disease as multifaceted as diabetes—and they can readily refer you to a range of specialists when you need them. So consider your primary-care physician your right hand, but expect to draw on the talents of a wide range of experts, including the following:

Your Diabetologist

This is a doctor who specializes in the management of diabetes, often with a board certification in endocrinology, the study of hormones and metabolism. A diabetologist will know more than your general practitioner about how to match your treatment to your blood-sugar, eating, and exercise patterns and is more likely to be up on the latest drugs and research. Talk with your GP about whether you need a diabetologist. If your main health problem is diabetes and you're finding it difficult to control your blood sugar, a diabetologist should probably be calling the shots as your primary-care physician. If, on top of diabetes, you're dealing with a range of other health problems, such as obesity, high blood pressure, or conditions not directly related to diabetes, you should stick with your GP and call your diabetologist when you have questions or issues your GP can't address.

Your Diabetes Educator

The 15 minutes you get with your doctor won't be enough to learn all the ins and outs of dealing with diabetes. That's where a diabetes educator, usually a nurse with a special interest in diabetes care, comes in. She can show you how to prepare and administer insulin and perform blood and urine tests, explain how to balance your eating and exercise with your blood-sugar readings, and tell you more about how diabetes affects your body. She's a walking diabetes library and may even offer classes on diabetes, at which you can get more background information and meet other patients. As such, your educator should have the right credentials. Look for the letters CDE—certified diabetes educator—after the name, which indicates that she has had special training in diabetes care and has passed an examination from the National Board for Diabetes Educators.

Your Dietitian

Controlling calories, counting carbohydrates, finding hidden fats, sorting out sugars, evaluating exchanges—your dietitian can help you with all of this. Meal planning (which involves everything just mentioned and more) is key to your care whether your main goal is to lose weight or to fine-tune your glucose intake. Usually a registered dietitian who may also be a certified diabetes educator, your dietitian will help you find both health and pleasure in what you eat by carefully matching your food to your drug or insulin use, your exercise habits, and your daily schedule. If anything about your treatment changes—or you get bored with your meal plan—your dietitian can help you adjust. Most of your contact with a dietitian will be at the beginning of your care, when you establish your meal plan, but checking in once or twice a year is a good idea.

Your Eye Doctor

Because diabetes is a leading cause of eye disorders and even blindness, you constantly need to guard against vision problems. The only person qualified to diagnose and treat eye damage from diabetes is an ophthalmologist—a medical doctor who special-

FISHING FOR PHYSICIANS

There are plenty of doctors out there. How do you find one who is right for you? Whatever specialty you're looking for, you can narrow your list of candidates if you:

■ **Ask around.** Start by getting recommendations from friends, other diabetes patients, and the doctors and nurses you already see. Ask what they know about any doctor they suggest: Does he listen? Does he work well with other people? Do his patients seem to do well?

■ **Schedule a visit.** When you hear of a promising doctor, book a getting-to-know-you visit. Keep your medical business to a minimum on the first appointment and focus instead on asking questions. Find out if the office takes your insurance, what tests you'd have to undergo, and how often you'd come back for follow-ups. Ask if the doctor is already plugged into a network of diabetes-care professionals.

■ **Check the sheepskins.** Both your primary-care physician and your endocrinologist should have board certification in endocrinology or internal medicine and also be members of organizations like the American Diabetes Association or the American Association of Clinical Endocrinologists.

■ **Ask about experience.** Even endocrinologists don't treat only diabetes, so be sure to find out how much your doctor works with people who have diabetes—particularly those with your type and at your age.

■ **Talk philosophy.** Does the doctor prefer sticking to well-established therapies or trying out new approaches? Neither way is necessarily better, but the doctor will probably have an opinion on the merits of one approach over another. Do you agree with his philosophy?

izes in the eyes. Don't rely on checkups by an optometrist, who is qualified to do vision screening and prescribe glasses or contact lenses but isn't an expert on eye diseases and can't do surgery to correct them. Plan to visit your ophthalmologist at least once a year, but don't wait for your annual exam if you notice changes in your vision or feel pain or pressure in your eyes—possible signs of damage that require immediate attention. When looking for an ophthalmologist, try to find one who specializes in diseases of the retina, especially if you've already developed eye complications.

Your Foot Doctor

High blood sugar makes you prone to foot problems partly because it hinders circulation: Blood has trouble getting all the way from the heart to the feet and back. Small sores and calluses, which are common with diabetes, can quickly become worse if you don't keep on top of them with the help of a podiatrist—

a medical doctor who specializes in foot care. Your primary-care physician should always check your feet when you go for an exam (and you should too, every day). But your podiatrist— known as a D.P.M., for doctor of podiatric medicine—is the best person to treat sores, calluses, corns, bunions, infections, or any other problem that may develop. He can also give you pointers on keeping your feet healthy. Ask your primary-care physician or endocrinologist to refer you to a podiatrist who has a lot of patients with diabetes.

Your Dentist

As every cavity-prone eight-year-old knows (or will eventually find out), bacteria thrive on sugar. Unfortunately, if you have diabetes, high blood sugar makes you prone to the destructive effects of gingivitis—infection of the gums—even if you faith-fully brush your teeth every day. There's no reason to change your dentist if you have diabetes; you just need to make sure you actually go for a checkup and a cleaning every six months, as everyone should (but usually doesn't). Do tell your dentist you have diabetes, however, and ask how you can improve your brushing and flossing techniques.

Your Pharmacist

You may know your pharmacist only as some-one who stands behind a counter and puts med-icines in bottles. But don't take this member of your team for granted. The special training that pharmacists receive about how drugs affect the body (in both good ways and bad) and how medicines interact with each other can make them an invaluable source of information. Try to find a pharmacist who works well with you; you may end up seeing this person more often than anybody else on your team. Then keep going back to the same pharmacy so the pharmacist can keep an up-to-date record of all your med-ications. Whenever you start a new drug— including over-the-counter remedies—or make a change in your prescriptions, your pharmacist can give you pointers on how your body may

WHAT THE STUDIES SHOW

How well your doctor relates to you through words and body language has an impact on your health. According to a recent review of 14 studies, doctors whose patients have the best outcomes are upbeat, supportive, and reassuring; share information openly; act friendly; and have a good sense of humor. They also tend to face their patients, lean forward, and nod when talking— and they don't cross their arms.

react. He can also give you a printout of all the drugs you take (along with their doses and side effects) to take with you when you see other members of your medical team.

Your Exercise Specialist

Your primary-care physician can approve an exercise plan, but he can't be your coach. If you're out of shape and haven't exercised since the Reagan administration (or just want a trainer's individual attention), you might want to design your fitness program with the help of an exercise physiologist. This person can custom-design a program that's safe for you, help you set realistic goals, and give you pointers on proper form and technique. Your exercise specialist could be a doctor (in this case, a Ph.D.) but doesn't have to be. You're looking for someone with graduate training (preferably at least a master's degree) in exercise science and a special interest in helping people with diabetes. She might be a certified diabetes educator or— ideally—someone certified by the American College of Sports Medicine. Start by asking your doctor to recommend a physiologist he's worked with before.

Your Counselor

Whether you need help handling the emotional aspects of diabetes is your call, but you should realize that it's not strictly a mental-health issue. People who are angry, depressed, or anxious are more likely to neglect their care, so emotional support can, in effect, help stabilize your blood sugar as well as your mind and mood. You have three basic types of mental-health experts from which to choose. A psychiatrist is a medical doctor who has received advanced training in psychological disorders and can write prescriptions for drugs, such as anti-anxiety medications or antidepressants. A psychologist doesn't have a medical degree (but usually has a Ph.D.) and can't prescribe drugs, but he can help you recognize and overcome destructive or self-defeating ways of thinking. A social worker usually has less training in mental health (typically a master's degree) but can help you cope with emotional troubles along with such practical challenges as dealing with insurance companies, hospitals, and government agencies.

Ready to Rumble

You know exactly what kind of opponent you're up against, you understand the tools at your disposal, you've formulated a battle plan and lined up a team to help you put it into action. So what will it take to win the fight? The same things it takes to succeed in just about any other worthy struggle: patience, strength, determination, good communication skills, the ability to cooperate with your team, and confidence that you will prevail. Last but not least, a sense of humor can't hurt.

An attitude of confidence may be the most important quality of all. It's easy to feel (especially right after your diagnosis) that diabetes has already won the battle: It's stolen your health and made you feel like a "diseased" or "damaged" person— a statistic. So what's the use of fighting when you know your essential condition won't change? Such bleak thoughts are the seductions of pessimism and defeatism. If you buy into them (and most people do—at least a little bit, at least some of the time), then diabetes really has won after all. Acknowledge these feelings when you have them, but don't let them linger. Just keep moving forward.

The truth is that diabetes is much like the classic playground bully who pushes you down and then turns his back because he doesn't expect you to get up and fight back. Standing up for yourself when diabetes lets down its guard means that you have refused to become a victim of the disease. And you'll find that diabetes often backs down in the face of diet, exercise, and drugs—though you don't ever want to turn your back on it.

If you're willing to fight, you'll find plenty of weaknesses in diabetes to exploit. And don't forget: You've got a gang of friends backing you up who know how to handle the meanest tricks diabetes can pull. But it's still your battle. Roll up your sleeves, make a fist, and prepare to knock diabetes off its feet.

2

Understanding Diabetes

You can't see it, you usually can't feel it—so what exactly is diabetes? It's a complex disease to be sure, one that affects your entire body, and it can seem difficult to get your mind around. But boning up on the basics braces you for battle with your condition. In fact, education is a cornerstone of care. The more you know about diabetes, the better you'll be able to use all the tools at your disposal to keep blood sugar in check and avoid complications that can compromise your enjoyment of life.

What exactly is diabetes? Unlike, say, high blood pressure, the term doesn't exactly paint a clear picture. Even doctors sometimes have a hard time describing it. Is it an endocrine disorder, a blood-related disease, a metabolic problem? Actually, it's all three—and then some.

If you don't understand what diabetes is all about, you're not alone. But it's worth finding out, because whenever you're faced with an important mission (and managing diabetes certainly qualifies), taking effective action means gathering good intelligence first.

Aside from being complex, diabetes is often the subject of misconceptions. For example, many people think it comes from eating too much sugar, but that's not really the case. It's also widely assumed that having diabetes means constantly jabbing syringes full of insulin into your body, but—while many people benefit from treatments involving injections—millions of others can control their disease by making relatively simple lifestyle changes.

And then there's the idea that people with the condition are defined by the term *diabetic*. This may seem like a small point, but it's worth making: You are not your disease, and your life isn't about diabetes, even if managing it demands your attention. Rather, diabetes is a condition that you can control day by day, so that you can celebrate, take part in, and enjoy the truly important aspects of your life that really define who you are.

A Hidden Fuel Spill

Imagine that the nation's intricate system of roads, streets, and highways is your body and that the millions of cars humming along this system are your cells. Every car needs regular replenishment with fuel, and, fortunately, gasoline is abundant. When everything is working normally, cars and gas come together, fuel tanks open, gas is dispensed, and the cars go about their business, brimming with the energy they need.

Now suppose something goes fundamentally wrong: The gas flows out of the pump, but there's nobody around to open the cars' fuel tanks. The gas spills all over, floods the roads, rushes down the gutters, and pollutes the entire system. That's the nature of diabetes.

In the real-life disease, the source of energy (that is, the "gasoline") is a substance called glucose, and the gas-station attendant who opens the tank is equivalent to a hormone called insulin.

Why Glucose Matters

Glucose, also known as blood sugar, is the major source of energy powering your brain, muscles, and tissues—all your body's functions. In fact, glucose is one of nature's great dynamos, providing an almost universal energy source for living things. Scientists know down to the molecule how it's made and what it does, but, interestingly, they have never been able to create it in a lab. Only plants can make glucose through the magic mix of sunlight, water, and other elements, and pass this energy along to other creatures through the food chain.

When you eat, your body breaks down the food into smaller, simpler components that move through the small intestine and into the bloodstream. Once in the blood, these nutrients are carried to cells throughout the body.

Different foods break down into different types of nutrients. Protein breaks down into amino acids, which are often used to build or repair tissue. Fat breaks down into fatty acids, which are mostly stored as energy reserves. Carbohydrates (including everything from bread and pasta to fruits and vegetables) mainly break down into glucose, which is used almost immediately for energy. In order to feel your best, you need enough glucose powering your cells at all times.

With diabetes, however, glucose in the blood doesn't make it into cells. The cells are deprived of energy, which explains why fatigue is one of the hallmarks of diabetes. And since the glucose can't enter cells, it builds up in the blood. High blood sugar wreaks havoc with the body. In the short term, for example, the excess glucose essentially soaks up water from the bloodstream, creating a paradoxical condition in which you need to urinate more often while feeling parched with thirst. Too much glucose can also hinder the immune system's infection-fighting white

blood cells, making you more vulnerable to illness. Over the long haul, persistently high blood sugar can lead to serious complications, such as damaged nerves, kidneys, eyes, blood vessels, liver, and heart.

A Wild Blood-Sugar Ride

Blood sugar fluctuates normally throughout the day, rising after you eat a meal. In people who don't have diabetes, these fluctuations stay within a span (measured in units of milligrams of glucose per deciliter of blood) that ranges from about 70 to 140 mg/dl. When you have diabetes, though, the patterns become more erratic:

▶ Blood-sugar levels spike to mountainous heights (rather than gentle hills) after meals.

▶ Levels drop more slowly as the body metabolizes the food you've eaten.

▶ Blood-sugar levels are, on average, higher than what is considered to be normal and healthy.

▶ The less you control your diabetes, the more likely your blood sugar is to swing wildly between highs and lows or simply stay high all the time.

The Blood-Sugar Problem

In uncontrolled diabetes, blood-sugar levels tend to spike after meals and remain high throughout the day. In healthy people, levels stay within the normal range, despite small fluctuations.

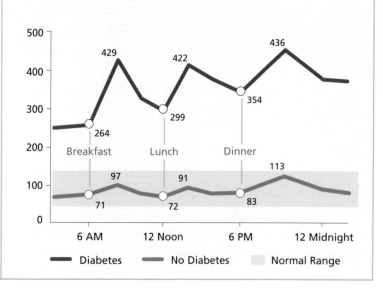

Insulin's Inside Job

Glucose may inflict the damage done by diabetes, but it isn't really to blame. Instead, the real troublemaker is the hormone insulin, manufactured by the pancreas. Insulin's job is to "unlock" cells so that glucose can enter. As glucose leaves the bloodstream and enters cells, blood sugar levels fall. When that happens, insulin levels also plummet so that blood sugar doesn't get too low—a condition called hypoglycemia.

When you have diabetes, the delicate dance of glucose and insulin is thrown out of step, either because the pancreas has trouble manufacturing insulin in the first place or because the body's cells have difficulty letting insulin do its job. The term that describes this latter condition is *insulin resistance*—a critical breakdown in the body's ability to utilize insulin properly. Insulin resistance is the underlying cause of the vast majority of diabetes cases.

Scientists are still struggling to understand exactly what goes wrong to cause insulin resistance. (In one recent medical textbook containing a diagram of how insulin may work at the cellular level, many steps in the process are simply illustrated with question marks.) But the sheer complexity of normal insulin function allows plenty of opportunity for things to go awry. It's possible, for example, that insulin resistance occurs when problems develop in the normal chain of chemical reactions that must occur to permit glucose to be transported through cell membranes. Or perhaps an intricate system of proteins in cells, sometimes called the metabolic switch, loses its ability to sense the presence of insulin and react accordingly.

Even if the biology is still a bit mysterious, however, it's important to remember that the factors known to raise the risk of diabetes are fairly well understood.

INSULIN OPPOSITES

Insulin isn't the only hormone that can affect blood-sugar levels. A number of others, sometimes called insulin antagonists, or counterregulatory hormones, have the opposite effect of insulin. These include:

■ **Glucagon**. Produced in the pancreas along with insulin, it blocks insulin's ability to lower blood sugar by causing the liver to release stored glucose when the body requires it.

■ **Epinephrine**. Also called adrenaline, this so-called stress hormone is released when the body perceives danger. Epinephrine raises blood sugar in order to make more energy available to muscles.

■ **Cortisol**. Another stress hormone, it can also raise blood-sugar levels.

■ **Growth hormone**. Produced by the pituitary gland in the brain, it makes cells less sensitive to insulin.

Typecasting: A Key to Understanding

Diabetes was long assumed to be one disease. But researchers have come to realize that it actually takes several forms, which, while fundamentally similar, differ in many important ways. The two main forms are known as type 1 and type 2. (Other types are far less common.) Both occur when glucose can't enter cells. As a result, they share many symptoms. These include:

Feeling tuckered. When cells can't get glucose and are deprived of energy, you can suffer from both physical and mental fatigue. The brain, in fact, is a glutton for glucose, using far more glucose for its weight than do other types of tissue. Mental fatigue can make you fuzzy-headed and emotionally brittle, while physical fatigue can make your muscles feel weak.

Frequent bathroom breaks. When the body is awash in blood sugar, the kidneys, which recirculate nutrients and filter out waste products, are among the first to know. When overwhelmed by glucose, they try to flush the excess out of your system by boosting production of urine, especially after blood-sugar levels reach or exceed about 180 mg/dl.

Unquenchable thirst. As urine is excreted, you lose fluid. To urge you to replace it, the body triggers a persistent thirst.

Snack attacks. The irony of diabetes is that although your body is overflowing with nutritional energy, your cells are starving. Deprived of sustenance, they tell the body's appetite system to send a call for more food—which only creates more glucose that can't be properly used.

Blurry vision. Diabetes can degrade your eyesight in two seemingly contradictory ways. In one, lack of body fluid due to loss of urine can dry out the eyes, constricting the lens and distorting vision. In the other, excess blood sugar can cause the lens to swell, also creating distortion. Both of these effects are temporary, although diabetes can cause other complications that may eventually result in serious visual impairment and even blindness.

More infections. Having too much glucose in your blood makes immune-system cells less effective at attacking viruses and bacteria that cause infection. To make matters worse, some of these invaders actually feed on glucose, making it easier for them to multiply and become an even bigger threat. This can result in frequent upper respiratory illnesses like colds and flu, as well as urinary tract infections, gum disease, and, in women, vaginal yeast infections.

Tingling hands and feet. High blood sugar can damage nerves, a condition that may first become noticeable in the touch-sensitive extremities as a tingling or burning sensation. Damage caused by excess blood sugar can also affect nerves in the digestive tract, provoking nausea, diarrhea, or constipation.

A PANCREAS PRIMER

The pancreas is a fist-size organ that resembles an overgrown tadpole. It lies just behind and below the stomach. In its "tail," cells known as beta cells (which are clustered in clumps called the islets of Langerhans) produce insulin and release it when needed. Other cells called acinar cells secrete enzymes that help break down proteins, carbohydrates, and fats.

Normally, the pancreas acts as a kind of glucose meter, closely monitoring levels in the blood and releasing insulin in spurts to mirror glucose levels. It also helps regulate a process in which the liver stores glucose as glycogen and then releases it back into the bloodstream to raise glucose levels when they fall too low. Certain diabetes drugs work to improve the function of the pancreas.

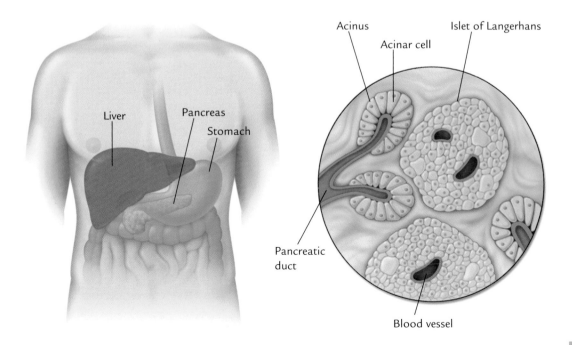

Liver

Pancreas

Stomach

Acinus

Acinar cell

Islet of Langerhans

Pancreatic duct

Blood vessel

Type I: An Insulin No-Show

So what makes the two types different? First, type 1 is much rarer, accounting for only 5 to 10 percent of all diagnosed cases of diabetes. With type 1 diabetes, the body's immune system destroys special cells in the pancreas that manufacture insulin. These cells, called beta cells, are the only places in the body where insulin is produced. Without them, the body lacks the insulin it needs to move glucose out of circulation and control high blood sugar. Other major characteristics of type 1:

Needles are necessary. Because the body can't produce insulin, type 1 patients need an outside supply of the hormone, self-administered by daily injections. That's why type 1 is sometimes called insulin dependent diabetes mellitus, or IDDM. This term is used less frequently today, however, because people with type 2 diabetes sometimes need to take insulin as well. But the fact that injections are an inevitable part of daily life for all type 1 diabetes patients remains one of the key characteristics of this form of the disease.

DIABETES AT A GLANCE

	TYPE 1	TYPE 2	GESTATIONAL
Characteristics	Sudden onset; pronounced thirst and hunger; frequent urination; fatigue; nausea and vomiting; weight loss	Slow, difficult-to-detect onset; pronounced thirst; frequent urination; fatigue; slow wound healing; tingling hands or feet; frequent infections; weight loss	Pronounced thirst; frequent urination; fatigue and other symptoms similar to those of type 2
Age at onset	Usually 20 or younger	Usually 40 or older, although rates are escalating among younger people	Child-bearing years
Physical condition	Usually lean or normal weight	Usually overweight	Pregnant
Cause	The immune system destroys the pancreas cells that produce insulin	Lack of exercise, poor diet, and resulting obesity; genetics	Hormones produced by the placenta hinder the function of insulin
Mainstay of treatment	Insulin injections	Lifestyle changes, possibly augmented by insulin and drugs	Lifestyle changes, possibly augmented by insulin injections

It strikes early. Type 1 diabetes often sets in during childhood, with about half of all cases developing before age 20. Most other cases begin in people up to age 30. It's very unusual to see a case of type 1 diabetes crop up in anyone over age 40. Because it's widely seen as a disease of the young (although you continue to have it your entire life), type 1 is sometimes called juvenile-onset diabetes. This term, too, has fallen out of favor, both because adults can get type 1 diabetes and because rates of type 2 diabetes in children are exploding.

It strikes fast. The onset of type 1 diabetes is rapid compared with type 2, which can take years to develop. If you (or your child) have type 1, such classic symptoms as fatigue, excessive thirst, and frequent urination will probably become worse over a period of just weeks or months.

There is a "honeymoon" period. In the first several months after type 1 is diagnosed and treatment begins, 20 percent of patients seem to improve as the pancreas temporarily begins to increase insulin production once again. This period of remission may last for as long as a year, during which blood-sugar levels become more stable and insulin injections may not even be necessary. While all honeymoons must come to an end, researchers see this period as a potential window of opportunity. One day it may allow yet-to-be-perfected therapies to preserve beta cell function before it's too late.

Blood sugar jumps wildly. With type 1, the pancreas loses its ability to monitor and control blood sugar. As a result, blood-sugar levels tend to spike and crash with greater volatility than in people who have type 2 diabetes, since their pancreatic function is usually less severely impaired. With type 1, the job of the pancreas essentially falls to you. You control your blood-sugar level with the timing and dosage of your insulin injections. This makes monitoring your blood sugar critically important (see Chapter 3).

What Causes Type 1?

Type 1 diabetes seems to appear out of nowhere and, as far as anyone knows, is not easily preventable—something that is definitely not true of type 2. So why does type 1 occur?

The bottom line is that researchers don't know yet. But clues can be found in the nature of the disease. Type 1 diabetes is

DID YOU KNOW

The discovery of insulin, a major breakthrough in understanding and treating diabetes, came in the 1920s, following the earlier discovery that when beta cells of the pancreas were missing, people developed diabetes. Building on this observation, a team of doctors led by researchers Frederick Banting and John MacLeod extracted insulin from beta cells and injected it into diabetes patients. When the patients improved, the researchers knew they had made a major discovery—one that brought Banting and MacLeod the Nobel Prize for medicine. Another 50 years passed, however, before researchers fully understood the distinction between type 1 and type 2 diabetes.

thought to involve a misguided attack by the immune system on the body's own tissue—specifically, the beta cells of the pancreas. This type of attack is known as an autoimmune response. Other autoimmune diseases include lupus, multiple sclerosis, rheumatoid arthritis, and Grave's disease.

Scientists are studying the different players involved with helping the body distinguish its own cells from foreign cells. Eventually they may be able to develop new therapies to prevent and treat type 1 diabetes. Meanwhile, the question still lingers as to why an autoimmune attack occurs in the first place. There appear to be a number of factors at work in type 1:

Genetics. Having a family history of type 1 diabetes may be the single most important risk factor in determining who will get the disease. Even so, the genetic connection is weak. It's actually uncommon to find two people in any given family who have type 1 diabetes. If you already have the disease, your children or siblings have only about a 5 percent chance of developing it. (For reasons that aren't well understood, men with type 1

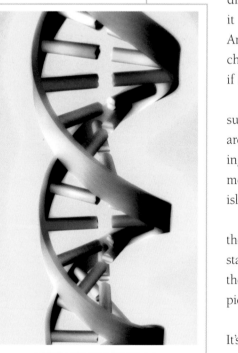

diabetes have a slightly higher chance of transmitting it to their children than women with type 1 do.) Among identical twins, there's only a 30 to 50 percent chance that the second twin will develop the disease if the first one has it.

Genetics does make certain ethnic groups more susceptible than others to type 1 diabetes. Caucasians are at the highest risk, as evidenced by studies showing that whites living in Hawaii get type 1 diabetes more than nonwhite Hawaiians who share the same island environment.

Even though genetics doesn't completely predict the disease, scientists are working to better understand the genes involved with type 1 diabetes, and they may someday be able to develop genetic therapies for people most at risk.

Viruses. Could type 1 be caused by an infection? It's possible. One reason researchers think so is that the onset of the disease appears to follow a seasonal pattern, with the fewest new cases in summer and the most in winter—when many viral illnesses are more common. A number of viruses have been implicated as suspects, particularly coxsackievirus, mumps, and rubella. Some studies have found that a high percentage of people newly diagnosed with type 1 have coxsackievirus antibodies in their blood, suggesting that the body has been fighting this viral infection. In the lab, a cousin of the coxsackie virus has been shown to produce type 1–like symptoms in animals.

Some researchers question whether the virus idea has any merit, but a number of theories explain how it might work. One hypothesis is that the immune system may have trouble telling the difference between certain viruses and the insulin-producing beta cells in the pancreas. After fighting off the virus, this premise goes, the immune system continues the battle by attacking the pancreas. Other theories suggest that viruses may change the beta cells in ways that make them appear foreign to the immune system. Or they may destroy proteins in the pancreas that manufacture insulin.

Cow's milk. This idea is mostly speculation and far from proven, but some research has suggested a link between feeding children cow's milk before three or four months of age and the risk of developing type 1 diabetes. People with type 1 sometimes have higher levels of antibodies that bind to both a protein found in milk and a protein sometimes found on beta cells, but the significance of this isn't clear. Other studies have failed to find any connection between cow's milk and type 1 diabetes. Still, the concern offers more reason not to wean a baby from breast milk or formula before 12 months of age, as recommended by the American Academy of Pediatrics.

Free radicals. These unstable molecules are formed as a by-product of natural bodily functions (such as breathing) that involve the use of oxygen. Free radicals have a single, unpaired electron instead of the usual pair, making them unstable. As they circulate around the body, they try to latch onto other molecules, inflicting damage on healthy cells in the process. Normally, enzymes in the body neutralize free radicals and keep this damage to a minimum. But toxins, such as air pollution and tobacco smoke, can boost their numbers to levels the body can't adequately handle. Studies suggest that the insulin-producing cells of the pancreas may be particularly vulnerable to free-radical damage because they are less well guarded by protective enzymes than other parts of the body are.

WHAT THE STUDIES SHOW

Harvard scientists using an imaging technique called X-ray crystallography recently obtained the first detailed, three-dimensional pictures of immune cells called T-cells attacking a foreign substance. The pictures revealed a previously unknown docking mechanism between cells that will help researchers better understand the rules of engagement in immune-system battles. Eventually, such knowledge may lead to therapies to help the body protect itself against specific kinds of attack. Meanwhile, researchers at the University of Illinois have discovered a way to improve the properties of T-cell receptors. This may open the door to manipulating the immune system in new ways to fight a variety of autoimmune diseases.

Type 2: A System Breakdown

Compared with type 1, type 2 is far more common, accounting for 90 to 95 percent of all cases of diabetes. It's also far more complex. High blood sugar is still the basic problem. But with type 2, the pancreas doesn't completely shut off insulin production. Instead, the body's use of insulin becomes impaired in any number of different ways.

▶ The beta cells of the pancreas are able to produce plenty of insulin, but they take their sweet time releasing it in response to the surge of glucose that follows a meal. Result: By the time the pancreas puts out the large amounts of insulin the body is waiting for, glucose levels have already built up in the blood.

▶ The number of beta cells is lower than normal, so the pancreas has trouble keeping up with insulin demand.

▶ There's plenty of glucose and insulin, but cells don't allow insulin to do its job—a condition known as insulin resistance. The problem can be caused by any number of things: A lack of proteins called insulin receptors on cells (think of insulin as a key and the receptor as a lock), a mismatch of insulin and receptors (the keys don't fit the locks), or flaws in the chemistry that lets insulin pass into cells. No matter what the problem, the result is the same: Glucose can't get where it needs to go and stays in the bloodstream instead.

▶ Excess body weight boosts the need for insulin and the pancreas can't keep up with demand.

Often, type 2 diabetes results from a combination of these factors, which tend to be interrelated. For example, obesity both creates more demand for insulin and promotes insulin resistance.

The major symptoms of type 2 mirror those of type 1, but type 2 is different in other ways:

It takes time. Unlike type 1, type 2 develops slowly over time, and symptoms don't show up right away. When you finally notice that something's wrong, you may already have had diabetes for many years. That can make type 2 diabetes seem a bit vague—if it appears so gradually, when does it actually begin? And once you're diagnosed, do you really, truly have it? Doctors admit that it's sometimes tough to say exactly when any given case of diabetes got started—especially after the fact. But exact criteria based on blood-sugar levels clearly define when you have diabetes and when you don't. Once you have it, you can control it to a remarkable degree, but it never goes away. There is no such thing as "a touch of" diabetes.

Adults suffer most. Type 2 diabetes is sometimes called adult-onset diabetes because it usually strikes after age 40 and is more likely to develop as you get older. One reason: Insulin resistance increases with age. In fact, more than 10 percent of people over age 60 have type 2 diabetes. But, as with other terms for diabetes, "adult onset" is becoming a misnomer because of the increasing prevalence of type 2 in kids.

Blood sugar is more stable. Because the pancreas still produces and releases at least some insulin when it's needed, glucose levels in the blood don't tend to swing as wildly as they do with type 1—even though, on average, unmanaged blood-sugar levels with type 2 are still too high.

What Causes Type 2?

The causes of type 2 diabetes have much more to do with lifestyle issues, particularly obesity. But weight doesn't tell the whole story. In fact, it's unlikely that type 2 develops because of any one thing. Instead, a number of factors appear to come together, potentially even magnifying each other, with unhealthy results. Among the factors that may come into play:

Genetics. Again, patterns in twins indicate how strong the genetic link is—and it's much stronger with type 2 than with type 1. In the case of type 2, if one identical twin has diabetes, the chances of the other getting it are as high as 75 percent. If one parent has type 2, there's a 20 to 30 percent chance the kids will develop it, too. (If both parents have type 2, the risk to children is about the same as that shared by identical twins.) This makes type 2 a serious concern for ethnic groups that seem predisposed to it—and those groups are not the same ones that are most susceptible to type 1. Whites are most likely to get type 1,

but type 2 is more prevalent among African Americans, Latinos, Native Americans, Pacific Islanders, and Asian Americans.

Inactivity. Physical activity improves the body's use of insulin. This happens for a variety of reasons. Muscle, for example, uses glucose more efficiently than other types of tissue, and exercise builds muscle. Unfortunately, the opposite is also true: Lack of physical activity makes cells more prone to insulin resistance. It also contributes to weight gain.

Poor diet. How much you eat matters. But what you eat is also important. And the fat-laden foods so common in the American diet are more likely to pack on pounds than comparable amounts of other, leaner foods.

Age. Type 2 diabetes becomes more common with age, in part because cells in older bodies tend to be more insulin resistant. But it's also true that people tend to become more sedentary with age. Their metabolism slows down, yet they eat just as much—or more. All of those elements are a prescription for an increased risk of diabetes.

Obesity: The Big Difference

Type 1 diabetes doesn't "look" like anything—there's nothing to distinguish a person who has it from anybody else. That's usually not true of people with type 2 diabetes, who are overweight or obese in 80 to 90 percent of cases. Being overweight is the single most important contributor to type 2 diabetes. It's no coincidence that the skyrocketing incidence of diabetes in recent years has been matched by obesity rates, which have doubled in the past 20 years. Having put on a few extra pounds doesn't automatically mean you'll get diabetes, but, according to the Centers for Disease Control and Prevention, more than 13 percent of Americans who are overweight have diabetes, while only about 3 percent of healthy-weight people do.

The potbelly peril. Not all flab is created equal, though. Research studies have made it clear that fat around the midsection—what scientists call visceral adipose tissue and the rest of us call a spare tire—contributes to diabetes more than fat located on the hips, thighs, or other parts of the body. To get an idea of your risk, just take a look in a mirror: If your shape resembles an apple (thickest around the middle) more than a pear (thickest below the waist), your disease risks are higher. It's not clear why this is true, but excess belly fat seems linked with high levels of fatty acids that contribute to insulin resistance—perhaps through processes involving the nearby liver, which stores glucose.

Other "diabesity" dangers. Diabetes isn't the only chronic disease linked to abdominal fat. A spare tire is also a critical risk factor for heart disease and a raft of conditions that go along with it, such as high blood pressure and elevated levels of such blood fats as cholesterol and triglycerides. In fact, obesity, insulin resistance, and risk factors for heart disease appear together so often, researchers are beginning to think of them as different expressions of a single disorder sometimes called syndrome X, or metabolic syndrome.

It isn't clear how the different components of metabolic syndrome affect one another, but in 2001 the National Cholesterol Education Program, part of the National Institutes of Health, for the first time defined how to diagnose it (see "Do You Have Metabolic Syndrome?" below). Using the new definition, researchers at the Centers for Disease Control and Prevention announced in 2002 that about a quarter of the population has metabolic syndrome. What does this mean to you? If diabetes goes hand in hand with heart disease, taking charge of your blood sugar can help protect you against both.

Do your genes make you look fat? Like diabetes itself, obesity seems to run in families. Scientists believe that genes play a role in how well hormones, enzymes, and other chemicals are able to control appetite by, say, signaling the brain to stop eating or establishing how heavy the body thinks it ought to be. Does that mean you're a victim of genetic fate and can't do anything

DO YOU HAVE METABOLIC SYNDROME?

According to the National Institutes of Health, you suffer from metabolic syndrome—and have a higher risk of both diabetes and heart disease—when any three of the following seven measures are true for you:

- Fasting plasma glucose: 110 mg/dl or more

- Waist size (men): more than 40 inches

- Waist size (women): more than 35 inches

- HDL cholesterol (men): less than 40 mg/dl

- HDL cholesterol (women): less than 50 mg/dl

- Triglycerides: 150 mg/dl or more

- Blood pressure: 130/85 or more

about your weight? Absolutely not. Genes may contribute to weight, but they don't tell the whole story. Some of the ethnic groups in which obesity and diabetes rates are highest, such as Native Americans and Asian Americans, are not historically heavy people. Only when they took up a high-fat, high-calorie diet and became more sedentary did they "adopt" obesity and diabetes, too.

You hold the key. If weight is such an important contributor to diabetes risk, that's actually good news because it's almost entirely within your control. You can manage your weight through diet and exercise—and you can control type 2 diabetes the same way. That may sound like a tough challenge, but it's an opportunity that type 1 patients don't have: to change the course of their disease just by making changes in the way they live.

Gestational Diabetes: A Disappearing Act

At first, gestational diabetes sounds innocuous. It occurs in about 2 to 5 percent of pregnant women during the second half of gestation (usually in the third trimester) as hormones guiding fetal development in the placenta interfere with normal insulin function. Basic symptoms mirror those of other forms of diabetes, but when the baby arrives, gestational diabetes—or GDM—usually goes away.

But don't be lulled into thinking that gestational diabetes is strictly temporary or isn't worth taking seriously. GDM increases the risk of miscarriage (although it makes a child no more likely to have birth defects or diabetes) and, because it often causes the child to grow large before birth, can contribute to complications at delivery. (Having given birth in the past to a child weighing nine pounds or more suggests you're at risk for GDM.) Just as important, most women who develop GDM do so because their pancreas is already weak (they're often overweight), making them vulnerable to getting full-blown diabetes later on—which occurs in a third to a half of cases.

SIZE MATTERS

According to the American Diabetes Association, you're at high risk for type 2 diabetes if you fall into the weight ranges listed below—even if you haven't reached the point of clinical obesity, as defined by the National Institutes of Health.

Height	At-risk weight (lb)	Obese weight (lb)
4'10"	129	143
4'11"	133	148
5'	138	153
5'1"	143	158
5'2"	147	164
5'3"	152	169
5'4"	157	174
5'5"	162	180
5'6"	167	186
5'7"	172	191
5'8"	177	197
5'9"	182	203
5'10"	188	209
5'11"	193	215
6'	199	221
6'1"	204	227
6'2"	210	233
6'3"	216	240
6'4"	221	246

THE KIDS ARE NOT ALL RIGHT

Type 2 diabetes is also known as adult-onset diabetes because it's a disease that starts in adulthood—that is, until recently. The past decade has seen an alarming increase in type 2 cases in children. Before the 1990s, type 2 accounted for less than 4 percent of diabetes cases in kids. Now it makes up about 45 percent, according to the American Diabetes Association (ADA).

Why is this happening? Researchers point to a dramatic jump in juvenile obesity. Today about 25 percent of American children are overweight—twice the number in the 1970s. In an attempt to clarify the diabetes risk to heavy kids, Yale researchers writing in *The New England Journal of Medicine* in March 2002 reported that, of 167 obese children and adolescents they studied, about a quarter were already glucose intolerant—one step down the path to diabetes.

"This is all very new, and we're still not exactly sure how to treat type 2 diabetes in children," says Sonia Caprio, M.D., director of Yale's Pediatric Obesity/Type 2 Diabetes Clinic. One emerging controversy is whether doctors should prescribe medications to treat kids who have type 2 diabetes or to prevent it in children who are glucose intolerant. Studies in adults suggest that drugs can significantly reduce risks, but the side effects of drug treatment in children are unknown. A National Institutes of Health study now being organized to examine the issue won't provide results until around 2008.

Less controversial are the benefits of addressing lifestyle issues that contribute to the obesity epidemic. "More food is available to children at any time of day than has ever been the case before," says Dr. Caprio. "We promote food consumption in kids, especially high-calorie snacks and soft drinks, which are available from vending machines in schools." Supersize portions are another problem. "Kids are used to immense servings in restaurants," she says. "They don't even think about it."

On top of that, children are far less physically active than they were in the past, according to Dr. Caprio. Because of distance and safety issues, children seldom walk to school, and physical education is losing ground to other curricula. According to the ADA, only 25 percent of high schools still have daily gym classes. Back at home, kids spend increasing amounts of time on sedentary activities, such as watching TV, using computers, or playing video games, says Dr. Caprio.

To counter these trends, she supports the decision by some schools to screen children for obesity and notify parents of health risks. The ADA recommends diabetes testing for overweight children with at least two other risk factors—for example family history, high blood pressure, or membership in an at-risk ethnic group (Native American, African American, Asian America, Hispanic American, and Pacific Islander). But parents are the real focus of change. "Parents need to learn more about proper nutrition and go outside to play more themselves—like most of our parents did 30 years ago."

Protecting Your Pregnancy

GDM isn't considered a severe form of diabetes, but it does require treatment, which is why obstetricians routinely test for it. In fact, blood-sugar goals with GDM are fairly tight—you're shooting for the normal glucose levels found in a healthy woman who isn't pregnant. Fortunately, this usually isn't difficult because the pancreas still makes insulin and glucose levels remain fairly stable. Your doctor may recommend that you:

▶ Ease insulin demand on the pancreas by spreading calorie intake out in smaller, more frequent meals. Of course, you still need enough calories to maintain a healthy weight.

▶ Lower blood-glucose levels with mild exercises like walking or swimming.

▶ Make use of insulin injections if you have trouble controlling blood sugar through diet and exercise.

Testing One, Two, Three

The most important thing to know about diabetes is whether or not you have it. Sounds like a no-brainer, doesn't it? But diabetes can take the smartest of us by surprise. And people with early signs of the disease need to monitor their condition closely because symptoms alone won't tell you if you've developed full-blown diabetes.

The American Diabetes Association recommends that everyone be tested for diabetes every three years after age 45—or more often if they face such risk factors as a family history of the disease. More testing is the only way to fix the fact that, of the estimated 16 million Americans who have diabetes, 5 million to 6 million don't know it. Millions more who are at risk for the disease and could stop it before it starts aren't taking preventive measures because they don't know they're in danger.

Fortunately, testing for diabetes is relatively easy and painless. All you need is one over-and-done blood test. The ADA suggests three tests that measure blood glucose in slightly different ways. Any one of them can give you the information you need.

Fasting Plasma Glucose Test

If you make an appointment to see your doctor today, this is the test he'll probably schedule for you. And scheduling is definitely necessary, because accurate results depend on your preparing for the test in advance.

How it works. First, you must fast for at least eight hours before the test, consuming nothing but water. That way, when blood is drawn, your gastrointestinal system has long since digested all food. As a result, your blood-sugar levels will be at their lowest ebb, providing the bottom measure of what's typical for you. If you're healthy, your reading will be 110 mg/dl or lower. If the reading is 126 mg/dl or higher, you have diabetes. If your reading crosses the line into a bad-news diagnosis, your doctor may want to repeat the test on a different day, just to be sure—though if your numbers are through the roof, this may not be necessary.

Why it's used. The fasting plasma glucose (or FPG) test is the preferred diagnostic tool because it's easy for both patients and doctors, it's relatively cheap, and it generally delivers consistent results—a nearly perfect balance of what you want in a test.

➲ **Take the test in the morning, not the afternoon.** When researchers at the National Institute of Diabetes and Digestive and Kidney Diseases (NIDDK) compared more than 6,000 morning test results with a similar number of afternoon results, the average readings differed by as much as 5 mg/dl. The researchers concluded that up to half the cases of diabetes that would be caught in the morning were being missed in the afternoon. One reason for the discrepancy: People tested in the morning typically go more than 13 hours on average without food, while those tested in the afternoon go only about 7 hours. The NIDDK is now suggesting that different diagnosis standards be developed based on when the test is taken.

Random Plasma Glucose Test

This test is also referred to as a casual plasma glucose test. Both "casual" and "random" refer to the fact that you can take the test at any time. No fasting is necessary.

How it works. The procedure is not very different from the fasting glucose test: Blood is drawn and sent to a lab. But when the results come back, the bar for diagnosis is higher because

WHAT THE STUDIES SHOW

A recent analysis found that women with menstrual cycles that are very irregular or long (more than 40 days) were about twice as likely to develop type 2 diabetes as women with normal periods. Obese women with irregular periods faced a nearly four-fold increase in diabetes risk. One possible reason: Women with menstrual irregularities are prone to polycystic ovary syndrome, a hormone disorder characterized by insulin resistance and thus linked to diabetes. The researchers advise women with irregular periods to reduce their risk with weight control and exercise.

it's assumed you may have had glucose from food in your blood. In healthy people, normal insulin response usually keeps blood sugar under 140 mg/dl even after eating. If a random plasma glucose test shows a blood-sugar level of 200 mg/dl or higher and you have such symptoms as fatigue, excessive thirst, or frequent urination, it's quite likely that you have diabetes.

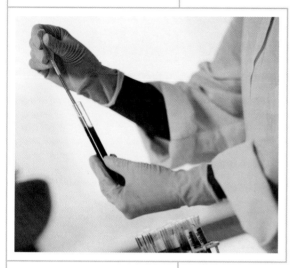

Why it's used. Because it requires no preparation, the random plasma glucose test is often done as part of routine blood draws. Your first hint at a diabetes diagnosis may emerge as the result of an annual physical and not from any special effort on your part.

➲ **Get confirmation.** Don't take a single positive result from a random plasma glucose test as the final word. Doctors will almost always insist on confirming such results using a more exact test designed specifically to detect diabetes.

Oral Glucose Tolerance Test

This test is regarded as the gold standard for making a clear-cut diagnosis of diabetes because it assesses blood-sugar levels under highly controlled circumstances, so the results are extremely reliable. But because it's so exacting (not to mention expensive and relatively time-consuming), patients and doctors alike sometimes find the oral glucose tolerance test, or OGTT, to be a less desirable one.

How it works. Again: you first fast for at least eight hours. But this time, that's only the start. When you get to your doctor's office, blood is drawn to provide a point of comparison for additional blood samples that will be drawn at one-hour intervals every hour for three hours. After the first blood draw, you drink a super-sweet solution containing about 75 grams of sugar (about three times sweeter than an average soft drink). Each subsequent blood draw helps plot out a picture of how your body handles glucose over time. Results are compared to a normal range at each measure, but the two-hour mark is especially critical: If your blood-glucose levels at that point are 200 mg/dl or higher, you have diabetes, final answer.

Why it's used. A more exact test is sometimes needed when results from other tests are less conclusive than your doctor would like. Let's say you have a strong family history of diabetes and are experiencing obvious symptoms but neither form of plasma glucose test has confirmed a diagnosis. Or a random plasma glucose test comes back over 200 mg/dl but you have no symptoms. In cases like these, your doctor will fall back on the gold standard for an unequivocal result. A version of the oral glucose tolerance test is also the preferred tool for detecting gestational diabetes, although the diagnostic criteria are slightly different for pregnant women.

➲ **Watch what you ingest before the test.** Because of the test's sensitivity, OGTT results can easily be skewed by foreign substances in the blood. In particular, let your doctor know if you're taking any kind of medication—including birth-control pills—or herbal or nutritional supplements, since they may boost blood sugar levels. For ideal results, some doctors recommend that you consume a lot of high-carbohydrate foods for three days before the test in order to mimic a standard diet.

Talk of Other Tests

The three tests summarized above (and in the box at right)—the fasting plasma glucose test, the random plasma glucose test, and the oral glucose tolerance test—are the trinity doctors commonly depend upon to make a definitive diagnosis. But you may have heard about other tests for measuring blood sugar. Some of these you'll read about in Chapter 3, but most are not—and in some cases, shouldn't be—relied upon to arrive at a diagnosis.

Glycated hemoglobin. Also called the hemoglobin A1c test, this is sometimes used after a

DIABETES BY THE NUMBERS

It's important to know for sure whether or not you have diabetes. Doctors make the determination based on any one of the following measures:

TEST: FASTING PLASMA GLUCOSE

What it does: Measures glucose in blood after an 8- to 10-hour fast

You have diabetes if: Your reading is 126 mg/dl or higher in two different tests taken on two different days

TEST: RANDOM PLASMA GLUCOSE

What it does: Measures glucose in blood at any time, including after eating

You have diabetes if: Your reading is 200 mg/dl or higher and you have symptoms of diabetes

TEST: ORAL GLUCOSE TOLERANCE

What it does: Following an 8-hour fast, measures blood glucose before and after you swallow a high-glucose solution

You have diabetes if: Your reading is 200 mg/dl or higher

diagnosis to get a better idea of your blood-sugar patterns, but it's most commonly used to monitor your condition as you continue living with your disease. Its main benefit: Rather than assess your blood sugar at a specific moment in time, it surveys what's happened with your blood-sugar patterns over two or three months by looking at glucose deposits on a specific type of cell. (See page 81 for more information.)

Urine test. Do doctors always have to use a needle? It's tempting to wonder why, if glucose appears in urine, they can't just measure that. High glucose levels in urine can indeed be an indication of diabetes. But the amount of glucose in the blood needed to raise glucose levels in urine varies from one person to the next, and sugary urine doesn't always correlate with high blood sugar. Bottom line: A urine test is not accurate enough.

Finger prick. Tests in which a small drop of blood is squeezed from a fingertip onto a special test strip that's read by a glucose meter are a mainstay of home monitoring that many people with diabetes know intimately. While these tests give reasonably accurate results for daily tracking, they don't offer the kind of precision needed to make a diagnosis that will affect the rest of your life. The American Diabetes Association has stated that these do-it-yourself monitoring devices are 10 to 15 percent less accurate than professional laboratory tests—a problem primarily attributable to human error. Older, nondigital devices in which the test strip is compared visually to a color chart are even less reliable. If a nurse-in-training gives you a finger-prick diagnosis at a health fair in your local mall, take it as a warning—then get to your doctor for follow-up tests to be sure.

WHEN TO TEST FOR DIABETES

Because risk increases with age, diabetes tests should be given routinely at three-year intervals for everyone starting at age 45, but they're not strictly reserved for older adults. The American Diabetes Association also recommends more frequent testing for younger people who are at high risk. This includes adults who:

■ are at least 20 percent above ideal body weight

■ have a parent or sibling with diabetes

■ are African American, Asian-American, Hispanic-American, Native American, or Pacific Islander

■ gave birth to a baby weighing more than nine pounds

■ had diabetes during pregnancy

■ have high cholesterol

■ have high blood pressure

■ have been identified with abnormal glucose tolerance

■ have polycystic ovary syndrome (POS), a hormonal disorder marked by insulin resistance.

To address the recent increase in type 2 diabetes among children, the ADA also urges testing every two years, starting at age 10, for overweight children who have two or more additional risk factors.

"Almost" Diabetes: Impaired Glucose Tolerance

The diagnostic cutoffs for diabetes seem so clear, so complete—and they are. However, there's a gray area in which blood-sugar numbers don't add up to diabetes but don't indicate normal glucose levels, either. This almost-but-not-quite state of affairs used to be called borderline diabetes, but some doctors don't like that term because it seems to dance around the critical yes-or-no question of whether or not you really have diabetes. Instead, in-between numbers are now considered a distinct condition called impaired glucose tolerance, or IGT—another way of saying your cells are becoming insulin resistant. You have IGT if:

▶ Fasting plasma glucose test results fall between 110 mg/dl and 125 mg/dl on two or more tests.
▶ Oral glucose tolerance test results at the two-hour mark fall between 140 mg/dl and 199 mg/dl.

Having IGT doesn't automatically mean diabetes is around the corner. Individual risks vary, with between 1 percent and 10 percent of people with IGT developing diabetes each year. What makes the difference? A strong family history or membership in an at-risk ethnic group raises your risk. But just as important, the more overweight and sedentary you are, the more likely it is that IGT will eventually turn into something more serious.

A chance for change. A diagnosis of IGT is really a window of opportunity; think of it as an early warning that not every person destined for diabetes gets.

The potential power of this opportunity was brought home with the publication of results from a major clinical trial, called the Diabetes Prevention Program, in early 2002. This study from the

National Institute of Diabetes and Digestive and Kidney Diseases tried two main approaches to prevent diabetes in people with IGT: lifestyle modifications—diet and exercise—and an oral medication (metformin) used to treat type 2 diabetes. A third group took placebo (dummy) pills instead of the real drug and made no lifestyle changes.

The result: Over the course of three years, people in the lifestyle group reduced their incidence of diabetes by an incredible 58 percent—about twice as much as those who made no changes, and far more than those who just took the drug. (Their incidence dropped by 31 percent.) These stunning findings show that taking action can reverse IGT and may allow you to avoid diabetes if you're at risk.

When Diabetes Becomes an Emergency

What if you simply decided to ignore your diabetes? Of course, you're not going to do that. But it's important to note that—while many complications of diabetes develop slowly over many years—blood sugar that's either too high or too low (due to treatment with insulin) can have immediate effects that may quickly prove dangerous and even fatal. Fortunately, these complications can usually be treated easily by either you or your doctor. And close monitoring of your blood-sugar levels can prevent them from sneaking up on you. Later chapters will discuss some of these subjects in more detail, but you'll better understand diabetes if you have a working knowledge of these three conditions.

Diabetic ketoacidosis. This is mostly a problem for type 1 patients, whose insulin deficit—barring treatment with supplemental insulin—allows no glucose at all into cells. In order to get energy, glucose-deprived cells instead start burning fat. The fat-burning process, however, produces highly acidic by-products known as ketones. When ketones build up in the blood (a condition known as ketoacidosis), they can cause shortness of breath, mental confusion, and vomiting. Eventually, diabetic ketoacidosis, or DKA, can put you into a coma and even cause death.

DKA is rare these days, thanks to insulin treatment and easy-to-use self-monitoring devices, but it's still a medical emergency when it occurs. To treat it, doctors immediately replace fluids to flush out acid and make sure you receive adequate insulin, which can quickly get you out of danger.

Hyperosmolar syndrome. This condition is somewhat similar to diabetic ketoacidosis in that it's caused by extremely high blood sugar. But it affects primarily people with type 2 diabetes who don't know they have the disease or aren't monitoring it effectively. With diabetic hyperosmolar syndrome (DHS), blood sugar becomes so concentrated it makes the blood thick and syrupy. As the body reacts by forcing sugar out of the body in the urine, you can become severely dehydrated and experience such symptoms as cramps, rapid pulse, confusion, and even convulsions and coma. Treatment involves fluid replenishment and insulin.

Hypoglycemia. Diabetes isn't always about high blood sugar. In fact, the most common acute complication of diabetes is blood sugar that falls too low—and that's what hypoglycemia is. It's most common in people with type 1 because blood sugar is most likely to drop from taking too much insulin. But hypoglycemia occurs in type 2 patients as well, when glucose levels ebb because of insulin or drug treatments, perhaps made worse by other factors, such as going too long without eating.

CAN DIABETES BE CURED?

Doctors often say you either have diabetes or you don't, based on your blood-sugar levels. But let's say you have type 2 and you do everything right. You change your diet, start an exercise plan, lose a significant amount of weight, and bring your blood-sugar numbers back to normal. Do you still have diabetes?

In one sense, type 2 diabetes can indeed be cured if all the measures that define it indicate that the condition at issue—high blood sugar—is no longer present. But this suggests that you can carry on with your life as if you never had diabetes—or that you won't have to worry about developing it in the future. And that would be a mistake.

Diabetes is considered a disease you have for life because, while you can keep it under control and live a normal life, the fact that you are controlling it is significant. The risk of having diabetes again never really goes away. If you were to stop controlling it—went back to a sedentary lifestyle and a poor diet—your diabetes would inevitably return. Even if you continue practicing your healthful habits, it's possible that your condition will change as you get older.

Think of it like parenting: Even when your kids grow up and move out of the house, you still have children. Likewise, even after you've managed to get your diabetes under control, you still have the disease.

Hypoglycemia is rarely life threatening in itself. But it's very unpleasant and potentially dangerous because its symptoms—including mental confusion, rapid heartbeat, sweating, and double vision—can severely impair your ability to drive a car, operate machinery, or do your job. Hypoglycemia must be dealt with immediately. Fortunately, most cases are mild and can easily be treated by getting some sugar into your system by, say, drinking a half cup of a non-diet soft drink.

The Agenda for Action

By now, two points should be clear. First, diabetes is a serious, complex illness that has the potential to degrade your overall health in a wide variety of ways. But second, it's well within your power to treat the underlying problem, prevent many—if not all—of the major complications, and live a stimulating, productive, and enjoyable life. In order to do this, you'll need to implement a big-picture plan in which you:

➲ **Become a control freak.** No, you don't need to obsess about your blood sugar. But studies have made it clear that using close monitoring to help you keep your blood sugar as near to a normal range as possible can dramatically reduce your risk of complications arising from diabetes.

➲ **Lose weight.** Just as being overweight is the biggest contributor to the vast majority of diabetes cases, dropping excess pounds is the single most important move you can make to assert control over your disease.

➲ **Eat smarter.** The right diet is the first step in controlling your weight. It's also a tool for managing your blood-sugar

SHOOTING DOWN DIABETES MYTHS

Considering all the factors involved with diabetes, there's plenty of room for misinformation. Some of the more persistent misconceptions:

Myth: If you develop diabetes, you can never eat sugar again.

Truth: People with diabetes can eat sweets, but sugary treats must be part of a careful meal plan (as they should be for people without diabetes).

Myth: I have just a touch of diabetes.

Truth: Either you have diabetes or you don't. Even if your type 2 case doesn't require insulin injections (type 1 always does), it still demands medical attention and careful lifestyle choices.

Myth: I feel fine, so my blood sugar's fine.

Truth: High or low blood sugar doesn't always produce symptoms. Regular monitoring is the only way to know for sure where you stand.

Myth: I'm a pro at self-management; checkups are just a waste of my time.

Truth: Your treatment program is never a done deal. Thanks to ongoing research, the medical community is constantly learning more about this complex condition and how best to deal with it. The best way to keep up is to keep up your regular doctor visits.

Myth: If I don't need insulin or drugs, my diabetes isn't serious.

Truth: Diabetes is always serious. Even if diet and exercise keep your blood sugar in check, your cells are still insulin resistant and your condition could get worse if you don't control it.

levels. This doesn't mean you have to stop eating your favorite foods or subscribe to an eccentric eating plan. Instead, you'll want to follow a balanced diet that provides a variety of foods in moderate proportions.

Get moving. Equally important to your weight and blood sugar is exercise. As with diet, nothing extreme is necessary. You just have to get your heart and muscles into action with moderate exercises that are relatively easy to do—and keep doing. Finding a routine you can stick with over the long haul is the key.

Take advantage of treatment. Insulin is an important—even lifesaving—beginning, but a wide range of other medications and treatments are available today that may even eliminate the need for insulin in some cases. While diet and exercise can go a long way, medical care can make the difference between slowing the progression of the disease and stopping it in its tracks.

In the following chapters, you'll find out how you can use all five of these strategies to bring down your blood sugar and help you lead a full and active life.

3

Monitoring and Measuring

Controlling diabetes is all about vigilance. You can't know if your blood-sugar levels are where they should be unless you check them regularly. The idea of taking several blood samples a day may seem dreary, but sophisticated tools make the task easier than you'd think, and they're getting better all the time. Along with results from other tests, your blood-sugar numbers are an all-important window on your disease and a key to managing it—and living with it—successfully.

Everything you do to treat your diabetes—whether it's exercising, eating a healthy diet, using insulin, or taking medications—all serves one primary objective: controlling your blood-sugar levels. But how can you tell if you're managing your blood sugar well? Some people rely exclusively on their symptoms to determine how well they're doing. For example, they watch for thirst and fatigue to tell them when their glucose levels are high, or trembling and dizziness to tell them when they're low. But gauging your blood sugar by symptoms alone is highly unreliable—and potentially dangerous. Blood sugar can easily soar too high or dip too low without sounding any obvious alarms, potentially leading to irreversible organ damage.

Fortunately, advances in blood-testing technology allow you to track your blood sugar in ways that weren't fully available to people with diabetes as recently as a generation ago. There are two basic methods, and both should be part of your management plan:

▶ Test your own blood at home (or anywhere else) using such convenient devices as test strips and blood-glucose meters—a method known as self-monitoring of blood glucose, or SMBG.

▶ See your doctor regularly for more comprehensive exams, especially a hemoglobin test that reveals blood-glucose patterns over weeks or months.

What you're after is crucial information, and the more precise it is, the better. The more you know about the way your blood sugar behaves under specific circumstances, and the impact it has on your health, the more power you wield—power to control your glucose levels and, in turn, your life as a whole. Working without this information is like walking in pitch darkness without a flashlight: It's tough to know when you're veering off course or heading for a fall. Conscientiously monitoring your own blood glucose—and following up with regular checkups—shines light on your diabetes, providing you with a clear perspective and allowing you to stride ahead with more freedom and confidence.

Worth the Effort

Without a doubt, regular monitoring and measuring take a certain amount of dedication and discipline. Some people find it difficult. A recent study of over 3,500 type 2 patients showed that more than a third never self-monitored their blood glucose. Yet numerous studies have shown that the people who fare best with diabetes are those who do the most to control their blood sugar with the help of careful monitoring.

One of the most important studies is the Diabetes Control and Complications Trial (DCCT), which ended in 1993. For 10 years, it followed more than 1,400 people with type 1 diabetes, comparing complications in those who closely monitored and controlled their blood glucose with those who took a less vigilant approach. The remarkable results: Close monitoring and control reduced the risk of developing eye disease by 76 percent, nerve disease by 60 percent, kidney disease by 50 percent, and cardiovascular disease by 35 percent. A more recent study in Great Britain called the United Kingdom Prospective Diabetes Study produced similar results in people with type 2 diabetes.

Inspired by these findings, doctors have developed a form of treatment known as intensive therapy, in which patients, particularly those taking insulin or other drugs, tightly control their blood sugar by carefully adjusting injections, food intake, exercise, and medications according to results from very frequent self-monitoring. It's a disciplined approach that may not be right for everyone (and in some type 2 patients, especially those not taking insulin, may not be necessary). But the idea that everyone with diabetes should monitor and control their blood sugar as best they can has gained wide acceptance. In fact, the DCCT and Great Britain studies show that any consistent reduction in blood glucose reduces the risk of complications.

No matter how much or little testing you do, every bit of information you gather is valuable. You can use this data to:

▶ See how different foods affect your blood sugar, allowing you to adjust your diet as needed to keep glucose in check.

▶ Detect (or rule out) hypoglycemia—that is, low blood sugar, the most common treatment complication—so you can deal with it quickly.

▶ Track the effect of medications so that you and your doctor can fine-tune dosages.

▶ Understand how blood-sugar levels swing when you're taking insulin or when you're sick, exercising, or drinking alcohol so you can take steps to bring them back in line.

▶ Provide your doctor with a history of day-to-day blood-sugar changes, allowing your entire medical team to give you better-informed treatment advice.

Setting Blood-Sugar Goals

What blood-sugar readings should you shoot for? The starting point is to recall what's normal. In people without diabetes, the pancreas releases just the right amount of insulin when it's needed, allowing the body's cells to sop up glucose from the bloodstream and thus keep blood sugar steady at levels that rarely fall below 70 mg/dl or go above 140 mg/dl, even after eating. When you have diabetes, blood-sugar levels can swing erratically from, say, the high 50s before a meal to around 500 mg/dl after eating—or points lower, higher, or in between, depending on the type of diabetes you have, how well your pancreas functions, and many other factors.

Your goal is to bring these wild swings under control and keep your blood sugar as close to a normal range as possible. According to the American Diabetes Association, you should strive to keep glucose levels at:

▶ 80 to 120 mg/dl before eating
▶ less than 180 mg/dl after eating
▶ 100 to 140 mg/dl at bedtime

These are average goals for adults that will probably work for you, but they may not be appropriate for everybody. For example, glucose targets for children are sometimes less stringent, while those for pregnant women may be tighter. Your goals may also depend on whether you're suffering from any complications. Bottom line: You need to work out objectives with your doctor.

How high is too high? The American Diabetes Association suggests that additional action be taken if your blood-sugar levels tend to be:

▶ higher than 140 mg/dl before a meal
▶ higher than 160 mg/dl at bedtime

These measures indicate that your blood sugar is too high even when you've gone several hours without a meal. You'll need to work with your doctor to decide what steps to take—you may have to work more closely with your medical team, start taking or adjust medication, or do more testing to get a better handle on your blood-sugar patterns.

What's the Frequency?

How often you need to test depends mostly on what type of diabetes you have and how you're treating it.

For people with type 1. If you have type 1 diabetes and take insulin, you're particularly sensitive to blood-glucose swings because, with the pancreas out of commission, you rely on your insulin injections to keep blood sugar in line. This dependence makes you especially vulnerable to hypoglycemia, so you should take blood-sugar readings several times a day, usually in tandem with insulin injections before each meal and at bedtime.

TAKE-CHARGE TIPS

Outside of your regular testing regimen, it may pay to do some extra self-monitoring at certain times to protect yourself from dangerous blood-sugar highs and, especially, lows. Consider taking additional self-samples:

➲ Before getting behind the wheel for a long drive on the highway.

➲ When you make a change in your diet, such as eating more or less food than usual at certain times of day.

➲ When you make a significant change in your insulin treatment.

➲ When you take a medication to treat something other than diabetes.

➲ Before you go into a meeting, make a presentation, or have a conference with your boss, clients, or colleagues.

A TESTING TIMETABLE

You'll need to work out a self-monitoring schedule with your doctor based on your individual needs, but these guidelines provide a place to start.

SITUATION	SUGGESTED TEST SCHEDULE
You have type 1 diabetes and take insulin.	Four times daily, before meals and at bedtime.
You have type 2 diabetes and take no insulin or medication.	Two times daily, when you get up in the morning and before dinner.
You have type 2 diabetes and take insulin.	Four times daily, before meals and at bedtime.
You have type 2 diabetes and take medication.	Three times daily, when you get up, before dinner, and at bedtime.

Why test before meals and not after? You already know food will make your blood glucose rise and that your insulin injection will handle it. By testing before the meal (and at bedtime), you can see how well the amount of insulin in your previous injection maintained blood-glucose levels between meals—the most important consideration. This doesn't mean you should completely ignore what happens after eating: Your doctor may also advise you to take readings after meals and, occasionally, in the middle of the night to gain added insight into your blood-sugar patterns.

For people with type 2. If you have type 2 diabetes, it's tougher to generalize about your testing needs. Talk it over with your doctor. If you're managing your diabetes with just diet and exercise, your blood-sugar levels are probably fairly stable and you may need relatively little testing—maybe twice daily, when you get up in the morning and just before dinner. (Avoiding tests is a good reason to do everything you can to manage your diabetes through lifestyle changes.) Once you understand your blood-sugar patterns, you may find that they don't change very much, and your doctor may let you scale back your testing even further—perhaps to three or four times a week.

If you're taking insulin, your testing schedule will probably need to mirror the pattern a type 1 person follows: four times daily, maybe more, depending on your situation. If you're taking medication, you should test at least twice a day. You may need to test more often, especially at the beginning of your regimen, when your doctor will want to track how the drug affects your blood sugar.

For people with gestational diabetes. If you have gestational diabetes or become pregnant when you have diabetes, keeping blood-sugar levels tightly controlled is especially important for both you and the baby. This means you'll probably have to test your blood often—including after meals.

Five Steps to Success

It's natural to want to see your blood-glucose levels immediately fall into a healthier range as soon as you start treatment. But while it's good to set ambitious goals, you also want to be realistic. Failing to hit your ideal blood-sugar goals may leave you feeling frustrated and even depressed, which can sap your motivation. To remove the failure factor:

1 Start with no specific goals in mind at all. Instead, just gather the numbers to show you and your doctor where your blood sugar normally falls and work from there.

2 If your typical range is excessively high, don't feel you have to aim for ideal numbers right away. If they're unrealistic for you, you won't meet them, which will erode your self-confidence and sense of control for the long term.

3 Work with your doctor to set goals that—even if they're higher than the average ideal for adults—are an improvement for you.

4 As you achieve greater control and start bringing your average blood-sugar levels down, consult with your doctor to set new goals, gradually working your way toward healthier numbers.

5 Don't expect to be perfect. Sometimes you'll get disappointing readings for no apparent reason—but it's the numbers that are bad, not you.

The Tao of Testing

Granted, the actual job of self-monitoring is not a lot of fun. New devices promise to make the task more pleasant someday in the near future, but for the moment, it's tough getting around the inevitable fact that you need to draw blood, and to do it you need to prick yourself—usually in the finger—with a sharp instrument. Still, most people with diabetes find that the process eventually becomes a no-big-deal routine. Here's how to do it.

1 Wash your hands before you prick your finger. Some doctors say this isn't crucial if your hands are reasonably clean because people almost never get infections from a finger prick. But washing is still a good idea in case there's something on the skin (sugar residue from a piece of chewing gum, say) that might throw off your results. Make sure you dry your hands thoroughly after washing, since excess moisture can also affect your results.

2 Prick your finger with a pinlike (but not all that painful) device called a lancet to draw a drop of blood. If you want to prick yourself at other sites instead, that's fine: The forearms and earlobes are sometimes used as alternatives. Most people, though, find the fingertips easier. One reason: You'll probably need to squeeze the targeted site to get a good drop of blood, and that's handy to do (literally) with a fingertip.

3 Let the droplet of blood fall onto the pad of a test strip or, if your meter has a built-in test strip, directly onto the meter's sensor. But avoid touching the pad with your finger because it may contaminate the strip with skin oils. (Some test-strip systems are designed to let you touch the blood to the strip if you have trouble keeping your hand steady enough for an accurate drip.) Follow the meter's instructions; with some meters, it's necessary to wipe the excess blood off the test strip.

4 Put the test strip into your blood-glucose meter (if it's not built in). Wait for the meter to make its calculations and—presto!—check your reading in the digital display.

5 Write down the number. You might find it easy to overlook this step, but it's probably the most important. If you're trying to develop a record and identify patterns, all the trouble you took to get the number isn't worth anything if you don't record it. Even if your meter automatically registers your results, it's a good idea to keep your own record. After all, anything can break.

FOREIGN POLICY

Americans never seem to measure things the way the rest of the world does. Miles instead of meters. Gallons instead of liters. Well, it's true for blood-sugar measurement as well. Americans use a system of milligrams per deciliter—metric, yes, but still out of step with the rest of the world, including Canada, which uses a measure called millimoles per liter. If you're traveling and your blood-sugar meter breaks, you need to consult a doctor, or you end up in the hospital, you may find it useful to know how to make the translation. To get the international value, simply divide the mg/dl number by 18. For example, average blood-glucose goals convert this way:

Before eating: 80 to 120 mg/dl = 4.4 to 6.6 mmol/L

After eating: less than 180 mg/dl = less than 10 mmol/L

At bedtime: 100 to 140 mg/dl = 5.5 to 7.7 mmol/L

Four Essential Testing Tools

This may sound odd, but there's never been a better time to have diabetes. One reason: There have never been more tools to help you monitor and manage your condition. The first self-monitoring tests didn't appear until the 1970s, and they consisted of test strips that indicated blood-glucose levels by changing into a color that you had to compare to a color chart for your result.

Anyone who's painted a room and found he misjudged the sample swatch will appreciate that a lot of guesswork could go into matching test-strip colors to color charts. This kind of color-match monitoring is still available and is useful in a pinch—say, if your digital monitor's batteries die. But for day-to-day monitoring, there's a better way. In fact, there's an array of devices to choose from. Don't be daunted by having to sort through them. Instead, rest assured that the basic task is not very difficult and the range of choices means you should be able to find equipment that will meet your specific needs.

Looking at Lancets

Technically, the lancet is the sharp instrument that punctures your skin, while the handheld unit that holds the lancet is called a lancing device. Lancets are disposable both for sanitary reasons and because they can get dull. Some experts recommend that they be thrown out after each use to ensure that you always use a sterile one, but many people with diabetes (including some doctors) think this is wasteful—not to mention expensive—and reuse their lancets. (An obvious point that's nevertheless worth making: You should never use somebody else's lancet.)

Many glucose meters come with a lancing device or even build them in, but you're not wedded to what the meter manufacturer provides. Instead, you should find an instrument that's comfortable for you. (Theoretically, you can use lancets by themselves, but a lancing device is not only easier to manipulate with either hand, it's less painful. The reason: Lancing devices are spring-loaded so that penetration is very quick.) Because your skin may not be as thick as, say, the callused hands of a construction worker, most devices allow you to make at least one or two adjustments to how deep the lancet penetrates your skin. Many people are partial to a model called the Softclix, which has 10 different settings.

A final word to the wise: Whichever unit you buy, you'll need to continually resupply your stock of lancets. Lancets are not always interchangeable from one device to the next, and costs can vary, so check out lancet price and availability before you buy the lancing device.

Buying a Blood-Glucose Meter

Meter technology and features change rapidly, and the range of choices can be bewildering. However, variety also means you should easily be able to find a unit that matches your particular needs and preferences.

Most blood-glucose meters work in one of two ways. Some are still based on a color-changing process in which glucose in

Manufacturers try to make every meter convenient, but what's handy for you might be an obstacle for somebody else. Here's how several major features stack up:

MAIN FEATURE	PROS	CONS
Built-in memory	Allows you to track your results over time. Some units also automatically average your numbers.	Some meters store as few as 10 readings—not enough if you test four times a day and see your doctor only once a month. Aim for at least a 100-reading memory.
Download capability	Can feed your readings directly into your doctor's database or into diabetes-management software, which can generate useful graphs and charts.	Unit may not be compatible with your doctor's software. May cost more than simpler meters.
It talks	A voice walks you through the self-monitoring process step-by-step to help make sure you use the proper technique for accurate results.	Annoying. Once you get the hang of it, the voice may prove unnecessary. May cost more than most silent meters.
Siphon-action test strips	Wicking blood up into the test strip is easier than dropping blood down onto it.	Test strips—the major expense in a glucose-monitoring system—may cost more.

the blood reacts with enzymes on the test strip. But now the meter goes on to read the intensity of the color and shows you a number in the unit's display window—no need to try to match colors by eye. Other meters work by detecting minuscule electrical currents created by the enzyme reactions, with the strength of electron flow depending on the amount of glucose present in the blood. Again, the results are displayed on the meter's digital readout.

To sort through the multitude of meters and find one that's right for you, check first with your doctor, who may steer you toward a particular unit based on experience, reports from other patients, or compatibility with his own record-keeping systems. Also find out if your health insurer requires that you buy specific meters. If you can, check out the annual resource guide in the December issues of *Diabetes Forecast* magazine, which is published by the American Diabetes Association and is available at many major chain bookstores or perhaps in your local health center's library. This guide doesn't recommend specific meters, but it does provide a comprehensive list of what's available,

METER MISCOMMUNICATION

Glucose tests your doctor does in the office (such as the fasting plasma glucose test) measure blood sugar differently than most home meters do. As a result, your home-based readings may be 10 to 15 percent lower than those your doctor comes up with. One set of numbers isn't better or more accurate than the other, but you should guard against confusion over the discrepancy, which—if you were to compare the numbers directly—could make you think that your glucose levels are better than they really are.

Why the difference? Many home-based meters measure whole blood—that is, blood that drips, unprocessed, straight out of your body and onto a test strip. Whole blood consists of several ingredients, including plasma (a fluid) and red blood cells. Lab tests at your doctor's office separate these elements and test only plasma for blood sugar. And blood sugar tends to be slightly more concentrated in plasma than in whole blood.

Some home meters now automatically translate whole-blood numbers into plasma numbers, but there's no need to worry if yours doesn't. When your doctor looks at your home-test numbers, he'll convert the readings so they're consistent and factor all this into your treatment.

along with information about all the units. When evaluating the choices, you should consider a number of factors, including:

Ease of use. Meters come in different sizes and shapes—some as small as credit cards—and you'll want to choose one that is comfortable for you to use. Some require bigger drops of blood for an accurate result than others do, which may be an issue if you have poor circulation. If you have vision problems, look for a meter that features larger displays.

The information you need. How much you need to know may depend first of all on which type of diabetes you have. If you're type 1 or type 2 taking insulin or medication, you'll probably be taking more readings than if you have type 2 and control your diabetes through diet and exercise. If you're testing a lot, you may want a meter that has a built-in memory to help you keep track of the dozens of results you'll accumulate between doctor visits. Some units also have data ports that allow you to download this information into diabetes-management software on a personal computer. On the other hand, if you're testing only a couple of times a day or even less, these bells and whistles may be superfluous.

Practical details. Points that seem trivial at the outset can become more important to you the more you use your meter. Some units, for example, use standard batteries you can find in any pharmacy or discount store, while others take less common (and often pricier) batteries that may be harder to find. Still others don't have replaceable batteries at all, so you have to get a new meter when yours dies. These units usually last for thousands of readings, but how many thousands will vary from one model to the next. Consider cleaning as well: Some meters are easier to maintain than others. Also find out how fast the meter spits out a reading: Most deliver in less than a minute, but the difference between, say, 40 seconds and 5 can seem significant if you're late for an appointment or on the job.

Cost. Most popular meters run in the $65 to $70 range, though prices can vary depending on features. Insurers will usually pick up the cost of a meter, but even so, manufacturers routinely offer deep discounts, rebates, trade-ins—even give them away free—to get a unit into your hands and move you ahead to the real expense: buying the test strips.

You'll find plenty of information about meters on the Internet but little in the way of objective reviews. In October 2001, however, *Consumer Reports* published its first evaluation of blood-glucose meters in five years. Of 11 best-selling units that were tested by a panel of diabetes patients and experts, 4 scored exceptionally well for ease of use, features, accuracy, and consistency. They were:

▶ The One Touch Ultra (made by LifeScan)
▶ The Accu-Chek Advantage (Roche Diagnostics)
▶ The Freestyle (TheraSense)
▶ The One Touch SureStep (LifeScan)

TAKE-CHARGE TIPS

Being a "good bleeder" is a blessing (strange as it sounds) that not everyone shares. If you find that getting blood out of your finger is akin to getting it out of a stone, try these steps to get the juice flowing better:

➲ Before testing, do some light exercise or take a warm bath to boost circulation to your fingertips. Or, if your hands are cold (which indicates low blood flow in your fingers), fill a basin with hot water and let your hands soak for a few minutes.

➲ If you have an adjustable lancet, set it for deeper penetration. There's no point trying

to save yourself pain with a low setting if you have to repeat the prick to get blood.

➲ Swing your arms to force blood toward your fingers, then dangle your arms at your sides and shake your hands.

➲ After pricking, don't try to squeeze blood out right away. Instead, hold your hand below the level of your heart and relax for a moment to let blood pool at the lancing site.

➲ As a last resort, try putting a rubber band on the base of your finger where it connects to your hand to prevent blood from flowing out—then take it off again as soon as you get the blood you need.

Replacing Test Strips

Test strips are an ongoing expense that can easily run to more than $1,000 a year if you test four times a day. (Usually, insurance pays the cost.) But they are the heart of the monitoring process. Most often, the strips are designed to work with your meter and are not usable with other devices.

When choosing your system, check first to make sure the test strips you need are readily available in pharmacies. Also find out whether your health-insurance plan limits payment for the strips, which can vary in price from 50 cents to almost $1 per strip. Choosing a pricier style of strip might put you over budget. Generic test strips are available for some systems, especially those based on color change.

Once you've started using your system, be aware that test strips have a limited shelf life; using them past their expiration date can give you inaccurate readings. When you buy replacements, you'll find them packaged in different ways—for example, individually or in packages of 50. Consider how often you use them. Bulk packages lower the cost per strip, but if you end up throwing some out because they expired before you could use them, it may be more cost-effective to buy the strips singly.

Logbook Enlightenment

Most self-monitoring systems "throw in" a logbook in which you can record your results, but it's not a throwaway item. Recording your blood-sugar levels so you can track patterns is one of the main reasons you self-test. If you don't like the log that comes with your meter, your doctor may have one that meets your needs better by, say, including space to write information about medication, insulin, or other tests. You can get new pages from your doctor or by writing to the meter manufacturer, using the address in your instructions. Or you can simply use a note-

TAKE-CHARGE TIPS

You can't completely avoid the nip of the lancet's tip, but you can minimize the discomfort if you:

➲ Use mild soap and warm water instead of alcohol to cleanse hands before testing. Mild soaps dry your hands less and ease stinging, especially if you tend to use the same site. Warm water brings more blood to your fingertips, making it easier to extract a drop.

➲ Use an adjustable lancing device so that you can set the penetration depth to match the toughness of your skin.

➲ Prick on the sides of your fingers, where there are fewer nerve endings but plenty of blood vessels.

➲ Finish up by putting a little bit of lotion on the prick site to soothe your skin and keep it moist and pliable.

book to record your numbers (although logbooks provide ready-made columns that may prove more convenient and legible). Whatever kind of log you use, the crucial thing is to get your numbers down on paper—including the date and time of each reading. Don't settle for just numbers, though. Remember, you're looking for patterns and associations, making yourself the subject of a little scientific study—and good scientists take lots of notes. Write down anything unusual about what you eat, how much you exercise, how sick you feel, how much stress you're under. These are the observations that even the best glucose meter can't store in its memory.

Bring your logbook with you when you see your doctor. She may not want to page through it all herself (especially if your meter downloads raw data into her computer), but if she has a question based on your numbers—"Was anything unusual going on two weeks ago Friday?"—your logbook might provide valuable clues.

Seven Steps to Reliable Results

To do their job, glucose-monitoring systems need to be accurate, but even more important, they need to be consistent. (Even if your readings are off by a certain amount, if you know this and the degree of error is always the same, you can still get a good sense of your blood-sugar levels.) To make sure you're getting reliable results, follow these tips:

1 **Calibrate.** Each batch of test strips you buy may have slight chemical variations from other batches, and these can affect your readings, so you need to match your meter to each set of strips before using them. Some meters do this automatically; others require that you go through a calibration procedure yourself every time you open a new box of strips. Check the directions for either your meter or your test strips to learn how.

2 **Check your strips.** If your readings seem off—strangely inconsistent from one day to the next or seemingly out of tune with how you feel—you may have a bum batch of test strips. Check the expiration date to see if they're too old and examine individual packages to make sure they haven't been damaged.

3 **Run a test.** Make sure your meter is accurate by periodically testing it with a solution whose glucose level is predetermined. If your meter is calibrated properly, its readings should closely match the expected result. (Most meters come with a control solution for this purpose, but if you lose it or run out, you'll find more at your local pharmacy.)

4 **Compare at your doctor's office.** Take your meter along with you the next time you have a fasting plasma glucose test at your doctor's office. The whole-blood reading from your meter shouldn't vary from the plasma reading by more than about 15 percent.

5 **Do a self-critique.** Are you the problem? Review the meter's directions and think about your technique. Is there anything you're doing that could throw off results? Are your hands clean? Are you touching the strip with your finger? Are you failing to mop up excess blood using materials specified in your meter's instructions?

6 **Check the meter.** Maybe your meter just needs a freshening-up: "Needs minimal cleaning" doesn't mean "never needs cleaning." Follow the directions regarding what materials to use (or not use) to clean the device, paying special attention to the slot where the test strip goes in. Then take the obvious but often overlooked step of checking the batteries to see if they're still fresh.

7 **Call the manufacturer.** If your metering results seem chronically out of whack and you can't resolve the problem on your own, call your unit's customer service hotline. In many cases, manufacturers will replace unsatisfactory meters at no charge.

Advances in Testing Technology

Self-monitoring technology has come a long way, but it's hard to be satisfied with a routine that's painful, no matter how much you might get used to it. Manufacturers have long sought ways to take the sting out of self-testing procedures and have recently made several advances. These don't necessarily eliminate the need for regular self-testing, but they can reduce the number of finger pricks you need or make them more comfortable.

Laser lancet. Instead of drawing blood with the sharp point of a pinlike lancet, a new device approved by the Food and Drug Administration (FDA) uses a laser beam to zap a small hole in the finger. Called the Personal Lasette, the device is available by prescription and is purported to be less painful than a standard lancet, although you can still feel it when the laser breaks the skin. The unit does have some drawbacks: It's relatively bulky, which made it seem inconvenient to panelists from *Consumer Reports*. But the deciding factor may be price: At last report, the device cost about $1,000.

Less-sensitive sites. Some meters require less blood than the globule you extract from your fingertip using a standard lancet, thanks in part to siphon-style (also known as capillary) test strips that you can touch to the blood. Because you don't have to squeeze out such a big drop of blood, the lancing devices that come with the meters (some units combine the lancing device and the meter into one product) allow you to break the skin in places, such as the forearm, that are less sensitive than the fingertips. Some diabetes-care professionals say alternate-site testing is less

accurate, though one such unit placed third in overall quality on the *Consumer Reports* list. The magazine's panelists reported that forearm testing was indeed a bit less painful but that blood samples were more difficult to get. The bottom line: Capillary test strips provide new options and make getting blood (especially from a finger prick) onto strips easier and less messy.

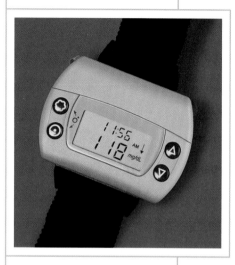

No-prick meters. The dream is to avoid drawing blood at all, and some devices have moved testing in that direction. The GlucoWatch Biographer, recently approved by the FDA, uses a sensor worn on the wrist to measure glucose as it's drawn right through the skin with the help of an electric current. Similar devices under development will draw out glucose using sound waves or chemicals. Still others will perforate the skin with tiny holes the diameter of a hair using lasers or a high-pressure blast of fine particles, then suck out the fluid surrounding the cells rather than blood for the reading. The GlucoWatch Biographer provides up to three glucose readings per hour for up to 12 hours and is useful for tracking trends. It can't, however, replace a regular meter altogether because it takes the watch 20 minutes to calculate a reading, and in that time blood sugar may change (especially if a medication is peaking in effect).

Implants. One new device, called the Medtronic MiniMed Continuous Glucose Monitoring System, logs a nearly continuous stream of information on blood-glucose levels through a sensor implanted under the skin. Over the course of three days, it takes a reading every five minutes, providing a complete picture of how your glucose levels behave in between normal testing times—even when you're sleeping. This data, which can be downloaded onto your doctor's computer, may help fine-tune your treatment or pinpoint problems that make it difficult to keep your blood sugar in line. Researchers hope they'll eventually be able to keep sensors in the body for longer periods without their being attacked by the immune system. That could pave the way for combined monitoring and insulin-delivery systems—in effect, an artificial pancreas.

Highs and Lows: Why They Happen and How to Fix Them

You wouldn't need to monitor your blood-sugar levels throughout the day if not for the inconvenient fact that they change. Figuring out what makes them go up and down is the key to keeping them under control.

Food: The Blood-Sugar Source

Glucose from food makes blood sugar go up within an hour or two of eating a meal, but the extent and speed of the rise can depend on what you eat and how much—and also on how insulin resistant you are. Testing will help you gauge your responses to different foods.

⊃ **Adjust your meal plan.** If the meals you've worked up with your doctor or dietitian fail to keep blood sugar under control, you may need to go back to the drawing board. You could be getting too many total calories in a sitting or eating too many sugars and starches—which raise blood glucose faster and higher than other types of food—at once. Mealtime monitoring will help you determine how your blood sugar changes in response

---

HANDLING HYPOGLYCEMIA

If monitoring reveals that your blood sugar has dropped below 70 mg/dl, your glucose levels are too low and you're in danger of hypoglycemia. Don't wait for such symptoms as mental confusion, rapid heartbeat, sweating, and double vision to occur before you act—they often don't kick in until blood sugar drops dangerously low. Instead, take immediate action.

Eat. Start by consuming 10 to 15 grams of a fast-acting carbohydrate to get glucose into the blood as quickly as possible. Examples:

- Three nonprescription sugar pills
- Two tablespoons of raisins
- Six or seven Lifesavers or jelly beans
- Half a cup (four ounces) of a regular (not diet) soft drink
- Half a cup (four ounces) of fruit juice

Rest. Take it easy for 15 minutes or so while the carbohydrate goes to work.

Test. Take another reading to see if your glucose levels have improved. If you're still below 70 mg/dl, eat another snack and rest again. Once your glucose levels have risen to an acceptable level but you have an hour or more before your next scheduled meal, eat another small snack (a few saltine crackers, for example) to help tide you over.

---

to what you eat, and this will provide your medical team with the information they need to guide you to better choices.

⊃ **Be consistent.** Using your monitoring data as a guide, try to identify foods that seem better at keeping your blood sugar within your target range. Then try to eat those foods in consistent quantities at the same time every day. The more you control the glucose going into your body, the more you'll be able to predict—and control—the rise and fall of your blood sugar.

⮑ **Limit alcohol.** If you drink, try to have only one or two alcoholic drinks a day, preferably with food. Alcohol lowers blood glucose, putting you at risk of hypoglycemia. And mixed drinks are usually high in sugar and calories.

⮑ **Consider medication.** If your meter readings indicate you're having trouble keeping your blood sugar in line through diet and exercise alone, you may be a good candidate for drug intervention, most likely with an oral antidiabetic drug, such as acarbose (Precose), as opposed to injections of insulin.

Exercise: The Glucose Gobbler

Moving your muscles revs the body's engine, boosting its fuel consumption. Result: Glucose levels tend to drop when you're physically active. Overall, this is a good thing, and monitoring can provide insight into ways in which you can strategically use exercise to lower your blood sugar. Be sure to work with your doctor to figure out how exercise should factor into your overall approach to diabetes management.

⮑ **Adjust your drug regimen.** Strenuous exercise can sometimes lower blood sugar for hours after your workout—even for as long as one or two days. If you're tightly controlling your glucose with insulin or medication, your postexercise monitoring may suggest that you lower your dosages to avoid hypoglycemia. Ask your doctor for specific advice with regard to your condition and activity levels in order to adjust your drug regimen accordingly.

⮑ **Tank up ahead of time.** If you're planning to exercise vigorously, you may want to eat more food earlier in the day or take less insulin to make sure you have enough glucose readily available to fuel working muscles. Aim to work out an hour or two after eating, when blood sugar will be naturally high.

⮑ **Keep well fueled afterward.** Depending on how strenuous your workout has been, it might be a good idea to increase your food intake for up to 24 hours after exercising to make sure blood-sugar levels don't fall too low.

○ **Use exercise as medicine.** If you're taking insulin and understand through monitoring how exercise affects your blood sugar, you may find that it's possible to use a workout essentially as an insulin substitute—specifically intended as a way to bring blood sugar down at certain times. (Talk to your doctor before adjusting your drug regimen.)

○ **Be alert to the unexpected.** Certain types of vigorous exercises—weight lifting, for example—that unlock glucose stored in muscles can make blood sugar go up rather than down. Your doctor can suggest how you might adjust insulin or drug treatments accordingly.

Insulin: Fine-tuning the Control

If you're taking insulin, the point is to keep blood sugar down, but hypoglycemia can occur if your injections bring your levels too low. On the other hand, you may experience hyperglycemia if your doses are improperly timed. Monitoring can help you figure out how to use insulin to keep glucose levels steady.

○ **Inject earlier to bring down highs.** Patients taking regular (intermediate- or long-acting) insulin normally inject it about 30 to 45 minutes before a meal. But if monitoring shows that your blood-sugar levels tend to be high either before or about an hour after you eat, you may want to add more time between injecting and eating to give the insulin a better chance to bring glucose levels down. You might also do some exercise for a similar effect. This advice does not apply to patients taking a rapid-acting insulin, such as lispro, which must be injected 15 minutes or less before eating.

○ **Wait a bit to raise up lows.** If your blood sugar tends to be on the low side 30 to 45 minutes before you have a meal, you may want to wait until you're closer to eating before injecting insulin to keep blood sugar from dropping lower before you've had a chance to get some food into your system. Again, this advice does not apply to people taking rapid-acting insulin.

○ **Add small snacks.** If insulin injections tend to produce hypoglycemia, you might want to eat a small amount of carbohydrate (such as a handful of raisins) around mid-morning and mid-afternoon to keep blood-glucose levels steady between meals. Or discuss with your doctor the possibility of adjusting your insulin regimen.

DID YOU KNOW

While most types of exercise lower blood sugar, some forms of physical stress, such as illness or even sunburn, can raise it. Be sure to wear sunscreen regularly, especially if you take certain diabetes medications, which can make your skin more sensitive to the sun.

Illness: You're Low, Sugar's High

Illness and the stress that sometimes precipitates it can boost blood-sugar levels by stimulating the release of hormones that work against the action of insulin and cause glucose to be released from storage sites in the muscles and liver. Naturally, you mainly need to treat the illness, but you also need to take some extra steps to keep your blood-sugar levels down.

⮑ **Drink more water.** If blood sugar is higher than usual, your kidneys are probably working harder and producing more urine. The result: You become dehydrated from the unusually high urine output. Therefore, keep yourself hydrated by drinking at least a cup of water every half hour or so.

⮑ **Avoid exercise.** Even if you think it might bring blood sugar lower, there's the possibility that exercise will cause the release of glucose from muscles. In any case, it's more important that you rest in order to fight the illness.

⮑ **Consider adjusting insulin.** If you're taking insulin, ask your doctor if and when you should take additional or increased doses while you're sick.

Morning: The Dawn Phenomenon

You'd think blood sugar would be low when you wake up. After all, you've gone an entire night without food. Often, however, blood sugar is high in the morning. The reason: Your body clock triggers the release of hormones that inhibit insulin so that more glucose is available to the body at the start of the new day. This is natural and not necessarily a problem. But if monitoring reveals that your blood sugar becomes excessively high in the morning, you may want to consult your doctor about what actions you can take.

⮑ **Take insulin later.** If you're using insulin and take an evening dose, you may find it works better to inject it closer to bedtime for longer-lasting control during the night.

⮑ **Skip the bedtime snack.** Try eating less food at night so there's not as much glucose in the blood when morning rolls around. You may also want to eat less at breakfast.

⮕ **Exercise in the evening.** Because the glucose-lowering effects of exercise can last for many hours, a workout shortly after dinner can help keep your blood-sugar levels under control the following morning.

Getting the Whole Story

Self-monitoring tells you a lot about how well you're controlling your blood sugar, but it doesn't give you the entire picture. Each reading you take is a snapshot that shows what your blood sugar was like at that moment. It could be different 10 minutes later. That's like knowing that a high-rise elevator was on a certain floor at a given moment when your real concern is that it should operate only within a certain range of floors. You need an indication of where the elevator is the rest of the time, too. That's where additional tests can help. The most important of these are:

Hemoglobin A1c. This test indicates what your average blood-sugar levels have been like over a period of two to three months, making it an invaluable tool. If you're taking insulin, your doctor may recommend that you take this test every three months; if you're not taking insulin, you may want to have it done every six months or so.

The test provides long-term results because it measures not blood sugar per se, but blood sugar's effect on a particular type of hemoglobin. Found in red blood cells, hemoglobin is a substance that carries oxygen through the bloodstream and clears away carbon dioxide. During red blood cells' roughly four-month life span, glucose gradually "sticks" to hemoglobin in a process known as glycosylation (the A1c test is sometimes referred to as a glycosylated hemoglobin test). The buildup of blood sugar in hemoglobin reflects how high your blood sugar has been on the whole during that time.

A caveat: Glucose attaches itself slowly, so any wild swings in blood sugar you might experience won't be detected—they'll just show up as tame-looking averages in this test. In other words, the hemoglobin A1c test doesn't tell the whole story, either. But together, self-monitoring and the A1c test provide a good overall view of your blood sugar.

Results from the A1c test are measured on a percentage scale that goes from 4 to 13. The American Diabetes Association recommends keeping A1c results below 7 percent. Be sure to discuss the meaning of your results with your doctor though: Different labs measure hemoglobin A1c in different ways, and results are not consistent from lab to lab. There's a movement afoot to standardize the numbers, but for now you'll need your doctor's guidance to interpret the results. You might also ask your doctor about a newly approved, pager-size device, available by prescription, that allows you to take hemoglobin A1c readings yourself at home.

Fructosamine. Like the hemoglobin A1c test, the fructosamine test looks at how much blood sugar builds up in components of your blood. But it uses proteins as a yardstick, particularly a protein called albumin. This test isn't used as widely as the A1c because the results are substantially similar, with one important difference: The fructosamine test measures blood sugar over a period of two to three weeks. It's a useful "bridge" between your short-term home glucose tests and the long-term A1c. Your doctor may order a fructosamine test for an intermediate check on your progress if you make a change in your insulin or medication, or if you're pregnant.

Four More Important Tests

While blood-glucose monitoring is a critical part of diabetes management, it's not the only way to keep tabs on your condition—and your risk of complications. These four tests provide important information about your diabetes and your overall health.

Urine ketones. If self-monitoring shows your blood sugar is over 240 mg/dl, it's possible you're at risk of ketoacidosis, the condition in which glucose-starved cells burn fat for fuel, releasing acidic ketones into the blood. A urine ketone test, which you can do at home, involves exposing a test strip to your urine. The results indicate whether ketones are present in your body. You should also do a urine ketone test if you experience such symptoms as deep or rapid breathing, nausea or vomiting, fever, or stomach pain. Ketoacidosis is a dangerous condition that's especially likely to occur in people with type 1 diabetes. If you get a positive result, call your doctor right away.

Lipids. At least once a year you should get this blood test, which measures a variety of lipids, or fats, in the blood that can raise your risk of cardiovascular disease when present in large amounts. Because people with diabetes have a significantly higher than average risk of heart disease, it's especially important to know your blood-lipid levels. The key lipids you're testing for are:

▶ **LDL, or "bad," cholesterol.** This waxy substance can accumulate and harden on artery walls, interfering with the flow of blood and eventually causing a heart attack or stroke. When you have diabetes, your LDL cholesterol should be 100 mg/dl or less, which is lower than the norm for people without diabetes.

▶ **HDL, or "good," cholesterol.** This beneficial form of cholesterol helps rid the body of the other form by scouring artery walls and ushering deposits of LDL to the liver and out of the body. High levels of HDL are good. (Don't settle for a test that gives you only total cholesterol, which won't reveal the critical ratio between good and bad cholesterol.) Your HDL should be at least 35 mg/dl for men and 45 mg/dl for women.

▶ **Triglycerides.** Most of the fat you consume is made up of triglycerides, a type of lipid that cells can store for energy later on. High triglyceride levels may contribute to hardening of the arteries. Yours should be less than 200 mg/dl.

WHEN TO TEST

To track your diabetes and its potential complications, you should have regular examinations that include relevant tests on this suggested timetable:

Every doctor's visit

■ Blood pressure

Once a year

■ Lipid workup (cholesterol and triglycerides)

■ Eye exam with pupil dilation

■ Urine microalbumin

Every three to six months

■ Hemoglobin A1c

As advised by your doctor

■ Fructosamine

Blood pressure. This familiar test—performed with a device consisting of a pressurized inflatable cuff that goes around your arm, an air pump, and a glass column filled with mercury—should be done every time you see your doctor. It indicates how hard your heart is working to pump blood throughout your body. If your blood pressure is high, your heart is having to work harder than it should, placing too much stress on your blood vessels. The complications that can result are similar to those of diabetes itself—including damage to the kidneys, nerves, and eyes. Blood pressure for people with diabetes should be below 130/85 millimeters of mercury (mmHg)—a two-part reading that reflects the force the heart exerts against the walls of the blood vessels when contracting (known as the systolic pressure, which is reflected in the high number of your blood pressure reading) and the residual pressure within the arteries between heartbeats (the diastolic pressure, indicated by the low number of your reading).

NUMBERS TO KNOW

Ideal blood glucose before eating: . . . . . 80 to 120 mg/dl

Ideal blood glucose at bedtime: . . . . . . 100 to 140 mg/dl

Blood glucose that indicates hypoglycemia: . . . 70 mg/dl

Blood glucose that merits a ketone test: . . . . . 240 mg/dl

A1c glycosylated hemoglobin target: . . 7 percent or lower

Low-risk LDL cholesterol . . . . 100 mg/dl or lower

Low-risk HDL cholesterol (men): . . . . 35 mg/dl or higher

Low-risk HDL cholesterol (women): . . 45 mg/dl or higher

Low-risk triglycerides: . . . . less than 200 mg/dl

Low-risk blood pressure: . . . . . . 130/85 mmHg or lower

Urine microalbumin. This test can detect kidney damage—a common complication of diabetes—at its earliest stages. The test looks for minuscule quantities of a protein called albumin, which normally remains within the bloodstream but shows up in the urine when the kidneys are having trouble filtering wastes properly. If you have type 2 diabetes, you should get a urine microalbumin test upon diagnosis and then every year after that. If you have type 1 diabetes and were past puberty at the time of diagnosis, you can wait five years after diagnosis before the first test because it's unlikely that your kidneys would have been silently damaged before that time.

A positive urine microalbumin result may qualify you as a good candidate for additional treatment—perhaps with a blood-pressure–lowing medication, since high blood pressure can narrow the arteries leading to the kidneys and damage the delicate blood vessels inside them.

PASSING THE TEST

Maggie Lopez, 41, had a family history of diabetes, so she knew she was at elevated risk. "When I noticed I was making frequent trips to the bathroom, and I was unusually tired for no clear reason, I made an appointment for a physical," says Lopez, of Port Orange, Florida. Not surprisingly (at least to Lopez, then age 37), blood tests led to a diagnosis of type 2 diabetes, a prescription for a glucose-lowering drug—and a wholehearted effort at self-education.

While gathering information from the Internet, Lopez read about the A1c test that reveals glucose buildup in hemoglobin over a period of time. "My doctor hadn't told me about the A1c yet—I asked him about it," says Lopez, who considers the test one of her most important tools for controlling her diabetes. Her first A1c result: a disturbing 8.9 percent, well above the recommended 7 percent. "That told me that I needed more than medication to control my diabetes," says Lopez. Having watched her mother suffer with numerous complications, including heart disease, she became determined to control her disease. While continuing to monitor her blood glucose each day, her goals focused on improving what, to her, was like a semester exam and report card all rolled into one: the A1c results. "I started taking changes in my diet and exercise habits more seriously."

A self-professed couch potato, she began using a treadmill and stationary bike, alternating gym days with 30 minutes of walking. She also took a hard look at the number of calories she consumed in foods like beans and rice—and decided she was getting too much of some good things. Once-heaping daily servings of rice, for example, she pared into a weekly ration.

"Six months later, my next A1c reinforced my work—it was at 5.7, which is better than normal," says Lopez. "I get the test every six months, and it continues to bolster my efforts."

Lopez is now something of a crusader for the A1c. "Every time I find out someone has diabetes, the first thing I ask is 'What's your A1c?' It seems to me that a lot of people just don't know about this test," says Lopez. One of her converts is her husband. He also has diabetes and keeps track of his A1c as well. "We don't use our dining room table for eating—it's covered with the glucose monitors we use for home and travel, plus our food diaries," says Lopez. "There are so many tools available to help stay on top of diabetes, and they're affordable. We just don't have any excuses for not using them."

4

Eat to Beat Diabetes

To a large extent, diabetes begins and ends with food, the body's glucose source. Having diabetes doesn't mean you can never enjoy your favorite dishes or desserts again. It does mean you'll have to strike a careful balance. By following a personalized meal plan, you'll cut calories, control your weight, and bring down your blood sugar. Systems like food exchanges and carbohydrate counting can help you make wise choices. Think of it not as a diet but as a permanent path to better health.

The fact that diet is a key part of managing diabetes is no surprise. After all, glucose comes from food, so it makes sense that what you eat plays a role in making your blood sugar go up. But you shouldn't think of food as the problem. Instead, consider it a big part of the solution.

Food as medicine? You bet. In fact, the right diet is such powerful medicine that, for people with type 2 diabetes, it could actually reverse the course of your disease. If you take insulin or other medication, it could help you reduce your dose or even eliminate your medication. For people with type 1 diabetes, the right diet can help you better manage your condition.

Fortunately, your food prescription doesn't have to taste like medicine. If you think having diabetes means a no-fun "diabetic diet" of flavorless meals, and all your favorite foods forbidden, think again. The truth is, a healthful diet for a person with diabetes isn't very different from a healthful diet for anybody else. Although for many years the medical establishment recommended a restricted diet for people with diabetes—especially when it came to sugar—research has shown that sugar is not the villain it was once thought to be. In 1994 the American Diabetes Association (ADA) loosened its dietary recommendations and expanded the options for healthful eating. The emphasis now is on choices—and some choices are better than others, whether you have diabetes or not.

Your "Eat to Beat" Game Plan

How do you eat to beat diabetes? The goal is to control blood sugar while getting the right balance of nutrients for great health. But exactly what that means for you will depend on a host of factors. To plot a strategy that will work for you:

⟳ **Consult a dietitian.** Your doctor can refer you to a registered dietitian, who will evaluate your current diet and make suggestions based on what, when, and how much you like to eat. Don't worry that a dietitian will only give you a list of rules and no-no's—a common fear. You may find instead that she actually provides you with more flexibility than you thought possible. For example, if you eat an ethnic diet that includes a lot of beans and rice—foods that raise blood-glucose levels—your dietitian can help make sure those staples remain a major part of your diet by, say, limiting per-meal portions or spreading your consumption out over the course of the day.

Many health-insurance and managed-care plans won't pay for ongoing consultations with a dietitian, but a diagnosis of diabetes will often allow you to schedule up to three visits. That's enough to establish a workable plan, which you, your doctor, and—per-haps occasionally—your dietitian can fine-tune as you go.

➲ **Keep a food diary.** Before you see your dietitian for the first time, keep a log of each morsel—no matter how small—that you eat every day for at least a week. Don't just simply note what you put in your mouth. Also write down where you ate a particular food and what you were doing at the time. Doing this will help your dietitian find patterns that may reveal the other "w"—*why* you eat. If, for example, you often go out with col-leagues after work, your dietitian won't want to eliminate this important social and business noshing, but she may suggest that you nibble on pretzels instead of beer nuts. Keeping a food diary doesn't help only your dietitian: Writing down what you eat will heighten your awareness of your eating habits, and this can help you recognize ways you can change.

For your diary, keep a small notebook handy throughout the day so you can jot down what you eat right away. Some people make their notes in digital planners like Palm Pilots. If taking notes at every sitting is inconvenient, you can try to reconstruct your food consumption at the end of the day; the record will be valuable even if you forget an item here and there.

➲ **Factor in your blood sugar.** Also show your dietitian your log of daily blood-sugar readings so she can compare your glu-cose levels to your eating patterns. Comparing the two will indi-cate how much your blood sugar tends to swing in response to food and will help determine when and how much you should eat. Some people with diabetes can manage simply by eating three balanced meals a day and cutting back on the empty calo-ries in sweets; others need to follow a more detailed plan speci-fying calories, grams of carbohydrate, or number of servings from different food groups.

⊃ **Put it all together.** Once you and your dietitian have a grasp of your eating and blood-sugar patterns, it's time to hammer out recommendations for specific foods you can eat at each meal or snack. This process is part negotiation and part analysis, and it involves other variables that have to be factored in:

▶ **Your weight.** The more excess pounds you carry, the more careful you'll need to be about what you eat.

▶ **Exercise habits.** Exercising typically makes blood sugar go down, so how much you do—and when—will affect the number of calories you should take in at each meal.

▶ **Insulin use.** If you're type 1, the content and timing of your meals should consistently balance the amount of insulin circulating in your blood from injections. If you're type 2 and using insulin, you'll need to factor this in on top of variables (such as weight and exercise) that affect insulin resistance.

▶ **Medication use.** Which medication you take, how much, and when its action peaks may affect your dietary choices. If you have type 2 diabetes, getting off medication may be a realistic goal for your meal plan.

▶ **Special considerations.** Be sure to inform your dietitian of results of tests for lipids (such as cholesterol), blood pressure, and microalbumin (for kidney function). If you already suffer such complications as poor cholesterol ratios, high blood pressure, and kidney damage, you may need to follow guidelines that specifically deal with those conditions, such as eating even less saturated fat, cutting back on salt, or avoiding excessive amounts of protein.

⊃ **Consistency is key.** Once you've developed a plan, you'll keep your blood sugar more stable if you eat about the same amount of food with the same balance of nutrients at about the same times each day. Don't figure you can be "bad" on some days as long as you're "good" on others: Eating in erratic patterns only causes blood sugar to seesaw. Instead, try to come up with a meal plan you can live with all the time.

⊃ **How's it working?** Self-monitoring your blood sugar will give you and your doctor a sense of how well you're able to control it with diet. From there, you can fine-tune your plan of attack by tinkering with your meal plan or changing your activity level, insulin dosage, or other variables. If you're type 2 and you're having trouble keeping your blood sugar in line through diet and exercise, that may mean you're a candidate for insulin or drug intervention. On the other hand, if you've succeeded at losing weight and controlling your blood sugar through diet and exercise, you may be able to stop taking insulin or medication.

Remember: Calories Count

If you have type 2 diabetes, how much you eat is just as important as what you eat—maybe more so. That's because one of the most significant goals of your diet plan will be to lose weight. To help you accomplish that, your dietitian will want to establish right away the number of calories you should eat in one day.

Weight control is essentially an energy-management issue that involves a simple law of thermodynamics: To maintain your current weight, you must take in only as much energy—measured in calories—as you burn. If you want to lose weight, on the other hand, you have to take in fewer calories, burn more calories, or both.

Dropping pounds is essential for people with type 2 diabetes because the more fat you carry on your body, the more your cells become resistant to insulin. When you lose excess weight, your cells' response to insulin actually improves, and they become better able to take in glucose and remove it from your blood. Just as vital, losing weight reduces your risk of cardiovascular disease by lowering blood pressure and improving your ratio of good to bad cholesterol.

A major clinical trial published in early 2002 clearly proved the importance of weight loss. Called the Diabetes Prevention Program, it studied more than 3,200 adults at 27 medical centers who had impaired glucose tolerance and therefore were at high risk of developing full-blown diabetes. Some of the subjects were given the blood sugar–reducing drug metformin (Glucophage), while others were put in a weight-loss group whose goal was to drop 7 percent of their excess weight. (A third group got a placebo.) The big news: The drug was helpful, reducing the risk of developing diabetes by 31 percent, but the weight-loss results blew the drug numbers away, reducing diabetes risk by an astounding 58 percent.

Studies suggest that you can make significant gains in blood-sugar control by losing as little as 5 percent of your body weight. For a person who weighs 175 pounds, that's between 8 and 9 pounds—a goal easily attained, especially if you combine dietary measures with exercise.

How Many Calories Should You Eat?

Everybody's calorie needs are different and based on a variety of factors, including how overweight you are, your body's metabolism, and your activity level. Your dietitian will come up with a calorie goal for you, but you can get a ballpark idea of how many calories you need to maintain your current weight by using the "Rule of 10."

Step 1: Multiply your weight by 10. For example, if you weigh 175 pounds, you get 1,750 calories. This is approximately how many calories your body needs to function when it's idle.

Step 2: To fill in roughly how many calories you're burning through physical activity, rate yourself on the following scale:

> ▶ If you're totally sedentary, give yourself a 3.
> ▶ If you're moderately active, give yourself a 5.
> ▶ If you're very active, give yourself a 7.

Step 3: Now take the number you chose and multiply it by 100, then add the result to the number from Step 1. For example, if your Rule-of-10 result is 1,750 calories and you're sedentary, add 300 (that is, 3 times 100) to 1,750 to get a total of 2,050 calories per day. Keep in mind that this is only a rough estimate. Figures for men and women, for example, will differ because men tend to have more metabolically active muscle.

So how many calories do you need to eat in order to lose weight? Consider this fact: A pound of fat contains about 3,500 calories. Obviously, this is not an amount you can expect to lose overnight—or even in a week. But a slow and steady calorie deficit that you achieve with diet and exercise can gradually trim away those unwanted pounds.

7 DIET MYTHS

Weight loss can be difficult, no thanks to popular misconceptions that have the ring of truth but can actually work against you. Among the more common myths:

❶ DESSERTS ARE FORBIDDEN

The truth is, there's room in your diet for any kind of food, especially the ones you love most—as long as you control your total caloric intake (and grams of carbohydrate, if you tally them). Denying yourself your favorite foods can lead to binge eating and, ultimately, discouragement.

❷ YOU HAVE TO LOSE A LOT OF WEIGHT TO MAKE A DIFFERENCE

The closer you can get to an ideal weight, the better, but small, sustained improvements at the beginning of a weight-loss program have the biggest impact on your health. Studies show that losing just 5 to 10 pounds can improve insulin resistance enough to allow some people with type 2 diabetes to quit medication or injections.

❸ WHAT YOU EAT MATTERS MORE THAN HOW MUCH

Both matter, but recent research finds that the number of calories in your food is more important than where they come from. Example: A bagel might seem healthier than a doughnut hole, but dense bagels have the calo-rie content of six slices of bread. As long as you're not eating too much fat in other foods, the doughnut hole wins.

❹ IF YOU WORK OUT, YOU CAN EAT WHATEVER YOU WANT

That's robbing Peter to pay Paul. You can't lose weight if you reduce calories in one way but increase them in another.

❺ SKIPPING MEALS MAKES YOU LOSE WEIGHT FAST

Actually, studies show that people who skip breakfast tend to be heavier than people who don't. And skipping meals tends to make you overeat later. If you have diabetes, it's important to keep up a steady intake of small portions of food throughout the day to keep your blood-sugar levels stable and reduce the risk of hypoglycemia.

❻ STARCHES ARE FATTENING

If you are insulin resistant, your body may find it easier to convert carbohydrate calories to fat than to burn it as energy, but the

fact remains that starches (and other carbohydrates) are less dense in calories gram for gram than other types of food. The main issue is calories, so if you load starchy foods with fat—sour cream and butter on a baked potato, for instance—or eat them in large quantities, the caloric load can add up.

❼ YOU SHOULD NEVER EAT FAST FOOD

Never say never. Fast food can be worked into your meal plan if you choose well. Opt for grilled foods instead of fried, avoid or scrape away high-fat condiments like mayonnaise, and share those French fries to keep portion size down.

What's on the Menu?

Surprisingly, all of the foods you eat, from apples to zucchini, fall into only a handful of basic nutrient categories that make up the building blocks of your diet. While total calories are a major consideration, it also matters which building blocks those calories are made of. Why? Because while food raises your blood sugar within an hour or two of eating, the height and speed of that increase depends on both how much and what types of foods you consume.

Should You Cut Back on Carbohydrates?

That would seem to make sense. After all, the major types of carbohydrate—sugars and starches—both break down into glucose and are the main source of blood sugar, making them an important target of dietary control. But carbohydrates are also the body's primary source of energy, so they play a critical part of any healthy diet. According to the American Diabetes Association, carbohydrates should account for up to 60 percent of your total diet. Why so much? It's mainly a calorie issue. One gram of carbohydrate contains only four calories, while a gram of fat contains nine calories. That means, gram for gram, you can eat more than twice as much carbohydrate as fat for the same number of calories. A carb-based diet allows you to eat larger quantities of food and therefore a greater variety of foods (both nutritionally and taste-wise) even if you're restricting your total calories.

But shouldn't sugars be avoided? The answer is yes, but only because they often come in packages that are high in fat and low in vitamins and minerals: desserts, candies, and baked goods, for instance. Otherwise, there's nothing inherently wrong with sugars (sometimes called simple carbohydrates because their chemical structure consists of only a few molecules that are easily broken down during digestion). Milk contains sugar (called lactose) and so does fruit (fructose), and there's no reason to ban these foods. There's even room for sucrose (table sugar) and sweets in your diet, as long as you eat them in small amounts.

That makes starches, or complex carbohydrates, the main staple of your diet. Starches lack the sweetness of sugars but are found in some of the most nutritious foods you can eat, including beans, potatoes, pasta, rice, whole-grain breads and cereals, and vegetables like broccoli, carrots, corn, and peas. Starches not only are energy powerhouses, they're rich in vital nutrients, such as vitamins and minerals.

Counting Carbs: An Easy Solution

One of the most useful tools for controlling your caloric intake and blood sugar at the same time is carbohydrate counting. This method has recently become a favorite of dietitians since researchers discovered that all types of carbohydrates, whether sugars or starches, are converted into glucose and released into the blood at about the same rate—within an hour or so of eating. (Fat and protein are eventually broken down into glucose too, only at a much slower rate.) So the level of glucose in the blood after a meal is determined primarily by the amount (not the type) of carbohydrate consumed.

This makes following a meal plan relatively easy because you can control the amount of glucose entering your body by simply counting the grams of carbohydrate you ingest—information that's printed on every package of food you buy. This approach is particularly useful to people with type 1 diabetes or those with type 2 who must take insulin because it allows more precise matching of insulin doses to glucose intake.

To start you out on a carbohydrate-counting plan, your dietitian will first come up with the number of carbohydrates that you should eat at every meal and snack based on your individual calorie needs. Ideally, carbohy-

CAN I EAT ALL THE SUGAR-FREE FOODS I WANT?

You'd think sugar-free foods like candy and soft drinks would have less impact on blood-glucose levels than regular candy or soft drinks. But you can't eat sugar-free foods with impunity.

The reason: Common sweeteners, such as maltodextrin, sorbitol, and xylitol, may not be sucrose (the technical name for regular sugar), but they do contain carbohydrate, each gram of which can raise blood glucose just as much as sugar does. Nonnutritive sweeteners like aspartame contain no carbohydrate or calories, but products that contain these sweeteners (such as yogurt and soft drinks) might.

The best advice: Pay no attention to "sugar-free" claims on the packaging. Look instead at a product's total carbohydrate count.

GETTING YOUR FILL OF FIBER

While food labels list grams of fiber for processed and packaged products, don't worry about "counting fiber" to get the recommended 25 to 30 grams per day. It's much better (and easier) to simply work as many grains, beans, and fresh fruits and vegetables into your diet as you can. Here are some smart strategies:

■ **Bump up beans.** Whether dried or canned, beans and other legumes are among the best fiber sources you can find. For example, half a cup of black beans provides about a quarter of your recommended daily fiber intake.

■ **Hail the whole.** Whole-grain foods contain far more fiber than more processed foods, in which such fiber-containing grain parts as the bran are thrown out. For example, whole-grain bread contains about twice the fiber as bread made with refined flour.

■ **Preserve the peel.** Routinely thrown away, the peel is often the most fiber-filled part of a fruit or vegetable. You're better off eating apples, carrots, and potatoes with the peel still on (be sure to wash them first if you eat them raw).

■ **Savor stems.** We also often toss out the stalky stems of vegetables like asparagus and broccoli, but that's where the plant's fiber is most densely concentrated. To make them less tough, chop the stalks into small pieces and cook them a bit longer, adding the florets slightly later.

■ **Use fibrous fixings.** Products like bran cereal, oat bran, and wheat germ make good condiments when sprinkled over oatmeal (which is high in fiber itself), applesauce, cottage cheese, or salads. In recipes that call for bread crumbs, try substituting oats.

drate should make up 50 to 60 percent of your daily calorie intake. You then have flexibility in choosing the foods you like in order to hit your target. A similar program of fat-gram counting can be helpful for people with type 2 diabetes who are trying to lose weight.

Your dietitian can provide carb-counting food lists, or you can find more extensive lists in books. But a general rule of thumb is that one serving of starch, fruit, or milk contains about 15 grams of carbohydrate; vegetables, 5; and meat and fats, none. Unfortunately, that doesn't mean you can load up on meat or eat the same three carbohydrates at every meal; you still need to aim for variety and balance. Try to spread your carbohydrate intake evenly throughout the day so the amount of glucose released into your blood is fairly consistent from meal to meal.

Why You Need Fiber

Fiber, an indigestible complex carbohydrate found in plant foods, such as bran, broccoli, oatmeal, and whole grains, should be part of your diet for a number of reasons—primarily because it slows the rise of blood sugar after a meal. Soluble fiber (one of two main types, found in oats, citrus fruits, and other foods) mixes with food and water to form a gooey gel that slows digestion and makes blood sugar enter the bloodstream more gradually. In one study, people with type 2 diabetes who got 50 grams of fiber in their diet every day for six weeks (after starting with six weeks of 25 grams, the amount recommended for the general population) brought their blood-sugar levels down by about 10 percent. In addition to lowering blood sugar, soluble fiber helps lower cholesterol, reducing your risk of cardiovascular disease. Insoluble fiber (the other type) improves overall digestive function by helping waste move through your system. What's more, fiber adds bulk to food, which makes you feel full without adding a single calorie.

Factoring in Fat

Fat is usually seen as a dietary evil, mainly because it's so dense in calories and a known contributor to heart disease. But fat also has important roles to play in the body, such as helping to form cell membranes, distributing fat-soluble vitamins, and insulating the body against heat loss. And there's an upside to fat for diabetics: It slows the digestion process, which means that glucose enters the blood more gradually. As a result, fat should play a bigger role in your diet than you might assume—making up as much as 25 to 30 percent of total calories.

But watch out—there's a caveat. The type of fat you eat makes a difference. According to the American Diabetes Association's 2002 dietary recommendations, less than 10 percent of your diet should consist of the kind of fat we're likely to eat most—saturated fat. Found in animal-based foods like meat and eggs and in dairy products like butter, saturated fat tends to raise levels of LDL ("bad") cholesterol and is associated with an increased risk of cardiovascular disease, thus magnifying the metabolic problems that worsen diabetes. What's more, foods that contain saturated fat are often loaded with cholesterol, which can also raise LDL levels.

CAUTION

Foods like beans and broccoli are notorious for producing gas in the intestines, but the effect is temporary and your body will adjust if eating more fiber becomes a habit. Meanwhile, you may feel more comfortable if you add fiber gradually over a period of weeks to give your system a chance to get used to it. Start by adding about 5 grams a day (about the amount in half a cup of kidney beans) until you reach the 25- to 30-gram daily target. Your body will also handle added fiber more effectively if you drink more water.

TEN TOP WAYS TO TRIM THE FAT

Fat is a beloved dietary staple because it's both tasty and versatile: It can be creamy, crunchy—and sometimes both at once (think fried ice cream). But while no one needs to forgo all of fat's pleasures, a lot of the fat in our diet comes hidden (and unbidden) in cooking or eating habits that can easily be changed without sacrificing taste.

1 CHOOSE LEANER LOINS

Oddly enough, "prime" meats are the ones you should avoid; they're loaded with saturated fat. The leanest grade is "select," followed by "choice." Lean cuts include flank steak, top round, and pork tenderloin.

2 CHILL OUT

Trimming obvious fat from meat quickly carves off lots of saturated fat. To do it better, put meat in the freezer for 20 minutes first; this will firm up the meat for closer cutting and make marbled fat more visible. When preparing soups or stocks, chill broth overnight and skim congealed fat from the surface.

3 GO FOR SAVORY SNACKS

Salty snacks like potato and tortilla chips can have as much saturated fat content as beef. Better options: low-fat chips, pretzels, or fresh-cut vegetables with salsa.

4 SWITCH TO SKIM

Whole milk gets almost half its calories from fat, while fat-free milk has almost no fat and fewer calories. If you don't like the taste of skim, blend varieties to start, progressively adding fat-free milk as you get more used to it. And use fat-free in recipes.

5 USE SPRIGHTLY SPREADS

Try low-fat versions of peanut butter, cream cheese, and other spreads or, better yet, use lower-fat alternatives like fruited yogurt, cottage cheese, honey, and jam.

6 SKIN YOUR CHICKEN

About half the fat in poultry is concentrated in the skin, which you can leave on while cooking to keep the meat moist but remove before eating—especially if you like drumsticks, which contain more than twice the fat of chicken breast, even with the skin off.

7 TAKE ADVANTAGE OF TEFLON

Why use butter or margarine to keep food from adhering to frying pans when nonstick pans eliminate the need? If you still want to coat the pan, use a cooking spray.

8 RETIRE THE FRYER

Even with healthier oils, frying adds fat calories you can do without. Better bets are baking

and broiling, which add little fat and bring out the flavor of beef, poultry, fish, and hearty vegetables like peppers and eggplant.

9 MIX YOUR MEATS

When recipes call for ground beef, cut the amount in half and bulk up the meat by substituting lower-fat ground turkey or shredded vegetables, such as onions, carrots, and green peppers.

10 REPAIR THE RECIPE

When baking foods like breads, cakes, muffins, and brownies, try using only half the amount of fatty ingredients like butter and oil and substituting an equal amount of applesauce or pureed fruit, such as prunes.

But if you eat only small amounts of saturated fat (easily recognized because it usually stays solid at room temperature), where should the rest of your fat calories come from?

The answer is monounsaturated and polyunsaturated fats, neither of which raise your levels of bad cholesterol. Monounsaturated fat is especially recommended because it actually raises levels of good cholesterol, making it the best source of fat in your diet. (Polyunsaturated fat, found in such foods as corn oil, safflower oil, and mayonnaise, ranks second because it's been shown to lower levels of good cholesterol.)

According to the ADA, monounsaturated fat may also reduce insulin resistance.

These fats are so good for you that the ADA says either monounsaturated fat or carbohydrates can be eaten in place of saturated fat. In fact, either one can make up as much as 60 to 70 percent of your total calories. This allows you even more

GREAT SOURCES OF GOOD FATS
- Olive oil
- Canola oil
- Peanuts and peanut oil
- Almond
- Avocados

latitude when planning your meals, especially if you eat an ethnic diet. For example, a person who eats an Asian diet may prefer a diet high in carbohydrates like rice, while someone who eats a Mediterranean diet may want more calories from foods like olive oil. Both are allowed. But remember: Even monounsaturated fat is rich in calories, so don't go overboard, especially if you're trying to lose weight.

Last and Perhaps Least: Protein

Getting the right amount of protein isn't difficult if you're already controlling your fat and carbohydrate balance—protein will account for the rest of your calories. You need protein to build and repair tissues and ensure the proper functioning of hormones, immune-system cells, and hardworking enzymes throughout the body. But it doesn't have to be the major dietary staple many people assume it should be. In fact, for most people with diabetes, only 10 to 20 percent of calories should come from protein. You can easily get all you need in just a few

servings of protein-rich foods, such as meats, fish, dairy items, and plant foods like beans, nuts, and soy products. Smaller amounts are also found in vegetables and grains.

Most Americans already get far more protein than necessary, which raises issues when you have diabetes. One concern is that because the body excretes excess protein, eating more than you need makes your kidneys work harder. Diabetes already increases your risk of kidney damage, and some doctors believe that eating too much protein can lead more quickly to kidney complications. A number of studies have suggested that this is the case, but a large study reported in *The New England Journal of Medicine* in 1994 found that a high-protein diet didn't impair kidney function any faster than a low-protein diet. Because the kidney question remains unresolved, doctors and dietitians are cautious about your taking in more than the recommended amount of protein.

When you do eat protein, about a third to half of it is converted to glucose for energy—far less than carbohydrates but more than fat. Protein is digested slowly compared to carbohydrates, causing a more gradual rise in blood sugar.

The Low-Carb Controversy

Not everyone agrees with the generally accepted recommendations about what your diet should look like. In fact, proponents of a number of popular diets argue that the picture is upside down for people with diabetes. If carbohydrates produce the largest and fastest increases in blood sugar, the argument goes, it doesn't make sense to eat more of them than of anything else. What's more, critics note, eating a lot of carbohydrates can contribute to obesity (as can eating too much of anything).

But if you take this message to heart and cut back on carbs, what should replace them? The answer, inevitably, is protein or fat, particularly monounsaturated fat. Proponents of alternative eating plans say that, contrary to popular opinion, people with diabetes can lose weight on such diets and keep blood sugar more stable. The popularity of the low-carb approach suggests that it works for some people—or at least appeals to their desire to eat more bacon, eggs, meat, and other favorites. But the consensus in the medical community is that you should view low-carbohydrate diets cautiously, with an eye to your unique needs.

Who should go low carb. The American Diabetes Association acknowledges that some people may legitimately need to lower their carbohydrate intake. For example, certain people who have type 2 diabetes and are insulin resistant may find that eating a diet rich in carbs raises triglyceride levels and brings down levels of HDL cholesterol. It's another reason the ADA's latest recommendations allow 60 to 70 percent of total calories to be distributed between carbohydrates and mono-unsaturated fat. If your main concern is keeping your blood sugar in check after meals and improving your triglyceride levels, eating more monounsaturated fats may be the way to go. If losing weight is your main concern, then according to the ADA, favoring carbs over fats (which contain more calories gram for gram) may be preferable.

Something to keep in mind: According to a recent U.S. Department of Agriculture report that evaluated a variety of popular diets, how much weight you lose depends more on how many calories you eat than where they come from.

Dangers of low-carb diets. Besides not offering significant advantages, low-carb diets may pose a number of problems:

▶ **They're more difficult.** Even a so-called high-fat diet doesn't give you free rein with the doughnuts and bacon. Instead, you're supposed to get more fat from foods like nuts, avocados, and olive oil, still keeping unhealthy saturated fat at 10 percent of total calories. In the meantime, carb-containing foods you might otherwise be able to enjoy are forbidden. One diet's "no-no list" includes all candies, pastries, and desserts except for sugar-free gelatin, along with beans, beets, breads, breakfast cereals, corn, carrots, potatoes, and most tomato products.

▶ **They can be nutrient-poor.** If you cut back on starchy foods rich in fiber, vitamins, and minerals, you may find it difficult to get all the nutrients your body needs.

▶ **They're less proven.** The generally accepted guidelines got that way—that is, generally accepted—from years of research that led experts to conclude that these are the best dietary approaches to beating diabetes. While popular low-carb diets draw on some of this research, they don't have the same level of scientific consensus backing up their conclusions.

▶ **They may be dangerous.** While the question of whether high-protein diets promote the development of kidney damage is unresolved, many people with diabetes already have undiagnosed kidney damage that would make extra exertion by the organs potentially harmful.

Getting Enough Vitamins and Minerals

As a rule, if you eat a wide variety of foods, you'll have no trouble getting all the nutrients you need. However, people with diabetes appear more likely to be deficient in certain micronutrients—something your dietitian can evaluate. Nutrients you may need more of include:

Vitamin C. Evidence for diabetes-related deficiencies is most clear for vitamin C, which, like glucose, requires insulin to help it enter cells. It's not hard to add more vitamin C to your diet. Just one cup of steamed broccoli contains 123 milligrams—a whole day's supply.

Magnesium. The most common mineral deficiency, especially in people with type 1 diabetes, is of magnesium. Getting too little of it may promote eye damage, a common complication of diabetes.

Vitamin E. An antioxidant, vitamin E may protect against such complications as eye, nerve, and kidney damage. But amounts in food tend to be small, so you may want to take a supplement. Check with your doctor first.

Vitamin B_{12}. Some diabetes medications, such as metformin, may interfere with the body's absorption of B_{12} from food, potentially leading to deficiencies.

Before taking any dietary supplements, check with your doctor. As a rule, if you suffer from deficiencies, you'll want to correct them by eating more foods containing the nutrients you need. Supplements are generally considered less desirable because some vitamins and minerals can be harmful in high amounts; in addition, supplements lack other nutrients or elements, such as fiber, that may make it easier for the body to absorb and use what it ingests.

WHERE THE NUTRIENTS ARE

Vitamin C

Citrus fruits, tomatoes, spinach, bell peppers, broccoli, and strawberries

Magnesium

Leafy green vegetables (like spinach), whole grains, dairy products, brown rice, apricots, and bananas

Vitamin E

Many nuts, such as almonds, Brazil nuts, and peanuts, as well as whole-wheat flour

Vitamin B_{12}

Poultry and a variety of seafood, including clams, crabs, scallops, and shrimp

Finally, there's one mineral you may need less of: sodium. High blood pressure is common among people with diabetes, and studies suggest that eating less sodium can help bring blood pressure down. Use table salt sparingly and avoid canned or packaged foods, which tend to pack a wallop of sodium. Rely more on herbs and spices when cooking.

What's the Glycemic Index?

How fast or slow your blood sugar goes up after eating can depend on what you put in your mouth, and in the 1980s, Canadian researchers developed a system to rate the glucose-raising effects of specific foods. It's called the glycemic index, or GI.

GI numbers are based on a comparison point of 102 grams of white bread, which is given a value of 100—a moderate effect. Foods with a higher glycemic index have a slightly greater effect on blood sugar, and foods with a lower index have a slightly lesser effect. Some people find glycemic-index lists (available from your dietitian, in bookstores, or on the Internet) helpful when choosing which foods to eat during meal planning.

Studies suggest that people with diabetes who eat a low-GI diet may tend to have lower blood sugar than those who eat higher-GI foods, along with lower triglycerides and LDL. Still, some researchers question the value of the glycemic index. One reason: Many healthful foods (such as potatoes and whole-grain breads) rate relatively high on the scale, yet they should hardly be avoided. But mainly, though it sounds simple, the glycemic index is actually fairly complex, and many dietitians find that it makes meal planning more cumbersome than carbohydrate counting.

Downsides of the GI

For one thing, everybody responds to food differently. Your blood sugar will not rise to the same extent as the next person's, even if you eat the same food. By itself, this isn't a big problem because GI numbers would still prove useful once you understand what they mean to you personally. But other factors make the glycemic index difficult to interpret. For example, the glycemic effect of food can vary as you get older or more insulin resistant. Perhaps most important, the GI of a food itself can change depending on how much it's been processed, what you eat along with it, and how it's prepared. Mashing, chopping, or

GLYCEMIC INDEX

Scientists have calculated glycemic indexes for hundreds of foods. Here's a sample of values for a range of different foods, from high to low GI:

Baked potato	121
Cornflakes	119
Pretzels	116
Waffles	109
Doughnut	108
Watermelon	103
Raisins	91
Oatmeal	87
Fresh apricots	82
White rice	81
Brown rice	79
Sweet corn	78
Banana	77
Sweet potato	77
Pumpernickel bread	71
Whole carrots	70
Peas	68
Spaghetti	59
Apple	52
Fettuccine	46
Skim milk	46
Kidney beans	42
Pearled barley	36
Soybeans	25

pureeing a food (which makes it easier to digest) raises its glycemic index—as can merely cooking it. Even ripeness can make a difference. For example, a green banana has a GI of 51, while an overripe one's value is 84.

If you eat a high-GI food (a bowl of cornflakes) with a low one (skim milk), the overall glycemic effect is a balance of the foods together. For that reason, many dietitians feel the GI becomes a moot point if you simply try to eat a balanced diet with a variety of foods.

Making the Most of Food Exchanges

Another tool your dietitian may bring into play is the food-exchange system, which looks beyond carbohydrates at the diet as a whole, organizing foods into several groups—generally breads and starches, fruits, vegetables, milk, meat and protein-based substitutes, fats, and other carbohydrates like sweets. While food exchanges are designed for people with diabetes, many nutritionists find them valuable for anyone trying to control calories, reduce fat, and eat a balanced diet.

The idea behind the exchange system is that every item within a given category is nutritionally equivalent to every other item on that same list—providing roughly the same amount of carbohydrate, fat, protein, and calories. Using the portion sizes laid out on the lists is important for making the system work. But the big advantage is that—as with carbohydrate counting—you have a lot of flexibility in choosing foods within each category, as long as they add up to the nutritional budget allowed in your meal plan. Fortunately, portion sizes for many of the groups tend to be similar, which helps give you an intuitive grasp of how much you should eat. One bread/starch exchange, for example, is usually measured in slices or half cups (as are many vegetable exchanges). One meat exchange is generally about one ounce—much smaller, by the way, than the two to three ounces that constitute a serving in the familiar USDA food pyramid.

Like the food pyramid, the exchange system strives to give you a range of nutrients from a variety of foods, but it does so with greater precision. Still, using the exchange system requires guidance. Your dietitian can help you figure out how many exchanges from each group you should eat.

The groupings themselves may take some getting used to because they're organized by calorie and nutrient content rather than source. Cheeses, for instance, are listed with meats rather than milk because their protein and fat makeup are more similar. Corn, green peas, and potatoes appear with starches rather than vegetables because of their high carbohydrate content. Once you're familiar with the system, however, its combination of flexibility and consistency can help you keep blood sugar down while providing enough nutrients.

RANGES OF EXCHANGES

Some exchange lists are subdivided into groups that specify exchanges of, say, very lean meats and substitutes (separate from high-fat meats), or nonfat-milk products (separate from whole-milk products). Foods within each category are nutritionally equivalent in the exchange system.

Starches

1 slice white bread
½ cup cooked lentils
½ cup cooked pasta
½ cup corn
1 small potato

Vegetables

½ cup cooked carrots
½ cup cooked green beans
1 cup raw radishes
1 cup raw salad greens
1 large tomato

Fruits

1 small banana
1 large pear
17 small grapes
2 tablespoons raisins
½ cup fruit cocktail

Very lean meats and substitutes

1 ounce skinless chicken breast
1 ounce canned tuna (in water)
1 ounce fat-free cheese
¼ cup low-fat cottage cheese
2 egg whites

Nonfat and very-low-fat milks

1 cup skim milk
1 cup plain nonfat yogurt
½ cup nonfat fruit-flavored yogurt
(containing nonnutritive sweetener)
½ cup evaporated nonfat milk
1 cup nonfat buttermilk

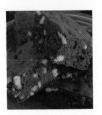

Other carbohydrates

1 two-inch-square brownie
2 small cookies
1 tablespoon 100% fruit spread
½ cup gelatin
5 vanilla wafers

Is Alcohol Off-Limits?

There are plenty of reasons to avoid drinking alcohol, starting with the obvious: inebriation and addiction. But assuming you're a responsible drinker, is there room for alcohol in your diet if you have diabetes? Most experts agree that the answer is a qualified yes. Alcohol may even have some benefits in terms of preventing cardio-vascular problems associated with diabetes.

A Harvard study published in the *Archives of Internal Medicine* in early 2002 found that women who have a few alcoholic drinks over the course of a week stand an almost 15 percent lower chance of developing high blood pressure than nondrinking women. Other studies in both men and women have shown that alcohol raises HDL ("good") cholesterol and thins the blood slightly, protecting against the formation of clots that can cause a heart attack or stroke.

Drawbacks of Drinking

There are a number of caveats. First, the line between healthy and unhealthy drinking appears to be very thin. In the recent Harvard study, women who had more than about 1½ drinks a day had a 30 percent higher risk of elevated blood pressure than nondrinkers did. Furthermore, alcohol's effects on the body are of particular significance when you suffer from diabetes. The main threat is hypoglycemia. Alcohol is processed in the liver, which also stores and releases glucose. Result: Wine, beer, and spirits hinder the liver's ability to release glucose, which can lead to hypoglycemia as much as a day after you drink. Moreover, symptoms of hypoglycemia can be similar to those of inebriation, making the danger harder to spot.

Another consideration is that alcoholic drinks have seven calories per gram—almost as much as fat—but provide no nutrition, making them a poor choice if you're trying to lose weight. And if you're taking medication, alcohol may be out of the question.

Should you drink? Talk it over with your doctor or dietitian. If you get the okay to imbibe, here are some basic guide-lines to keep in mind.

↪ **Keep it to one.** Most studies find few risks and possible benefits from one drink a day or less. "One drink" is defined as a 12-ounce beer, 5 ounces of wine (about a half cup), or a 1½-ounce shot of distilled spirits, such as scotch, whiskey, or vodka (mix only with sugar-free soda or water).

↪ **Eat something.** Food slows the absorption of alcohol into the bloodstream, allowing the liver to better process glucose while handling the alcohol. Also try to nurse your drink over a couple of hours to further ease the burden on your liver.

↪ **Sidestep the special stuff.** In addition to their calories from alcohol, sweet wines and liqueurs pack extra amounts of carbohydrate. Likewise, sugary sodas and other sweet mixers added to distilled spirits can boost the calorie quotient.

↪ **Exchange cautiously.** As a rule, doctors and dietitians would prefer that you not drop a nutritious item from your meal plan to make room for alcohol. But for the record, alcoholic drinks (except for beer) count as two fat exchanges, which may be consistent with your dietary goals. Beer counts as one and a half fat exchanges and one starch exchange.

Making Weight Loss Work

Knowing what your ideal diet should be is one thing. Putting it into practice—especially if you're trying to cut calories—is quite another. Anyone who's tried to lose weight can attest to the fact that it's easy for the best-laid dietary plans to go awry—at least temporarily. Not to worry. This is a long-term project, and occasional lapses are to be expected. In the meantime, a few smart strategies can help you peel off those unwanted pounds.

Control the Calorie Crunch

Researchers have recently noticed what seems to be a curious trend: According to a number of national surveys, the proportion of fat in the average American diet has actually gone down, even as rates of obesity have gone up. This has come to be called the "American paradox." Does this mean fat isn't the villain we've been led to believe it is? No. The explanation: While the percentage of fat in the diet may be dropping, the sheer amount of fat we consume as a nation is going up because we're eating larger portions of *everything*.

Controlling your calorie intake is the bedrock of all weight-loss plans. But how can you stay the course when food is abundant and the temptation to overindulge is strong? Start by making a few small adjustments to your dining and snacking habits. For instance:

▶ **Keep food off the table.** If you portion out servings on plates at the stove or kitchen counter and don't set food out on serving platters, you'll be less tempted to take more once your plate is empty.

▶ **Don't eat from packages.** It's all too easy to lose track of how much food you've gobbled if you're nibbling straight from the box. Instead, portion out crackers, pretzels, and other snacks on a plate to give yourself a visible sense of what you're consuming.

▶ **Downsize your dishes.** Smaller plates and bowls make portions appear larger.

▶ **Take it slow.** It takes about 20 minutes for the brain's appetite-control center to register that there's food in the stomach. To wait it out, put down your fork between each bite and take small sips from your drink.

▶ **Work for your food.** Eating foods that require some effort—peeling an orange, cracking open crabs, or cutting open a baked potato, for example—slows you down even more, giving food a chance to make you feel full.

▶ **Socialize outside the kitchen.** People seem to congregate in the kitchen, but you'll be less tempted to nosh if you move the action to the living room.

Shop Smarter in 10 Easy Steps

You came, you saw, you shopped. But then you got home from the supermarket and started unloading fatty snack items and deli meats. What went wrong? You fell back into the habit of shopping like an average American rather than a person with a dietary purpose. In an enticing palace of eating designed to lead you astray, here's how to stay on track:

➲ **Make a list.** The meal plan you develop with your dietitian will help you figure out which foods you should be buying. Before you shop, write down what you need to reduce the chances of buying what you don't.

➲ **Limit your trips.** Make your shopping list long so you have to make only one or two trips to the store per week. Besides being more efficient, doing this provides less opportunity to make impulse purchases.

➲ **Avoid shopping on an empty stomach.** When you're hungry, you're more likely to grab high-fat snacks and desserts.

SIMPLE SUBSTITUTIONS

Cutting calories is surprisingly easy when small changes add up to big savings. Here's how a variety of foods measure up—and what you can save by making smart choices.

INSTEAD OF	TRY	DIFFERENCE
1 cup frosted flakes (159 calories)	1 cup regular cornflakes (93 calories)	66 calories
1 doughnut (198 calories)	1 English muffin (134 calories)	64 calories
1 cup whole milk (149 calories)	1 cup nonfat milk (86 calories)	63 calories
1 tbsp. butter (100 calories)	1 tbsp. jam (48 calories)	52 calories
1 tbsp. butter (100 calories)	1 tbsp. low-fat cream cheese (35 calories)	65 calories
12 oz. regular cola (153 calories)	12 oz. diet cola (4 calories)	149 calories
12 oz. canned fruit punch (117 calories)	12 oz. sports drink (60 calories)	57 calories
3 oz. chunk light tuna in oil, undrained (254 calories)	3 oz. chunk light tuna in water, undrained (89 calories)	165 calories
4 oz. lean choice round ground beef (316 calories)	4 oz. ground turkey (266 calories)	50 calories
1 slice salami (143 calories)	1 slice beef bologna (72 calories)	71 calories
4 oz. lean choice T-bone steak (232 calories)	4 oz. lean ham (164 calories)	68 calories
Batter-fried chicken breast (728 calories)	Roasted skinless chicken breast (284 calories)	444 calories
Quarter-pound hamburger with cheese (530 calories)	Grilled-chicken sandwich without mayo (340 calories)	190 calories
1 oz. potato chips (160 calories)	1 oz. pretzels (110 calories)	50 calories
1 cup vanilla ice cream (265 calories)	1 cup low-fat frozen yogurt (229 calories)	36 calories

◗ **Follow the walls.** Limit browsing to the perimeter of the store, where you'll find the freshest, most healthful foods: raw produce, low-fat dairy products, fresh lean meats and fish. Venture into the interior aisles only when you're after specific foods, such as pasta and dried beans, to avoid picking up extra items not included in your diet plan.

◗ **Pay attention to portions.** Those cookies look great—and hey, eating them only costs you 12 grams of carbohydrate. But check the serving size: one cookie. Eating "them"— say, three cookies—brings your total carb count up to 36 grams, more than the flesh of a baked potato.

◗ **Ignore the pictures.** Golden sunshine glows on heaps of freshly harvested grains—an image of good health that signifies nothing. Look at the side of the box instead for the facts, and choose foods that are high in fiber and low in fat and calories.

◗ **Grade your grains.** Want high-fiber bread? Look for the words "whole grain," "100 percent whole wheat," or "stone-ground" on the label. Breads labeled simply "wheat"—even if they are brown in color—may not contain whole grains. True whole-grain bread contains at least two grams of fiber per serving.

◗ **Watch the language.** Beware of foods labeled "no sugar added"—the wording is carefully chosen because the product may be loaded with natural sugar. You'll find the real story on the label, under "Sugars."

◗ **Add some spice to your life.** Instead of creamy condiments, load up on such spices as basil, chives, cinnamon, cumin, curry, garlic, ginger, horseradish, nutmeg, oregano, paprika, parsley, and Tabasco sauce. They're so low in carbohydrates, fat, protein, and calories that they're considered "free" items in meal planning.

◗ **Keep your eye on the cashier.** You're waiting in line, nothing to do—a captive audience. It's no accident that supermarkets pile their impulse items next to the registers. Keep a couple of items from your basket in your hands: It'll stop you from reaching for the candy bars.

Exercise: Your Secret Weapon

To shed a pound a week, you need to subtract 3,500 calories from your current total, or 500 calories a day. But that doesn't necessarily mean you have to eat 500 fewer calories. Instead, you can eat 250 fewer calories and burn the other 250 through physical activity. In fact, studies show that combining diet with exercise is the surest way to lose weight and keep it off for good. Burning additional calories allows you to eat more and still meet your weight-loss goals.

Recent research finds that you need at least 40 minutes of moderate physical activity—or, better still, 60 minutes—every

ARE ARTIFICIAL SWEETENERS SAFE?

For people trying to reduce their calorie and carbohydrate intake, artificial, "nonnutritive" sweeteners have been a godsend, allowing a wide variety of foods and drinks to taste more delectable without sugar or added calories. But two of the most popular artificial sweeteners, saccharin and aspartame, have been battered by storms of controversy regarding their safety. Should you worry?

■ **SACCHARIN.** Back in the 1970s, the Food and Drug Administration banned saccharin (marketed as Sweet N' Low) after studies indicated that high doses of it caused cancer in rats. At the time, no other artificial sweetener existed, and the public, feeling the threat was overblown, clamored successfully to bring it back. But products that contained it had to be labeled with a warning. Since then, studies have suggested that differences between rat and human anatomy make the rats' risk inapplicable to people, and in 2000 saccharin was taken off the official list of cancer-causing compounds. Some consumer-advocate groups and nutrition researchers are uneasy about the change and claim the evidence of a cancer risk still warrants caution. Still, even they admit that if a risk exists, it's very small.

■ **ASPARTAME.** Heated debate preceded aspartame's FDA approval in 1981, partly because investigators found research by the manufacturer to be riddled with inconsistencies and errors. An outside advisory board recommended withholding approval, but was overruled by the FDA, which felt (after an audit) that the evidence proved aspartame (sold as NutraSweet) to be safe. Even after approval, skeptics charged that aspartame interfered with normal brain chemistry, triggering headaches, seizures, and (it was feared) brain cancer. However, numerous studies over the past 15 years have found these concerns to be groundless, and even strong advocacy groups, such as the Center for Science in the Public Interest, no longer sound alarms about aspartame.

■ **THE BOTTOM LINE.** The consensus is that in the amounts they're usually consumed, both saccharin and aspartame are safe. In addition, other nonnutritive sweeteners (such as sucralose and acesulfame-K) have come on the market, allowing food makers to blend sweeteners together, thus diluting the potential impact of any one compound.

day to lose weight and keep it off. Don't let those numbers scare you. You can break up your activity into 10- or 15-minute sessions and still get results.

Exercise—especially strength training—offers another big bonus: a faster metabolism. A pound of muscle burns about 45 calories a day, whereas a pound of fat burns fewer than 2 calories a day. So by building up your muscle mass, you can turn yourself into a virtual calorie-burning machine. Researchers at the University of Alabama found that middle-aged adults who worked out with weights three times a week for six months built enough muscle to raise their resting metabolism by 80 to 150 calories a day—the equivalent of a 20- to 40-minute workout.

Turn to Chapter 5 for more information on how—and why—you should exercise when you have diabetes.

Attitude Makes the Difference

Some researchers say that losing weight and following a meal plan are as much a psychological challenge as a physiological one. And one of the primary tasks is accepting that your health can improve—but maybe not by tomorrow.

Diets that promise quick results seem to be everywhere. But it's counterproductive to expect change to happen quickly. While it's true that some diets can take pounds off fast, few can guarantee that the weight will stay off. For that to happen, you need to view dietary change as a permanent adjustment in the way you live. Some researchers, for example, refer to the "100/100 rule": If you eat 100 fewer calories a day (the amount in half a candy bar) and burn 100 more calories a day (by walking 15 to 20 minutes), you'll lose almost half a pound per week, or 20 pounds a year. It's not fast, but it's easy, it works—and it's significant.

Accepting good eating habits as a permanent part of life protects against a number of other attitude snags that can hinder your progress. For example, if you see your diet as a temporary measure you take until you drop a certain number of pounds, you'll tend to think of yourself as either "on" or "off" your diet. That promotes a sense that dieting demands special willpower and that eating a food you like or an occasional item that's not in your meal plan means you've cheated or failed. You'll have better results with a more forgiving attitude that lets you make mistakes and quickly move on to make better choices next time.

Divide (meals) and Conquer (Diabetes)

It sounds strange, but Carolyn Glosup, 57, can thank her diabetes diagnosis for making her a fitter, healthier person than she was several years ago. "I weighed about 280 pounds, my back hurt, and I often felt dizzy, so I used a tripod cane to get around," says Glosup, of rural McGehee, Arkansas. She was treated for a double ear infection but continued to feel faint when standing up, so her doctor looked for another cause—and found that her blood-sugar level was over 250 mg/dl.

"The day my doctor said I'd have to go on insulin, I went right out and found a nutritionist," says Glosup. "My mother had diabetes but wouldn't stay on a diet. She'd eat cheese puffs instead of a decent meal. She needed at least one shot a day, plus a urine test every morning and four finger pricks throughout the day. She hated it, but wouldn't do anything about it. I knew I didn't want to get to the point where I'd hate my lifestyle, so something drastic had to change."

Back then, Glosup skipped food but would sip all day long from a jug of sugared tea, then dig into a megameal at bedtime—an eating style that wreaked havoc with her blood sugar and piled on pounds. "I'd have a big hunk of meat equal to about three burger patties, sometimes deep-fried chicken—and I loved the skin," she says. Today, Glosup divides three square meals so she's eating several times a day. Breakfast might be a bowl of cereal, followed in a couple of hours by a slice of toast. Lunch is half a sandwich, the other half later. Supper is now lean beef or chicken that's been broiled, grilled, or baked—not to mention skinned—and a balance of vegetables. "My husband and I went from four loaves of bread a week to less than one," she says. She still carries that jug of tea—but it's sweetened with sugar-free lemon-lime soda.

Glosup refers to her new eating habits as "food modification" rather than a diet, and it's led to other happy changes in her life: Her blood sugar is usually around 110, and she's lowered her blood-pressure and cholesterol levels. She's lost 80 pounds—and the cane. "I walk in place for 30 minutes every day or just chase my dog around," says Glosup. "I used to wear baggy sweat suits all the time, and now I live in jeans. My husband says I look so sexy!" And he's doing well himself, having lost 10 pounds and improved his blood-pressure and cholesterol levels as well.

"But the best part is that I feel good," says Glosup. "I'm not on shots. I'm handling my diabetes, and I know I'm doing the best that I can."

5

Exercise as Medicine

Getting active trims fat from your body and helps you tip the scales in the right direction—two key ways to control diabetes. But there's more: Exercise is almost like insulin in its ability to bring down blood sugar. It also helps the body use insulin. That makes physical activity one of the single most effective ways to control your diabetes, not to mention slashing your risk of a heart attack or stroke. Adding workouts to your schedule doesn't have to take a lot of time or effort. It can even be fun!

Let's say a dramatic treatment hit the market that could drop your blood sugar from 386 to 106 mg/dl, help you lose 100 pounds in 14 months, and squelch any ideas of using insulin. Would you be interested? Joseph Grossmann of Albany, New York, sure was—and those were his results. But it wasn't a powerful new drug the 53-year-old took. In fact, he's off all medication. His secret weapon? Exercise.

Grossmann walks his three dogs four to five miles a day, does pushups and sit-ups, digs in his garden, and lifts boxes at his job in a floral shop, and he rounds out his "treatment" with a meal plan of fresh vegetables, fish, and chicken. "I feel like a new person," he says. "I'm proof that if you take a hold of exercise and diet, you really can control your diabetes and make your whole life a lot better."

You've heard for years that exercise is good for you. But it has specific benefits for people with diabetes—a fact that healers in ancient cultures like India's and China's recognized centuries ago. Since then, scientists have discovered exactly how exercise works its magic. Here's what it does:

Lowers blood sugar. Putting your muscles into action is like hitting your car's accelerator: It instantly boosts the demand for fuel—namely, glucose. Once your muscles exhaust their own supply of glucose, they clean out the stores in your liver, then draw glucose straight from the bloodstream, lowering your blood sugar. When you're done exercising, your body gives top priority to replenishing glucose stores in the liver and muscles rather than the blood, which means that your blood sugar will stay lower for hours—perhaps for as long as a couple of days, depending on how hard you worked out.

Boosts insulin sensitivity. If you exercise regularly, you can actually lower your level of insulin resistance. That's because exercise forces muscles to use glucose more efficiently by making cells more receptive to insulin. It's as if getting physical gives your cells a kick in the pants: If they absolutely *must* have more glucose, they'll work harder to get it. Exercise also boosts the number of insulin receptors. Do it regularly and you'll perpetuate good blood-sugar control. In fact, the effect won't entirely fade away unless you go for about 72 hours without a workout. Even if you've been a die-hard couch potato for years, you can ratchet up your insulin sensitivity with exercise in as little as one week.

Burns fat. What happens when muscles tap out the glucose in the liver and blood? After about 30 minutes of continuous exercise, the body turns to fatty acids both in flabby storage sites throughout the body and in the blood. Using fat for energy helps clear the blood of harmful fats, such as LDL cholesterol and triglycerides. It also boosts "good" HDL cholesterol and helps trim abdominal fat, which is linked to a higher risk of diabetes and complications.

Shaves pounds. The more active you are, the more energy you use, and if you control your diet as well, you'll end up with a calorie deficit that eventually tips the scales in a favorable direction. A bonus: Exercise also builds up your muscle mass, and since muscle burns energy faster than other types of tissue (especially fat) do, that means you'll burn more calories all the time—even when you're lounging in front of the TV.

Protects your heart. Exercise cuts your chances of having a heart attack, stroke, or other cardiovascular problem linked with diabetes by helping to improve your risk profile. In one study, type 2 patients who took part in an aerobic-exercise program lasting only three months saw their triglyceride and HDL cholesterol levels improve by about 20 percent, along with a significant drop in blood pressure. And the benefits aren't limited to those with type 2 diabetes. Researchers at the University of Pittsburgh found the risk of dying from cardiovascular illnesses to be three times higher among sedentary people with type 1 diabetes than among those who regularly burn about 2,000 calories a week through exercise.

Makes you feel good. This isn't a minor point. Dealing with a chronic disease day after day can sometimes feel discouraging, stressful, or even depressing. Exercise helps by producing feel-good chemicals in the brain that can boost your mood, relieve stress, and alleviate the blues. It also does wonders for your sense of confidence and self-esteem. When you finish a workout, you're justified in feeling that you've accomplished something important. You might feel that if you can do this, maybe you really can get your health under control. And you'd be right.

Makes you look better. It's not the most important health benefit, but it sure is a strong motivator. Without a doubt, if your

DID YOU KNOW

Muscle weighs more than fat, so it can take patience to lose weight by toning up. The pounds may seem to melt away slowly, but they will disappear—and they'll be less likely to come back than if you diet without working out. People who diet but don't exercise tend to lose a lot of weight (perhaps 15 pounds in a few months) but often lose muscle along with fat, which slows their metabolism. Maybe that's why they have trouble keeping the weight off. People who just exercise, on the other hand, may lose only a pound or two in the same amount of time, but they are more likely to sustain their "losses"—and build on them over time.

fitness improves, your appearance does, too. You lose flab and gain muscle, strength, and energy, which make you seem livelier, more capable, and maybe even younger. What's not to like?

Fringe Benefits

Exercise helps control diabetes and reduce the risk of heart attack and stroke. As if that weren't enough, it also:

▶ Helps prevent certain malignancies, such as colon cancer.

▶ Improves or maintains blood flow to sex organs, potentially enhancing sexual function and enjoyment.

▶ Preserves cognitive functions, such as memory.

▶ Retards bone loss that can lead to osteoporosis.

▶ Boosts the ability of immune-system cells to fight invaders.

▶ Slows physical decline that accounts for most impairments associated with aging.

▶ Eases arthritis pain by strengthening and stretching the muscles, tendons, and ligaments that support joints.

▶ Guards against back pain by strengthening muscles that support the spine.

▶ Aids digestion and helps prevent such ailments as irritable bowel syndrome.

▶ Promotes good sleep.

Tailor-made Training

Exercise is so powerful it's almost like taking medicine. But a prescription that works for you won't be ideal for everybody with diabetes. That's why it's important to work with your doctor to customize your exercise plan to fit your circumstances, starting with which kind of diabetes you have and how you're treating it now.

Whichever strategy you choose, you'll want to bring blood sugar down—but not too far. To keep close tabs on it, test an hour before your workout, then again a half hour later to find out if your levels are rising or falling. If they're falling and on the low side, you may want to eat about 15 grams of carbohydrate before you start exercising. If your blood sugar is high and rising, you may need more insulin. Once your blood sugar becomes more stable, your doctor may allow you to monitor less often, but self-testing following a workout is always a good idea.

The readings you get will help clarify how exercise should work into your overall diabetes-management plan, which will vary from one situation to the next.

If You Have Type 1 Diabetes

People with type 1 diabetes need to approach exercise with extra caution. If you work out too soon after taking insulin, the glucose-lowering tag team of insulin plus exercise can be too much of a good thing and lower your blood sugar to dangerous levels. On the flip side, having too little insulin in your blood while you exercise can make blood sugar build up and potentially cause ketoacidosis. To ensure your safety, check with your doctor about taking steps like the following:

⊃ **Avoid peak hours.** Try to time your workout so that you're not exercising when insulin activity peaks, often within the first hour or two of an injection, depending on which type you use.

⊃ **Adjust your dose.** You may be able to drop your daily insulin requirements by as much as 20 to 30 percent if you cut your dose before a workout. Ask your doctor how much of an adjustment to make based on your current dosage and how hard you exercise—then be sure to actually do your workout.

⊃ **Exercise after eating.** You're less likely to be hit by hypoglycemia if you wait to work out until an hour or two after a meal, when your blood sugar will be naturally high and plenty of glucose will be on hand to fuel your muscles.

⊃ **Inject into the abdomen.** Problem: If you inject insulin into muscles you'll be using, they will absorb it faster and send your blood sugar plummeting. Solution: Unless you're going straight into sit-ups, inject into the softer folds of your midsection. If you're working your abs, wait to exercise until about an hour after your injection to give the insulin a chance to disperse throughout the body.

⊃ **Have a snack.** Eating a small, low-fat snack containing about 20 grams of carbohydrate (two rolled fruit snacks, for

example) during your workout can help keep blood sugar from falling too low, especially during vigorous exercise or workout sessions lasting an hour or more.

If You Have Type 2 and Use Insulin

The great promise of exercise for people with type 2 diabetes is that—unlike with type 1—it can actually throw the condition into reverse. Boosting your insulin sensitivity could bring your blood sugar back into the normal range, especially if you're controlling your diet as well, and could permanently reduce the amount of insulin you need—or even get you off insulin altogether. Some practical advice:

➲ **Proceed with caution.** While keeping your eyes on the prize—less insulin or none at all—remember to keep your goals reasonable at first. If you're taking insulin, you stand the same risk of hypoglycemia during exercise that a type 1 person does. Take a look at the above list of recommendations for people with type 1—they also apply to you.

➲ **Try not to snack.** If you're in danger of hypoglycemia during exercise, you may need a snack to bring your blood sugar back up. But this solution can ultimately work against you because it adds calories you're probably better off avoiding. So instead of relying on snacks to head off hypoglycemia, be diligent about planning to exercise after a meal so blood sugar is high during your workout.

➲ **Stick to your meal plan.** If you do eat an unplanned snack during your workout, don't make up for it by subtracting calories from your after-exercise meals. It's just as important to keep calories up after a workout as before, since exercise can make blood sugar dip dangerously for as long as a day.

If You Have Type 2 and Use Medication

If you take a drug like metformin to control your blood sugar, you may be able to get by with less—or stop taking it altogether—by adding more physical activity to your life. Once you figure out how exercise affects your blood sugar, you'll want to talk with your doctor about how to adjust your drug regimen accordingly. Keep in mind, though, that exercise and diet aren't automatic substitutes for diabetes drugs—and taking drugs doesn't excuse you from working out. In fact, drugs often work their best only when combined with other measures, such as meal planning and exercise. Some advice:

➲ **Time your workouts.** If you're using medication, avoid exercising when the drug is reaching its peak effectiveness so that your blood sugar doesn't drop dangerously low. If you're working to cut back on or eliminate your drug use, your doctor may start by having you take less (or none) before your workout. In effect, you may be able to exercise in place of taking your medication if the effects on blood sugar prove to be similar.

➲ **Be alert to side effects.** Some diabetes medications can cause muscle ache or fatigue, while others can make you dizzy or nauseated. Be sure you and your doctor are clear about how intensely you intend to exercise and how your medication's side effects may limit your activities.

➲ **Drink plenty of water.** It takes about eight 8-ounce glasses of water a day to keep the body hydrated—and you'll need more when you're sweating. Don't wait for thirst to hit before drinking; that's a sign of high blood sugar and could bring your workout to a halt while you check for hyperglycemia. Instead, drink one to two cups 15 minutes before exercising, at least a half cup every 15 minutes during your workout, and another one to two cups afterward.

THE EXERCISE–BLOOD SUGAR PARADOX

Why does blood sugar go down sometimes but go up other times after exercise? Muscles use glucose for energy, so as a rule, blood sugar goes down when you're active, as the body moves glucose from the liver and bloodstream into the cells. But that assumes there's enough insulin on hand to help with this transfer. If you take insulin and your dose is too low, glucose can build in the blood during exercise and cause hyperglycemia. That's why it's important to consult your doctor for advice on exercising and to check your blood sugar before and after (and perhaps even during) exercise to understand how physical activity affects you.

If You Have Impaired Glucose Tolerance

The best evidence for exercise's effectiveness against diabetes comes from research in people with impaired glucose tolerance. In one University of Pennsylvania study, every 2,000 calories burned per week through exercise dropped the risk of diabetes by 24 percent, with people at greatest risk gaining the most benefits. To take advantage:

➲ **Get started immediately.** Just because full-blown diabetes lies "out there" over the distant horizon doesn't mean you have time to spare. If you don't start making changes now, insulin resistance is only likely to get worse. But if you jump on the

WHEN TESTING MEANS RESTING

As long as your blood sugar is under control, there's no bad time to exercise. But blood-sugar testing can tell you when it might be better to hold off, at least until your glucose or insulin levels can meet your muscles' demands. Some guidelines to follow:

■ To protect against hypoglycemia, don't exercise if your blood sugar is below 100 mg/dl. Instead, have a piece of fruit or other snack containing at least 15 grams of carbohydrate, then test again in about 20 minutes. Keep snacking until blood sugar rises above the 100 mg/dl mark.

■ To protect against hyperglycemia, test for ketones (using a urine ketone test strip) if blood sugar before exercise is above 240 mg/dl. If the test detects ketones, don't start exercising until you've taken more insulin to handle glucose uptake during your workout.

■ If ketones are absent, don't exercise if blood sugar is above 400 mg/dl if you have type 2 diabetes or 300 mg/dl if you have type 1 diabetes.

exercise bandwagon right away, you can boost your cells' insulin sensitivity within a week, even if you're obese, giving you a good chance of dodging a diagnosis of diabetes.

⊃ **Track your blood sugar.** Don't assume that because you haven't developed diabetes you don't have to worry about blood sugar. You may not need to test as often as a person with a diabetes diagnosis, but you should still keep track of your glucose levels with self-monitoring and regular checkups to make sure your condition remains under control.

⊃ **Keep it up.** It's just as important for you to keep workouts regular and consistent as it is for a person with diabetes. Controlling the risk of developing the disease will never be easier than it is now—and you should aim to keep it that way.

How to Sweat Safely

You'll avoid most hypoglycemia problems with proper planning (by matching exercise to your drug, insulin, and meal regimens) but you should always be prepared for surprise bouts of low blood sugar.

⊃ **Know when to stop—now.** The second you detect symptoms of hypoglycemia, such as confusion, shaking, lightheadedness, or difficulty speaking, stop immediately—not after "just one more minute." Be alert to all symptoms, and understand that some of them overlap with natural responses to exercise, such as sweating and rapid heartbeat.

⊃ **Carry a snack.** A quick snack can rapidly bring dropping blood sugar back up in an emergency—but only if you remember to bring one along.

⊃ **Get a partner.** It's not always obvious when hypoglycemia is setting in, so it's wise to work out with somebody else or in a place where other people are available if you need help, especially if you're exercising vigorously.

⊃ **Pack ID.** Even if you're with a friend, you should carry identification with your name, address, and phone number— and those of your doctor. Also have the name of someone to call in an emergency as well as your insulin or drug dosages.

➲ **Stay alert afterward.** Blood sugar can continue to fall long after you've exercised, so don't let your guard down for signs of hypoglycemia until 24 hours after your workout.

The Aerobic Prescription

Quick: How will you spend the next 20 minutes? Sprawled in front of the TV? Parked at a computer? Chatting on the phone? Passive pleasures, to be sure, but consider an alternative: Twenty minutes of walking around the neighborhood or riding a bike can scour your arteries, muscle your blood sugar into line, and nip fat off your belly.

Aerobic exercises like these should be the mainstay of your exercise program for a number of reasons. By definition, they keep the body moving for sustained periods of time, which taps all of its glucose stores and does the most to bring blood sugar down. They also pump up your heart and breathing rate, which boosts blood circulation and oxygen delivery throughout the body and helps keep your heart and blood vessels in good shape. And they're the most efficient way to burn body fat.

Aerobics generally involves repetitive movement of large muscle groups, like the legs, that demands lots of oxygen (the term *aerobic* means "with oxygen"), and any activity that gets your pulse going and quickens your breath qualifies. That includes those activities that probably pop into your mind first, such as running, biking, and swimming. But you can also get an aerobic workout through hobbies that you may find enjoyable, such as hoeing your garden, hiking amid fall foliage, or dancing the night away.

Getting started on an aerobic-exercise program isn't difficult—just getting off the couch and out the door is a great beginning. But if you want to put together a more meaningful plan, follow the FIT formula—Frequency, Intensity, and Time.

Frequency: The Calendar Consideration

How often should you exercise? Unless you're undergoing vigorous training that requires time for rest and recuperation, the sky's the limit, and you should feel free to exercise as often as you can (if your doctor okays it). But holding yourself back is probably not the issue. As a rule, you should exercise at least three to five days per week. If you're just starting a program and this seems overwhelming, rest assured that any increase in activity will do you good. Studies find, in fact, that if you're totally sedentary, you can improve your cardiovascular condition significantly with as little as one workout a week. Once you get into a groove, though, it'll take at least three workouts a week for you to challenge your muscles consistently enough to continue improving.

Intensity: How Hard to Push

The exercise you do needs to be intense enough to give your body a good workout, but not so intense that you can't keep it going for a sustained period of time. Naturally, your intensity tolerance will be different from the next person's. Some people can run a mile in 10 minutes, while others might feel winded by

TAKE-CHARGE TIPS

To know if you're hitting your target heart rate, you'll need to take your pulse during your workout. Here's how:

➲ Locate an artery either on the palm side of your wrist or at either side of your neck just under your jawbone.

➲ Press lightly with your index and middle fingers to feel your pulse.

➲ Timing with your watch, count the number of beats you feel in 10 seconds.

➲ Don't bother counting for a full 60 seconds: The longer you stop to count, the slower your heart will beat, which skews your reading. Instead, multiply the 10-second count by six to find your beats per minute.

➲ Alternative: Calculate in advance how many beats should occur within 10 seconds by dividing your target rate by six. For example, if your target rate is 90 to 153 beats per minute, you should count 15 (90 divided by 6) to 25 (153 divided by 6) beats in 10 seconds. If you remember the target 10-second numbers, you can skip doing the math during your workout.

➲ A totally math-free alternative: Take the talk test. If you're sweating steadily and somewhat short of breath while exercising but can still carry on a conversation without gasping for air, you're probably within your target heart-rate range.

CALCULATE YOUR TARGET HEART RATE

AGE	25	30	35	40	45	50	55	60	65	70	75	80
Maximum heart rate	195	190	185	180	175	170	165	160	155	150	145	140
50% of max (low intensity)	97	95	92	90	87	85	82	80	77	75	72	70
85% of max (high intensity)	166	162	157	153	149	145	140	136	132	128	123	119
Beats per 10 seconds at 50%–85% of max	16–27	16–27	15–26	15–25	15–25	14–24	14–23	13–23	13–22	13–21	12–20	12–20

a walk around the block. It's important to find the level of exertion that's right for you and your current physical condition, not only to gain the most benefit for your health but also to make sure you don't overdo it.

The gold standard for measuring how hard you're working is your heart rate, or how fast your heart is beating. Shoot for a heart rate that's 50 to 85 percent of your maximum—the point at which your heart can't pump any harder. At the beginning of your exercise program, you should start at the low-intensity end of this spectrum and gradually work toward a more vigorous workout as you become better conditioned.

Maximum heart rate tends to be fairly consistent from one person to the next, although it declines gradually as you get older. That makes it easy to come up with a target heart-rate range that's specific to your age. To calculate your target heart rate:

▶ First figure out your maximum heart rate by subtracting your age from 220. For example, if you're 40 years old, subtract 40 from 220 to get a maximum heart rate of 180 beats per minute.

▶ Multiply this number by .50 and .85 to get the lower and upper limits of the 50- to 85-percent range. In this example, a maximum heart rate of 180 results in a target heart rate of 90 (180 x .50) to 153 (180 x .85) beats per minute.

Be sure to confirm with your doctor that the target heart rate you calculate is safe for you. Then check your pulse when you exercise (see "Take-Charge Tips" on the previous page). If it's in your target range, every pump of your heart is beating back your diabetes and its potential cardiovascular complications. But don't feel that less strenuous activity has no value: Even small bouts of exertion help to burn calories (though to a lesser extent), and any amount of activity is better than none.

Time: The Long and Short of It

The third FITness factor is how long each workout should last. As a rule, you should shoot for 20 to 40 minutes—long enough to give your heart and lungs the workout they need to improve, but not so long that you get tired and start to slow down. The more conditioned you become, the longer you should be able to go.

It's not all or nothing, however. If you don't have 20 to 40 minutes, try cutting your workout in half but doing it twice—once in the morning and once in the evening (or any other time that's convenient for you). Researchers have found in a number of studies that you can get almost as fit with shorter bouts of activity sprinkled throughout your day as with a single session. For example, in a study at Stanford University, men who exercised three times a day for 10 minutes reaped similar gains in oxygen uptake (a measure of cardiovascular fitness) as men who exercised for 30 minutes straight. A University of Pittsburgh weight-loss study of women produced comparable results—and also found that people who exercised in shorter sessions were better at sticking with their programs.

That means you have tremendous flexibility in exercising when it's most convenient. If you vacuum the floor in the morning, take a walk around the block at lunchtime, and rake some leaves at sundown, you can satisfy a day's workout requirements without ever changing into gym clothes or needing to take a shower.

CALCULATE YOUR CALORIE BURN

Here's the approximate number of calories you'll burn in 30 minutes of various activities, based on your weight.

ACTIVITY	140 LB	170 LB	200 LB
Aerobics, low impact	139	155	166
Bicycling, outdoors (moderate pace)	223	245	266
Bicycling, stationary (moderate pace)	195	215	233
Cleaning, general household	97	110	117
Dancing	125	140	150
Digging in garden	139	155	166
Golfing	125	140	150
Horseback riding	111	125	133
Jumping rope	279	310	333
Mowing the lawn	153	170	183
Ping-Pong	111	125	133
Raking	111	125	133
Rowing, stationary (moderate pace)	195	215	233
Running (12-minute mile)	223	245	266
Stair-stepping machine	167	185	200
Swimming	167	185	200
Tennis	195	215	233
Walking (20-minute mile)	97	107	117
Weight lifting (moderate intensity)	84	92	100

Some scientists still feel the evidence showing benefits from exercise "short takes" is sketchy, and experts agree that you'll reap the greatest gains in blood-sugar control, insulin sensitivity, heart health, and overall fitness if you work out for longer periods of time. But again, something is better than nothing. And if you lace up your shoes for a short walk, who knows? Once you're up and out the door—and your body remembers how good exercise feels—you might find yourself circling the neighborhood and not just the block.

Getting the Right FIT

Don't feel like pushing yourself today? Did you skip a workout last week? Not a problem. If you happen to change one of the FIT variables, just adjust another one to make up the difference. For example, if you exercise at a lower-than-usual heart rate (less intensity), you can add to the duration of the workout (more time) to essentially come out even. If you miss a workout (less frequency), you can boost either the intensity or the time during your next session, as long as you don't overdo it.

Put the Muscle on Blood Sugar

If you're going to give priority to one form of exercise, it should be aerobics. But there's another weapon in the exercise arsenal that's worth launching against diabetes: resistance training, also known as weight lifting. While aerobics builds endurance, resistance training builds strength and muscle mass—important because just like bigger cars, bigger muscles burn more fuel, which lowers your blood sugar. It also boosts your metabolism, even when you're at rest. And when you're stronger you'll look better, be less prone to injury, and simply find it easier to do daily tasks, from hauling groceries to climbing stairs.

Unlike aerobics, resistance training—so called because muscles work against a resisting force, such as the weight of a dumbbell—involves exercises that make muscles tire quickly.

(Continued on page 130)

GOOD WAYS TO GET GOING

No one exercise is inherently better than another. Your only goals are to move your body, pump up your heart rate—and have fun doing it. What you choose is a matter of preference, though some aerobic activities may be more appropriate for you than others in light of your complications (if you have any). Here's what some of the most popular exercises have going for them.

WALKING

Benefits

It doesn't cost anything and won't beat up your joints, and you can do it virtually anytime, anywhere—down your street, at the mall, or in a park. Its low intensity makes it a good starting point for any exercise program, but if you pick up the pace (especially on hills), it delivers a solid cardiovascular workout.

Tips

Start by just heading out the door. Breathe the air. Let your mind wander. Try to walk for at least 10 minutes at first, and gradually lengthen your walks as you feel more comfortable. Keep the pace easy until you hit the 20- to 30-minute mark, then start cranking up the intensity. Work toward a pace of about four miles per hour, which will bag you a mile every 15 minutes. A simple gadget called a pedometer, available at sporting-goods stores, can keep track of your mileage for you.

A WALKING PLAN FOR BEGINNERS

Not used to exercise? Walking is an easy, nonintimidating way to start. Try this six-week plan to get you going. By week six, you'll be walking enough to help control your blood sugar.

	DURATION	INTENSITY	FREQUENCY
Week 1	10–15 minutes	As slow as you want	3–5 times
Week 2	15 minutes	50–60% of your maximum heart rate	3–5 times
Week 3	20 minutes	50–60% of your maximum heart rate	5 times
Week 4	20 minutes	60% of your maximum heart rate	5 times
Week 5	25 minutes	60–70% of your maximum heart rate	5 times
Week 6	30 minutes	60–70% of your maximum heart rate	5 times

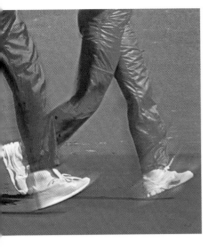

JOGGING

Benefits

It's almost as inexpensive and convenient as walking. Because it's more intense than walking, you can get a better workout in less time. It also feels (and looks) more serious than walking, which can bolster your sense of accomplishment.

Tips

Instead of a run, set out for a "wog"—a walk-jog. Start out by walking briskly, then progress into a run. When you feel winded, walk again. As you become better conditioned, you'll find yourself jogging more and walking less. If your joints start to bother you, rest for a day or two or go back to walking. To minimize the risk of injury, avoid hard pavement and opt, whenever possible, for soft, even surfaces, such as running tracks at schools and smooth expanses of grass.

BICYCLING

Benefits

Biking delivers fitness benefits plus a bracing rush of speed—at least if the bike is real, not stationary. Both types exercise your heart and your leg muscles without putting undue stress on your knees.

Tips

Start at a moderate pace of about 50 revolutions per minute (rpm). Digital readouts on stationary bikes often show the rpm; on a real bike, count the number of times one pedal reaches the top of its arc in 30 seconds, then multiply by two. When it feels comfortable, gradually boost your rpm to somewhere between 60 and 90. From there, you can adjust the program on your stationary bike for more resistance or (on a real bike) start shifting into higher gears or head for the hills.

SWIMMING

Benefits

By taking the load off joints, swimming is one of the exercises least likely to injure you, especially if you're overweight. It's also highly aerobic, depending as much on heart and lung capacity as muscle power.

Tips

Start at a leisurely pace with strokes that keep your face out of the water. When your aerobic conditioning improves, you can start holding your breath more. Make it a goal to do 10 laps without stopping. You might also decide to take a water-aerobics class if one is offered at a gym near you.

ROWING

Benefits

Works both the arms and the legs (along with most of the body's other muscles) while providing an excellent aerobic workout.

Tips

For proper form, use your arms and legs simultaneously, sliding back in the rolling seat without throwing your back into the action. Once you've got the motion down (if you're at a gym, ask a trainer for instructions), start with short 5-minute sessions and gradually work up to the 30-minute target, then adjust the resistance to make the exercise more difficult.

Therefore, they can't be sustained for more than a brief period. The idea is to consistently stress muscles, adding resistance as you become stronger to build them up even more.

Don't assume that pumping iron is only for hardbodies with rippling muscles or that you're too old to hit the weights. Studies find that even adults approaching their 90s can firm up their muscles with resistance training, reaping bonus benefits like stronger bones and more vitality.

How to Make a Muscle

Resistance exercises don't work the entire body at once, as aerobic exercises do. Instead, you need to do different exercises that target specific muscle groups. If you go to a gym, you'll find machines designed to help you do this. But you can also do resistance training at home, using basic exercises like push-ups and pull-ups and possibly some hand weights, or dumbbells, which you can get from any sporting-goods store. (If you don't want to buy dumbbells, you can improvise your own using everyday objects like milk jugs filled with water or sand.) How much weight you need depends on what you can comfortably lift, and that will vary from exercise to exercise, so you'll need more than one set of dumbbells. Sets of 3, 5, and 10 pounds should do the trick.

Use the exercises on page 134 and 135 to get started. And follow these basic principles:

⮕ **Lift to fatigue.** Rather than building endurance, with weight lifting you want to quickly make muscles so tired they just can't do much more. As a rule, you should have enough resistance during any exercise to make muscles feel fatigued after 8 to 12 repetitions. At the beginning of your program, start with light weights that you can easily lift for 12 repetitions until your muscles get accustomed to being worked.

⮕ **Make gradual progress.** Don't try to do too much at once: Building muscle is a long-term construction project that moves ahead slowly. Tackling more weight than you can comfortably handle will only make muscles sore and discourage you from continuing your workouts. If you can easily lift a given weight 12 times, add weight to make 8 repetitions easy, but

12 hard. (Don't add more than five pounds at a time.) Then, keeping to that amount of weight, gradually add more repetitions to your workouts until 12 repetitions feels easy. At that point, add more weight so that 8 reps are easy but 12 are hard...and so on.

⟳ **Move slowly.** Avoid quick, jerky movements with weights, which can stress muscles, ligaments, and joints. Slow and controlled movements ensure that you're working muscles at every point in your range of motion and not letting momentum do any of the work for you. A general guideline: Take two seconds to lift the weight and four seconds to let it down again.

⟳ **Breathe evenly.** Don't hold your breath when lifting weights—you need to keep oxygen flowing to working muscles. Breathe out when you lift and in when you let the weight down.

⟳ **Go from big to small.** Work large groups of muscles like the chest, legs, and back first, saving smaller muscles, such as the biceps and triceps, for last. That way, you won't tire smaller muscles that support the bigger muscles during their workout.

Taking the First Steps

If you're a stranger to exercise, the idea can seem intimidating. And starting anything new requires motivation. If you're having trouble getting going, take the easiest action possible—stepping out the front door for a walk. Once you conquer inertia, you can start to think about a more structured exercise plan.

Experts have discovered that people go through several distinct stages when they make fitness a fixture in their life. In the beginning, there's ignorance or lack of interest—exercise is simply off your radar—followed by a period of "contemplation," in which you're interested but take no action. Next comes "preparation," in which you begin to get moving but aren't physically active enough. It's common in this stage for barriers—everything from lack of time to lack of confidence—to hold you back. The mantra is often "I could never do that." And "that" could be anything from exercising for 20 minutes straight to joining an exercise class. But the question is, What can you do? Can you be physically active for two minutes by, say, walking around instead of

sitting down while waiting for someone at the mall? Then start there. The more you move, the more easily you'll progress to the next two stages: "action," in which you exercise regularly as a new habit, and "maintenance," in which you reinforce that new habit to make it stick.

Planning for Action

Crossing the line into the action phase can be so gradual, you may not be sure when you've arrived. One sign: You feel a need to organize your efforts. All your exercise doesn't have to be written into your calendar, but scheduling it can ensure that the time you need doesn't get swallowed up by other activities. It can also help you work toward specific goals that will keep you improving. The ideal plan is a mix of aerobic workouts lasting at least 20 to 30 minutes three to five days a week and resistance training at least two days a week. That sounds like a lot of exercising, but here are two basic strategies for fitting it all in.

Alternating workouts. Do your aerobic exercise three days a week, but keep a day open between each workout. Use the two open days to do your resistance training. That way, you can fit a comprehensive fitness plan into a five-day schedule, giving you two days off. This plan will also give muscles—which are worked differently in aerobics than in resistance training—a day to rest between each form of exercise.

Combination workouts. If you can squeeze in workouts only a few days a week, do one workout that incorporates both aerobics and resistance training. (Just don't do it two days in a row.) These sessions will be longer than if you worked out five days a week, but many people find that once they've

BEFORE YOU JOIN A GYM

Potentially, the world is your workout facility. But if you want access to high-quality resistance machines, aerobics classes, and trained staff, a gym may be worth the money—especially if it helps you stick with an exercise program. But gyms make their money because many of the people who pay for them rarely show up to use them. To make sure you'll get your money's worth:

■ Find a gym that's no more than 15 minutes from home or you'll have trouble getting there regularly.

■ Take a tour before signing anything, and ask to have a trial workout. If possible, snag clients out of your tour guide's earshot and ask their opinion of the place.

■ Make sure club supervisors have at least a bachelor's degree in exercise science, and look for staff certifications from organizations like the National Strength and Conditioning Association or the Aerobics and Fitness Association of America.

■ Check out the crowd, especially at times you're most likely to be there. Is it hard-core or low-key? Will you be comfortable working out with these people?

■ Be clear about your needs. Some clubs offer just fitness equipment and classes, while others go a step beyond with tennis or racquetball courts, swimming pools, and even social activities. Don't sign on the dotted line if you think you might want something different in six months.

committed a block of time to exercise, adding another 20 to 30 minutes is not a huge hurdle. Start with aerobics, which will warm and limber up muscles, and follow with resistance. (Exhausting muscles with weights first would make your aerobics workout more difficult.) If you're really strapped for time, skip the resistance training on one of the days.

Seven Steps to Success

When you start an exercise program, it's common to feel nagging doubts—that it's too hard, you're no good at it, you're too out of shape. To help yourself stay focused and boost your confidence:

1 **Make it fun.** Some people think exercise has to be unpleasant to do any good. Don't be one of them. You're more likely to stick with activities you enjoy—maybe because you like seeing what's going on in the neighborhood during your walks, you feel like a kid when gliding on your bike, or you enjoy spending time with your workout partner.

2 **Forget the old days.** You may have been a star quarterback or track standout in high school, but say thanks for the memories and move on with reality. Dwelling on how your body's changed will only make you see setbacks. Instead, focus on how you can change again—for the better.

3 **Set firm goals.** It helps to have goals, especially clear, immediate ones. Keep your goals specific and oriented toward what you will actually do, not where you'll end up if you do it. Saying "I'll run five minutes longer next time" is better than "I want to be able to do five miles by the holidays."

4 **Be your own benchmark.** Pay no attention to the next person's washboard abs or lack of cellulite. What you're doing has nothing to do with anybody but you. Stay focused on your goals. If you achieve a small success, even if it's just walking three times this week instead of twice, then celebrate!

5 **Make a note of it.** Tracking your progress in a notebook can help you realize how far you've come—or haven't. If you're walking or running, record your time or distance. If you're resistance-training, jot down how much weight you're lifting and how many repetitions you're doing.

(Continued on page 136)

WHAT THE STUDIES SHOW

Short on time for strength training? Twice a week should be enough. Researchers at the University of Arkansas had one group of women do a weight workout three times a week and another group only twice a week. The twice-a-week group lifted slightly lighter weights and did six more repetitions of each exercise, spending about five extra minutes on their workout. Result: The twice-weekly group reaped almost the same benefits as the other women after eight weeks, boosting strength by at least 15 percent and losing more than 2 percent of their body fat.

AN ALL-YOU-NEED ROUTINE

These seven exercises provide a full-body workout that targets all the major muscle groups. To start, do just one set of each exercise. Once your muscles get used to it, do at least two sets to gain the most benefit. Eventually, you may want to add or substitute exercises with help from a trainer or a good fitness book. Again: Be sure to have your doctor approve any exercise program to make sure it's safe for you.

LEGS
Lunges
1. Stand with your feet shoulder-width apart. Keeping your back straight, take a large step forward with your right foot so that your right leg is bent at a 90-degree angle and your knee is aligned over your right foot but not beyond your toes. Your left foot should remain in the starting position, though your left knee can bend to within a few inches of the floor and the heel can come off the floor.

2. Push yourself back firmly with your right leg to return to the starting position, then repeat with the left foot, and so on.

CHEST
Dumbbell chest press
1. Lie faceup on a bench with your knees bent to protect your back. Grasping a dumbbell in each hand with palms facing each other, exhale as you press the weights straight above your chest until your elbows are straight, but not locked.

2. Inhaling, slowly lower the dumbbells to your chest, with your elbows just below the level of your torso.

Safety pointer: Maintain a firm grip on each dumbbell, with fingers wrapped around one side of the bar and your thumb around the other, to keep weights under control at all times.

BACK
One-arm dumbbell row
1. With your left knee resting on a bench or low table, place your left hand on the bench and your right foot on the floor, knee slightly bent. In your right hand, hold a dumbbell straight down at your side, eyes facing the floor and back straight. Exhale as you draw the weight to your torso.

2. Inhale as you lower the dumbbell back to the starting position. When you finish your set, repeat the exercise on the other side of your body.

Safety pointer: Keep your back straight and your torso motion to a minimum to avoid straining your back, especially as you get tired.

TRICEPS
Dumbbell Kickbacks
1. Rest your right knee on a bench or low table, your right hand on the bench, and your left leg extended behind you, knee slightly bent. To get the weight to the starting position, hold a dumbbell in your left hand, palm toward your body, and bend your arm at a 45-degree angle.

2. Without moving your elbow, straighten your arm, extending the weight behind you. Then return to the starting position. Repeat on the other side.

BICEPS
Biceps curl
1. Sit on a chair, feet flat on the floor a little wider than shoulder-width apart. Grasp a dumbbell in each hand, with your arms straight at your sides, your palms facing your legs.

2. Keeping your elbows pressed against your sides, raise the weights in an arc toward your shoulders, turning your wrists so that your palms face your shoulders. Then lower the weights until your arms are straight, but elbows are not locked.

ABDOMINALS
Crunches
1. Lie faceup on the floor or an exercise mat, knees bent and feet on the floor about six inches apart. Point your toes up to provide extra back support. Lightly hold both hands behind your head or ears. Starting with your head a few inches off the floor, exhale as you curl your upper torso toward your thighs, raising your shoulders up but keeping the small of your back pressed against the floor.

2. Hold briefly, then, inhaling, slowly lower your upper body to the floor, keeping your head lifted a few inches at your lowest position.

SHOULDERS
Lateral raises
1. Stand with feet shoulder-width apart. Grasp a dumbbell in each hand with arms at your sides, elbows slightly bent and palms facing your body.

2. Keeping your back straight and tensing your abdominal muscles for back support, raise both dumbbells straight out from your sides until they're at shoulder level. Keep your elbows unlocked and your wrists, elbows, and shoulders in a straight line. Pause, then lower the weights.

6 **Get friends involved.** Try to enlist likable companions as workout partners: With a buddy to back you up, you'll feel validation, support, and maybe even a bit of competitiveness to spur you on. You're also more likely to stick to an exercise schedule if skipping a workout means letting down a friend. And don't forget the value of having someone at your side if your blood sugar crashes.

7 **Keep your priorities straight.** Life is about choices. And what's really more important: scrubbing the bathtub or fulfilling your exercise quota for the day? In the long run, exercise can save your life. In the short run, it can make you feel great. While scrubbing the bathtub might seem critical at the moment, it may not seem important a week from now.

How to Be a Perpetual-Motion Machine

If you can't swing a steady schedule of workouts, don't feel you've failed. Instead, look for opportunities to make movement a part of everyday life—you'll find them. Studies show that taking a lifestyle-based approach to exercise can improve fitness almost as much as a program of gym workouts, with sedentary people able to gain 30 minutes of activity five days a week just by sneaking it into their regular day. Some ways to achieve this:

➲ Next time you go to a sporting event, don't stay on the bench. Get up and walk around between quarters. Circle the stadium at halftime. Climb the stairs during time-outs—and stay clear of the hot dog stand.

➲ Why tap your feet waiting for the elevator? Hit the stairs instead—you may actually get where you're going faster.

➲ If you're going to sit in front of the tube, make it a stationary-bicycle seat. Aim to pedal your way through a 30-minute program. If you don't have a bike, do jumping jacks or march in place during the commercials.

➲ Instead of fighting for parking close to the door, head for the open spaces farther out and walk the rest of the way.

➲ Take the dog (if you don't have one, borrow the neighbor's pooch) for a stroll or run. Let him decide where to go, and follow wherever he leads.

➲ Get up to change channels instead of using the remote.

➲ Instead of meeting a friend for coffee, skip the java and get your jolt of energy from a walk in the park.

WALKING AWAY FROM DIABETES

When Deborah McMahon, 53, was hospitalized for dehydration during a bout of the flu, she didn't expect to receive a diagnosis of type 2 diabetes—but she did. With her blood-sugar level topping 300 and her A1c result a sky-high 11.7, her doctors didn't expect her to be off medication just four months later—but she was. The Des Moines resident's blood sugar now holds generally steady at a very healthy 82, and her A1c is now below 6. It seems McMahon has literally walked away from diabetes.

"When I received the diagnosis, I said, 'Okay, this isn't terrible. This is something I can live with,'" she recalls. "My doctor agreed, telling me that some aspects of treatment were in my control, especially diet and exercise. He mentioned walking as the easiest exercise—all you need is a good pair of shoes." The following day, after McMahon was discharged, she walked into a bookstore to gather information on diabetes care—and she's been walking ever since.

Each day, McMahon straps on a pedometer (a device that counts footfalls) and hikes about 10,000 steps (about five miles). But she doesn't limit exercise to one walking workout a day; McMahon also follows exercise experts' advice to incorporate more movement into everyday activities. "I have to park a few blocks from work, and that used to bother me. Today, I'm glad for the built-in opportunity to get more steps."

To learn more about diabetes management, McMahon attended classes at her hospital's diabetes-education center, and it was there that she stated her goal: to get off medication, which she was taking twice a day. "I was warned that this would be very hard to do," she says. "But I decided I was going to take charge of diabetes, and not let it take charge of me."

By combining regular exercise with a healthful eating plan (her favorite treats are now blueberries and low-fat granola bars), McMahon cut her daily dose of medication in half within a couple of months. Two months after that, she was down to none. And about two months after that, she achieved another health goal: She had pared 62 pounds from her at-diagnosis weight of 214 pounds.

McMahon's all-out efforts to cut out medication (and cut herself down to a healthier size) took place during the winter, when Iowa weather can make outdoor exercise tough. "When it's really cold out, I'll simply pace around the house," says McMahon. "My family thinks I'm nutty, but I tell them, 'You just do whatever you have to do.'"

6

Drugs and Surgery

Less than a century ago, there was not a single treatments for diabetes. Then came insulin and the first medications for type 2. Now new treatment options offer unprecedented flexibility, with shorter- and longer-acting forms of insulin to choose from and an assortment of drugs that can be mixed and matched to meet your own specific needs. Meanwhile, new devices deliver insulin without needles, and surgery, though not risk-free, offers a solution for some.

You're eating right, you're working out—but your blood sugar is still too high. What now? Diet and exercise go a long way toward controlling blood sugar, but there will be times when you'll need some extra help. For people with type 1 diabetes, the power assist of insulin is actually a key to survival. People with type 2 can benefit from insulin, too, but injections may still be a long way down the road if you can get a grip on glucose with pills.

In the not-so-distant past, the medical options for controlling diabetes were limited. Initially, there was just insulin and, starting in the 1950s, a single class of oral medications (known as sulfonylureas) that could help bring down blood sugar. It wasn't until the mid-1990s that new classes of drugs began to emerge. Now if you have type 2 diabetes, you and your doctor can choose among several types of oral medications—all of which attack high blood sugar in different ways. This has vastly expanded your treatment options, not only because each type of drug represents an advance in itself but because the various types can be used together in dozens of different combinations that best suit your individual needs.

It's important to note, by the way, that diabetes pills are not simply oral forms of insulin. Acids in your digestive tract would break insulin down and render it useless before your body could use it, which is why insulin has to be injected instead of swallowed. And pills don't work for people with type 1 diabetes because such medications often rely on the ability of the pancreas to produce at least some insulin—which simply doesn't happen with most type 1 patients. In fact, being able to use oral medications as a first line of medical therapy is a key distinction between type 2 and type 1 diabetes.

Medications have helped millions of people with type 2 diabetes lead healthier and more fulfilling lives, but they're not a cure for type 2 diabetes any more than insulin is a cure for type 1. And you certainly can't put aside your meal plan or regular exercise just because you're taking medication. If anything, the reasoning goes the other way: If your doctor prescribes drugs, achieving better glucose control with diet and exercise may get you off meds again.

When Do You Need Medical Help?

Whatever the miracles of medication, controlling blood sugar naturally with good old diet and exercise will always top your doctor's orders. Drugs, after all, often have side effects. Yet sometimes doctors put patients on medication right after diagnosis. What makes you a candidate for drugs?

It all begins with your blood sugar. Remember that a diagnosis of diabetes kicks in when fasting blood glucose is 126 mg/dl and you're trying to bring it down to around 120. Beyond that, your long-term hemoglobin A1c test results should come in below 7 percent—and many endocrinologists say 6.5 percent is a better goal. These are the benchmarks your doctor will consider first.

There are no hard-and-fast rules about when to start taking medication because everybody's body is different and each case must be treated individually. But doctors tend to follow some rough guidelines, as outlined below.

Deciding Who Needs Drugs

Generally, doctors will let you try to bring blood sugar under control with diet and exercise alone as long as your fasting glucose is 140 to 150 mg/dl or less. But here's where the A1c results come in. If your hemoglobin number is holding at around 7 percent, there's a good chance you'll succeed with just lifestyle changes. If this number creeps up to 7.5 or above, however, you'll likely need extra help. Still, at this level your doctor will usually let you try diet and exercise alone for a three-month trial period. Then, if your A1c number is still above 7 percent, you'll probably need to take medication.

If you start off with fasting blood-glucose levels higher than 150 mg/dl or your A1c results hit 8 percent, your doctor may put you on drugs from the get-go. But that doesn't mean you'll stay on them forever. Often, doctors prescribe drugs to gain immediate control over blood sugar until diet and exercise have a chance to produce results. After that, it's possible you won't need drugs anymore.

Blood-sugar numbers aren't the only factor that dictates whether you need medication. For example, let's say your numbers suggest that diet and exercise alone would help you, but you're not overweight (true of 10 to 20 percent of people with type 2) or you're already eating a good diet and working out. In each case, it's unlikely that eating one fewer cookie or exercising an extra 10 minutes will make a significant difference, so your doctor may prescribe medication sooner than he would someone with similar numbers who is overweight and sedentary.

On the other hand, your doctor may steer clear of ordering certain drugs if you have complications or other health problems that make them poor choices for you. For example, metformin, one of the most popular diabetes drugs, can cause a potentially fatal buildup of lactic acid in the blood (a condition called lactic acidosis) in people who have kidney, heart, or liver disease, and it shouldn't be taken by these patients.

Bringing in the Big Gun: Insulin

Even after you're on medication, your doctor will keep a sharp eye on your blood sugar. If one prescription isn't working adequately, he may try other drugs or drug combinations. You might go through five or six different regimens before he calls in the bigger guns. Once it's clear that drugs, diet, and exercise aren't doing enough to keep your blood sugar under control, your doctor may add an evening or bedtime dose of insulin to offset the glucose released by the liver at night.

For some people with type 2 diabetes, it makes sense to go straight to insulin therapy. Doctors may advise this strategy when their patients don't tolerate drugs well, have diseases of the kidneys or liver, or have a greater need for insulin due to injury, infection, or severe stress.

People with type 2 diabetes often don't need to give themselves as many injections as people with type 1 because the body is still able to manufacture insulin (or use the insulin it produces) to some extent. But the longer you have type 2 diabetes, the less your body can do on its own, generally, and the more likely you are to need insulin. This doesn't mean you've failed at managing your diabetes. It means simply that your disease has progressed to a point at which other types of therapy can't help you as much as they should.

The Medication Menu

No fewer than 15 basic drugs for diabetes are now available, and they are grouped according to how they work. Some make the body produce more insulin, others make cells better able to take in glucose or slow the release of glucose into the blood, and still others do several things at once.

Choosing which drugs to use can be a complicated business, and you'll need to trust your doctor to help you make the right choices. But you should educate yourself in order to weigh in on these decisions and understand your options if the drugs you're prescribed don't work well for you.

Bear in mind that medication works best in people who have had diabetes for less than 10 years. That's because drugs build on the body's ability to produce some insulin, but this ability tends to dwindle as diabetes progresses. You can also expect drugs to become less effective the longer you take them. That's why it's good to have choices; often your doctor can add a different drug to your regimen.

Sulfonylureas: The Old and the New Guard

Sulfonylureas are the granddaddies of diabetes drugs. Some of them have been around for almost 50 years and are still among the most widely prescribed treatments. For many years, there were four sulfonylureas, referred to as first-generation drugs. More recently, second- and third-generation drugs have been added.

All sulfonylureas bring blood sugar down in the same way: They bind to beta cells in the pancreas and stimulate them to produce more insulin. They differ from each other mainly in how much of them you need to take, how often you take them, how quickly they work, and how long they last. For example, the second-generation drugs are far more powerful than their first-generation siblings, so much lower doses are required. They are also less likely to interact with other medications.

Side effects. Most people do fine on sulfonylureas, but it's possible that these drugs will upset your stomach or cause skin reactions as a result of increased sensitivity to the sun. Let your

SULFONYLUREA DRUGS

First-generation drugs in this category are tried-and-true and widely prescribed. But the newer, second-generation sulfonylureas can deliver powerful effects with less medication, so your doctor may start you off with one of them.

DRUG	BRAND NAME	COMMENTS
FIRST-GENERATION DRUGS		
Acetohexamide	Dymelor	Takes effect in about an hour and lasts about 12 hours.
Chlorpropamide	Diabinase Glucamide	Lasts longer than other first-generation sulfonylureas, staying active in the body for 24 hours or more. Approach this drug with caution because its extended action can cause prolonged hypoglycemia. It can also contribute to water retention and cause your face to flush if you drink alcohol.
Tolazamide	Tolinase	It's absorbed very slowly; it doesn't take effect for about 4 hours and lasts for about 20 hours.
Tolbutamide	Orinase	The fastest-acting sulfonylurea. Kicks in after about an hour. A good choice if you have a very hard time keeping blood sugar down after meals.
SECOND-GENERATION DRUGS		
Glipizide	Glucotrol Glucotrol XL	Takes effect in one hour. Usually taken before meals to control after-eating glucose spikes.
Glyburide	Diabeta Glynase Micronase	Intermediate-acting. Stays active in the body for 12 to 16 hours.
THIRD-GENERATION DRUGS		
Glimipiride	Amaryl	Long-acting. Usually needs to be taken only once, at breakfast, to keep blood sugar steady throughout the day.

doctor know if these problems persist. Some people are allergic to sulfa drugs (which include sulfonylureas and some antibiotics), so, though these effects are rare, be on the lookout for skin rashes, hives, or swelling, especially of the airways. You'll also want to steer clear of sulfonylureas if you have liver or kidney problems or if you're pregnant.

Mighty Metformin

Since its introduction in the United States in 1994, metformin (Glucophage) has become the best-selling diabetes drug in the country—and it's no wonder, when you look at the amazing diversity of effects packed into each two- to three-times-daily pill. Metformin reduces the amount of glucose released from storage sites in the liver. This keeps blood sugar low not only after eating but between meals and during the night as well. It also hinders the absorption of glucose from food. By itself, metformin will not cause hypoglycemia because it doesn't make cells draw glucose out of the blood. And because it attacks the problem from a different angle, it makes a perfect companion to sulfonylureas. Combining the two is one of the most common forms of drug therapy.

Another plus: People often tend to lose weight when taking metformin, though it's not entirely clear why. It may reduce the appetite by irritating the gastrointestinal tract or by giving food a strange taste (often with a metallic tang). Whatever the reason, this makes metformin a boon to type 2 patients who are overweight and need to shed a few pounds anyway.

And there's more: Metformin brings down LDL ("bad") cholesterol and triglycerides (while raising "good" HDL cholesterol) and may make muscles more insulin sensitive. It works so well, in fact, that it cuts the risk of diabetes in people with impaired glucose tolerance by 31 percent, according to a major study called the Diabetes Prevention Program.

Side effects. Metformin sounds like a miracle medicine, but it's not perfect. Besides the unappetizing taste it lends to food and such gastrointestinal symptoms as nausea, bloating, and gas, some patients find it causes skin rashes. These side effects often disappear after several weeks and are less likely to crop up if you start on low doses and take the drug with food. You should avoid metformin if you're pregnant or have kidney disease, severe liver disease, or congestive heart failure—conditions in which the drug can promote lactic acidosis, a potentially fatal buildup of lactic acid in the blood. Drinking a lot of alcohol while on metformin can also promote this condition, so be up-front with your doctor about your alcohol intake when considering this drug.

Sensitivity Training for Cells

Another class of drugs gets the tongue-twister award for its scientific name: thiazolidinediones. But the idea behind these drugs is simple: They attack high blood sugar from a third angle—by boosting the insulin sensitivity of cells so that they're better able to take in glucose and clear it out of the blood. This makes the drugs especially useful for keeping blood sugar down

DID YOU KNOW?

The sulfa-drug class includes antibiotics that were new to battlefields during World War II. When a French army doctor noticed that the antibiotics made some patients act as if they had low blood sugar, he wrote about it to a colleague, who began experiments that showed sulfas could bring down blood sugar in animals. From these discoveries, the first oral medications to treat diabetes, the sulfonylureas, were developed and made available in the decade after the war.

immediately after a meal, so your doctor may add it to your regimen if other drugs fail to do this. If you're type 2 and use insulin, these medications (usually taken once a day) may also allow you to reduce your dose.

Sometimes called glitazones, thiazolidinediones have had their share of controversy. Troglitazone, the first of these drugs to become available, was forced off the market by the Food and Drug Administration (FDA) in 2000 after some patients taking it developed serious and even fatal liver disease. The FDA still requires that doctors closely monitor patients for liver damage if they're taking these drugs, especially during the first year, but this hasn't proved to be a problem with the two drugs still on the market, rosiglitazone (Avandia) and pioglitazone (Actos).

Don't expect instant results: It takes several weeks and even as long as three months for muscle and fat cells to fully respond to these drugs. Like metformin, however, they may bring down cholesterol and triglyceride levels and won't cause hypoglycemia.

Side effects. It's no surprise that metformin is more popular than thiazolidinediones. These drugs make many people gain weight and often cause swelling from water retention, especially around the ankles. They may also cause such gastrointestinal problems as nausea and vomiting, yellowing of the skin, and headaches. As with most drugs, you shouldn't use thiazolidinediones if you're pregnant. And you should use caution if you're trying *not* to become pregnant: Thiazolidinediones may improve fertility (probably because insulin resistance, which the drugs help correct, makes you less fertile), and pioglitazone can render hormone-based contraceptives less effective.

The Sugar Stoppers

The drugs acarbose (Precose) and miglitol (Glyset), technically known as alpha-glucosidase inhibitors, work to prevent enzymes in the intestines from breaking down carbohydrates into glucose, leaving the carbs to be digested later by bacteria lower down in the intestine. This slows the release of glucose into the bloodstream and restrains the rise in blood sugar that follows a meal. Usually taken at the start of each meal, they may be a good choice if you have trouble keeping blood sugar steady after eating, especially if thiazolidinediones don't work well for you. Hypoglycemia isn't a problem with these drugs unless you combine them with other drugs, such as sulfonylureas. If you do experience a bout of hypoglycemia while on these drugs, however, it's best to treat it by taking glucose tablets, which are less responsive to the medication than the sucrose found in a sweet snacks or fruit drinks.

Side effects. Because they leave carbohydrates to be fermented by bacteria in the lower gut, the drugs produce a lot of gas, bloating, and other GI problems, including diarrhea, and some people find them intolerable for those reasons. In many cases, however, these effects will ease up over time. It helps to start on a low dose and gradually take more as your body adjusts. Still, these drugs are a poor choice if you have a GI condition like irritable bowel syndrome or ulcerative colitis or if you suffer from liver or kidney disease.

Me-Too Meglitinides

Though chemically different from sulfonylureas, the two drugs in this category, repaglinide (Prandin) and nateglinide (Starlix), work the same way as the old standbys do—by wringing more insulin out of the pancreas. One difference: Repaglinide and nateglinide take effect more quickly than sulfonylureas, so you can take them with your meal (or up to half an hour beforehand) to keep blood sugar down after eating. And their effects are short-lived. For instance, nateglinide's concentration in the blood drops sharply as soon as 90 minutes after taking it. For that reason, these drugs are less likely to cause hypoglycemia. And because they go to work so quickly, they give you the freedom to eat impromptu meals. They are often combined with metformin for longer-term control.

Side effects. Like sulfonylureas, these drugs can cause hypoglycemia, but because they are designed to work when

---

DODGING DRUG INTERACTIONS

Before your doctor prescribes a diabetes drug, make sure to tell him about any other drugs you're taking. Likewise, make sure doctors treating other conditions know you have diabetes: Many drugs can make diabetes worse by raising blood sugar. Others can lower blood sugar and may need to be factored into your dosage. Among the medications to watch out for:

DRUGS THAT MAY RAISE BLOOD SUGAR

Blood-pressure drugs: beta-blockers, calcium channel blockers, minoxidil, thiazide diuretics

Drugs for HIV: megesterol acetate, pentamidine, protease inhibitors

Antipsychotics: lithium, phenothiazines

Tuberculosis medications: isomazid, rifampin

DRUGS THAT MAY LOWER BLOOD SUGAR

Pain relievers: aspirin, acetaminophen

Blood-pressure drugs: alpha blockers, angiotensin-converting enzyme (ACE) inhibitors

Infection fighters: cibenzoline, gancyclovir, mefloquine, pentamidine, quinine, quinolones, sulfonamides, tetracyclines

Antidepressants: doxepin, MAO inhibitors, tricyclics

WHAT THE STUDIES SHOW

Should drugs like metformin be used on children? It's a controversial question because drugs commonly used safely in adults can be dangerous for kids. Definitive studies to resolve the question are underway, but some preliminary research is already at hand. In a University of California study, children who took metformin reduced their fasting blood glucose by an average of 42 mg/dl without side effects beyond those typical for adults. Researchers concluded that metformin is both safe and effective for kids.

your blood sugar is already high after eating, this tends to be less of a problem than with the older drugs. You might also experience nausea, minor weight gain, itching, and skin flushing, but these effects are usually mild. You shouldn't take repaglinide or nateglinide if you are pregnant or nursing, and you should be cautious about using them if you have liver or kidney damage.

Medication Marriages

Sometimes two drugs are better than one, especially if they work in different ways. In fact, one popular combination, metformin and a sulfonylurea, is now available in a single pill (Glucovance), which simplifies the drug-taking regimen. Studies suggest that the new combo drug works even better than taking the two medications separately.

Here are some of the drug combinations you and your doctor might consider, especially if taking one drug alone does not sufficiently control your blood sugar. Be aware that when you take a combination of drugs, you have to watch out for side effects from all the active ingredients.

▶ **Metformin plus a sulfonylurea (Glucovance)**
   Why you might use it: To make the pancreas produce more insulin while keeping baseline blood sugar low. It's the most popular—and probably most effective—drug combination for diabetes, which is why it's now available as a single pill. **What to watch out for:** Hypoglycemia, gastrointestinal troubles (mild diarrhea, stomach upset).

▶ **A sulfonylurea plus a thiazolidinedione**
   Why you might use it: If first-line sulfonylureas begin losing their ability to prod your pancreas into stepped-up insulin production, it can be helpful to bring in rosiglitazone or pioglitazone to boost insulin sensitivity. **What to watch out for:** The dual action of producing more insulin and making cells more receptive to it makes you especially susceptible to hypoglycemia.

▶ **A sulfonylurea plus an alpha-glucosidase inhibitor**

Why you might use it: Using acarbose or miglitol to keep glucose from being absorbed can help keep blood sugar low after meals if the sulfonylurea can't manage to accomplish this on its own.

What to watch out for: Digestive discomfort, hypoglycemia.

▶ **Metformin plus an alpha-glucosidase inhibitor**

Why you might use it: Not every drug combination has been subjected to detailed study. However, this one has, and results show the two drugs together are better than metformin alone at keeping blood sugar under control, especially after eating.

What to watch out for: Mainly gas, bloating, and other effects from bacterial breakdown of carbohydrates.

▶ **Metformin plus a thiazolidinedione**

Why you might use it: This combination may be especially

Drugs and Their Dosages

Most drugs come in a variety of dosages, so your doctor can fine-tune your regimen according to your condition and how well you respond to what you take. Expect to start on a low dose and move to higher doses the longer you stay on the drug.

CLASS	DRUG	BRAND NAME	DOSES
Sulfonylurea	Acetohexamide	Dymelor	250 and 500 mg
	Chlorpropamide	Diabinase, Glucamide	100 and 250 mg
	Tolazamide	Tolinase	100, 250, and 500 mg
	Tolbutamide	Orinase	250 and 500 mg
	Glimipiride	Amaryl	1, 2, and 4 mg
	Glipizide	Glucotrol, Glucotrol XL	5 and 10 mg
	Glyburide	Micronase, Diabeta, Glynase	1.25, 2.5, and 5 mg
Biguanide	Metformin	Glucophage	500, 850, and 1,000 mg
Thiazolidinedione	Rosiglitazone	Avandia	2, 4, and 8 mg
	Pioglitazone	Actos	15, 30, and 45 mg
Alpha-glucosidase inhibitor	Acarbose	Precose	25, 50, and 100 mg
	Miglitol	Glyset	25 and 50 mg
Meglitinide	Repaglinide	Prandin	0.5, 1, and 2 mg
	Nateglinide	Starlix	60 and 120 mg

useful if sulfonylureas have lost their effectiveness, particularly if being overweight has made you insulin resistant.

What to watch out for: Gastrointestinal problems.

▶ **Metformin, a thiazolidinedione, and a sulfonylurea**

Why you might use it: If you're taking metformin plus a thiazolidinedione, or metformin plus a sulfonylurea, and your blood sugar is still too high, a third drug may be added to your regimen.

What to watch out for: Hypoglycemia.

Insulin: Who Needs It?

Insulin can be a lifesaver if you have diabetes, and it's considered one of modern medicine's true breakthroughs. When it first became available in the 1920s, there was only one kind of insulin, still known as "regular" insulin. Today there are many more options—some of them available just since the 1990s.

Whether it comes from a vial or from insulin-producing cells in the pancreas, everybody needs insulin, of course—not just people with diabetes. But if your pancreas has pooped out, you need to take over its job yourself. That's not only a task for people with type 1 diabetes. In fact, 30 to 40 percent of people with type 2 need insulin as well, usually because the beta cells of the pancreas can't manufacture enough insulin to meet the body's needs (even with medication) or cells become more insulin resistant.

Normally, the pancreas pumps just the right amount of insulin necessary to help cells take up the glucose in your blood. Though a healthy pancreas constantly makes subtle adjustments, there are two basic insulin patterns you need to mimic artificially whether you have type 1 or type 2:

▶ A continuous, low-level baseline of insulin to keep blood-sugar levels stable between meals (this is sometimes referred to as basal insulin).

▶ Extra bursts of insulin (known as boluses) when blood sugar rises above this baseline level, especially after a meal.

If you have type 1 diabetes, you'll typically take doses of different insulins throughout the day to cover all your needs. If you have type 2 diabetes, the number of doses you take (and the type of insulin you use) will vary according to how well your pancreas is functioning.

Choosing the Right Insulin

Insulin has improved in both quality and variety over the years, starting with the way it's made. Until recently, most insulin was extracted from animals, such as cows and pigs, and purified for use in humans. It worked well for most people, but others had allergic reactions, such as redness, itching, swelling, or pain at the injection site. While still available, animal insulin is being used less and less thanks to the wonders of genetic engineering. Today scientists can insert human DNA with insulin-making instructions into bacteria to make them crank out bona fide human insulin as they reproduce.

What matters most about insulin, however, is how it behaves. Available today are insulins that differ in how fast they start working, when their action peaks, and how long they stay active. Insulins are organized into four categories based on how long their effects last.

Short-acting insulin. Regular insulin is now officially classified as "short-acting." This means that it starts to work quickly but doesn't last very long. You can use short-acting insulin to provide a burst of glucose control when you need it, particularly in time for a meal. Regular insulin kicks in after 30 to 60 minutes, peaks in three to four hours, and lasts for a total of 6 to 8 hours.

Rapid-acting insulin. Don't want to wait a half hour to eat while your injection takes effect? No problem: Two new insulins (sometimes considered a subset of short-acting insulins) have been chemically altered to work even faster. Lispro (Humalog) and insulin aspart (Novolog) start to lower blood sugar in about 5 to 15 minutes, peak in 60 to 90 minutes, and last three to five hours—a pattern closer to what you'd experience after eating if you had a healthy pancreas. Besides allowing you more freedom to eat when you want, rapid-acting insulin is less likely than regular insulin to cause hypoglycemia because it doesn't stay in your system after the glucose from your meal is used up.

Long-acting insulin. At the opposite extreme is long-acting ultralente (Humulin U) insulin, which takes as long as 6 hours to crank up, peaks after 12 to 18 hours, and lasts for up to 24 hours before gradually fading out. This provides the sustained, low-grade background insulin you need with only one injection a day. People with type 1 diabetes need to supplement this type of insulin with a faster-acting agent at meals. But for type 2 diabetes, a long-acting insulin may be all you need, especially if you can still use medication.

In 2000 the FDA approved another insulin called glargine (Lantus), which offers distinct advantages. It lasts all day and night, offering relatively constant action with no pronounced peak over 24 hours. In other words, it closely mimics the pancreas's background insulin production by holding insulin levels steady over the long haul.

Intermediate-acting insulin. The effects of these insulins fall in between short-acting and long-acting insulin. Their peaks tend to be higher than long-acting peaks, so they might be better for you if your insulin needs are greater. The two offerings in this category, NPH (neutral protamine hagedorn) and Lente (Novolin L and Humulin L) both contain additives that slow its release—zinc in the case of Lente and a protein called protamine in the case of NPH. Cloudy in appearance because of the additives, these insulins start bringing glucose down after about 2 hours, peak in 6 to 12 hours, and keep working for up to 24 hours. They are designed to give you good half-day insulin coverage and are often combined with short-acting insulin.

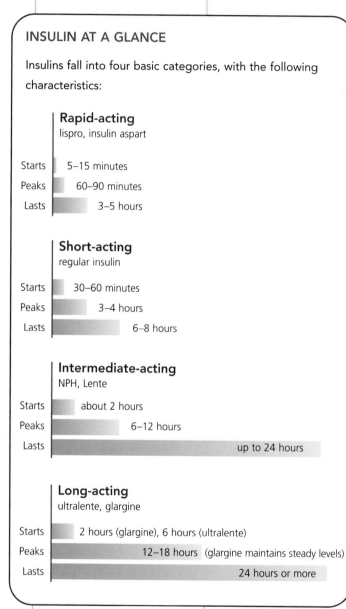

INSULIN AT A GLANCE

Insulins fall into four basic categories, with the following characteristics:

Rapid-acting
lispro, insulin aspart

Starts	5–15 minutes
Peaks	60–90 minutes
Lasts	3–5 hours

Short-acting
regular insulin

Starts	30–60 minutes
Peaks	3–4 hours
Lasts	6–8 hours

Intermediate-acting
NPH, Lente

Starts	about 2 hours
Peaks	6–12 hours
Lasts	up to 24 hours

Long-acting
ultralente, glargine

Starts	2 hours (glargine), 6 hours (ultralente)
Peaks	12–18 hours (glargine maintains steady levels)
Lasts	24 hours or more

The Ins and Outs of Insulin Therapy

You can combine different types of insulin, just as you can mix drugs to take advantage of their different effects. The plan that you and your doctor work out together will have to factor in a lot of elements—including how much you exercise (and when), what's on your meal-plan menu, and whether you're able to eat meals at a regular time each day.

Expect there to be a certain amount of guesswork at first. Everyone's body responds to insulin differently, so your personal onset, peak, and duration times may be slightly different from the averages. You'll always need to keep close tabs on your blood sugar with self-monitoring to find out exactly how you respond to the therapies you try.

Ultimately, though, deciding on an insulin plan comes down to two fundamental concerns:

▶ Making sure your body has enough insulin readily on hand to respond to blood-glucose levels as they rise and fall throughout the day

▶ Making sure you don't get caught with too much insulin in your system during times when your blood sugar is low—a surefire recipe for hypoglycemia

It's a tricky balance, but one that's worth striving for. Remember that the breakthrough Diabetes Control and Complications Trial found that people who kept their blood sugar in tight control reduced their risk of such complications as eye, kidney, and nerve disease by half or more. But the study also underscored the fact that tight control makes it easy for blood sugar to plummet too low.

To trick to keeping blood sugar low but not too low largely comes down to timing. The insulins you choose need to peak when your blood sugar is high. There are a number of ways to achieve this, and the plan you choose depends partly on how many shots you want to administer each day. Naturally, you're not jumping up and down for more shots. But better control—which equals better health—requires more injections as a rule. Here's how insulin plans can vary, depending on how often you inject.

One Shot a Day

Frankly, you can call this the "dream on" plan. One injection is sometimes adequate for people with type 2 diabetes, but it simply won't be enough to meet your needs if you have type 1. Consider your theoretical options:

▶ A short- or rapid-acting insulin at breakfast would kick in quickly and handle the glucose from your orange juice and cereal, but it would pass its peak by lunch and leave your blood sugar unacceptably high for the rest of the day and night.

▶ An intermediate-acting insulin at breakfast would become active in time for lunch but leave you with zero coverage for breakfast—unless you like eating in the midmorning. By evening, the dose would be fading, and you'd still have the whole night ahead.

▶ Taking a long-acting insulin at the beginning of the day wouldn't provide enough "oomph" to keep your blood sugar from spiking after you eat.

▶ You could mix short-, intermediate-, or long-acting insulins in the same syringe (check with your doctor for the proper procedure), but you'd still find yourself short at some point later in the day or night.

Two Shots a Day

With twice the shots comes twice the coverage—but there are still some gaps you'd be better off filling. Your doctor may advise against settling for a two-shots-a-day plan, but your success depends on how well you comply with your regimen, and the choice is ultimately up to you.

The split dose. With a "split dose" program, you inject yourself with intermediate-acting insulin twice: once in the morning (half an hour or more before breakfast) and again in the evening (half an hour or more before dinner). That way, as the action of the first dose is fading, the second dose is ramping up. Unfortunately, this means there's a point at which neither dose is up to full power—typically just about dinnertime, when you could use more, not less, insulin. Still, because the second dose peaks in the evening, you'll get the nighttime coverage you need, although the insulin starts to get thin as dawn approaches. Again, breakfast may need to wait until the insulin starts taking effect.

The mixed split dose. For better coverage, you have a second option called the "mixed split dose," which follows the same injection schedule as the split dose. The difference is that instead of taking just an intermediate-acting insulin like NPH, you add some short-acting regular, lispro, or aspart insulin to your syringe. It will keep blood sugar under control when you inject at breakfast (which means you can eat sooner) and dinner, while the intermediate peak covers lunch.

You can mix the short- and intermediate-acting insulins in any combination you want. This allows you to adjust the proportions according to your responses or needs—say, if your blood sugar is extra high before a meal or you want to have a second piece of pie and need more insulin to handle it. For the sake of convenience, some insulin products come premixed, typically combining 70 to 75 percent NPH with 25 to 30 percent regular or lispro.

In theory, these plans sound good. In practice, however, few patients who use them are able to achieve good enough blood-sugar control to meet currently recommended glucose targets. And although they free you from more injections, they can seem limiting in other ways—particularly by locking you into specific mealtimes every day.

Three Shots a Day

This really is the minimum standard of care for type 1 diabetes. More shots means more control because you can use short-acting insulin to counteract the effects of a meal or snack, you have more freedom to eat when you want, and you can quickly correct blood-sugar highs revealed to you by self-testing.

Three-shot plans take a number of different forms that you'll want to discuss with your doctor. One is similar to the mixed-split-dose plan except that you take the second dose of intermediate-acting insulin at bedtime instead of dinner for better coverage at night. At dinner you take a third shot of short-acting insulin. Another alternative is to use long-acting insulin in the morning to cover your basal needs for the rest of the day and night, plus a short-acting insulin at every meal.

Intensive Therapy

Even people who take three shots a day often find themselves adding a fourth or even a fifth injection to achieve ideal control. This is the pinnacle of insulin treatment, sometimes referred to as intensive therapy or management. It's not for everyone because of all those shots, plus the extra finger-sticking glucose monitoring that goes along with them. But if you're intent on doing all you can to show your diabetes who's boss, these regimens usually work the best.

Freedom and flexibility. The aim of intensive therapy is actually to make your life easier, not more difficult. The underlying assumption is that you're not a robot following a regimented program of eating and activity that's exactly the same every day. Rather, you might actually have a late lunch if you've been out shopping, eat a bit more with your coffee when the in-laws come to visit—even (gasp!) skip a workout. Intensive therapy lets you do it all without throwing off your program because responding to what's actually happening in your life *is* the program.

One traditional approach to intensive therapy is to take an intermediate-acting insulin (typically NPH) twice a day: in the morning (with a short-acting insulin to cover breakfast) and at bedtime. Added to that are two short-acting insulins that you inject whenever you choose to eat. The exact dosages of the four shots should be adjusted according to how physically active you are or how much carbohydrate you eat. Many doctors now favor replacing NPH in this plan with the new long-acting insulin glargine, which covers early-morning insulin needs better and maintains a steady "peak-free" basal insulin that's closer to what you'd get with a normal pancreas.

Pumping up your options. Not keen on injections? Consider an insulin pump, which provides a continuous infusion of insulin. These pagerlike devices, which can be hung on a belt or worn around the neck, hold a small reservoir of insulin that's dispensed through a catheter in your abdomen. (See "Insulin Pumps" on page 160.)

Intensive therapy's main drawback is the added risk of hypoglycemia that comes from keeping blood sugar consistently lower. You'll need to be alert to signs of dropping blood sugar (sweating, nervousness, rapid heartbeat) and be prepared to treat them in the short term with carbohydrate snacks. If you have persistent problems with hypoglycemia, see your doctor about adjusting your insulin dosage.

Insulin and Type 2

Studies find that intensive blood-sugar management is just as helpful in preventing complications with type 2 diabetes as it is with type 1. Fortunately, the experience will probably feel a little less intense if you have type 2 because you'll likely be able to get by with fewer insulin injections, at least to begin with.

Remember, if you have type 2, the pancreas is usually still able to pump out some of the insulin your body needs, so injections are most often started as a last resort after diet, exercise, and drugs no longer suffice. But you may want to talk with your doctor about starting insulin before your blood-sugar control deteriorates to that degree: Some research suggests that taking it sooner can help preserve the function of insulin-producing beta cells in the pancreas.

If you follow standard treatment patterns, though, your insulin therapy will typically begin with an evening dose of intermediate- or long-acting insulin, often combined with a sulfonylurea to cover your daytime needs—a therapy sometimes called BIDS, for "bedtime insulin, daytime sulfonylurea."

Eventually, most people with type 2 will need to step up their insulin regimen so that it resembles treatment for type 1, although this may not happen until you've had diabetes for 15 or 20 years. Most likely, treatment will then consist of two injections a day—usually a mix of short- and intermediate-acting insulin at breakfast and bedtime. If that's not enough to meet your blood-sugar targets, you'll need to work out a multiple-injection plan with your doctor. Because blood sugar naturally tends to be more stable with type 2, your risk of hypoglycemia with intensive therapy isn't as great as it is with type 1.

A WEIGHTY SIDE EFFECT

Intensive therapy gives you tight control over your blood sugar and therefore is the best way to ward off complications. You may, however, have to deal with an effect you hadn't counted on: weight gain. Why? Because close glucose control makes cells better able to use glucose for energy (read: calories), so the body pours less of it out in urine. This effect can be more of an issue with type 2 people who are already struggling to keep their weight down.

The first thing to be aware of with the weight issue is that the benefits of better blood-sugar control far outstrip any harm from a few extra pounds. Studies find, for example, that even when insulin therapy causes weight gain, cardiovascular risk factors like blood pressure either don't change or, in the case of cholesterol and triglycerides, actually get better. If metformin still works for you, its weight-reducing properties can help. So can adding one workout per week to your exercise plan or adjusting your meal plan.

Calling the Shots

Injections can seem scary at first, but most people quickly get used to them. The thin, small-gauge needles available today are specially coated and extremely sharp, so they slide easily into the skin with minimal pain. With a little practice and attention to a few details, shots soon become just another problem-free part of your daily routine.

When it comes to deciding where to inject, you have plenty of options. Anyplace that you have a layer of fat just below the skin is fair game—the abdomen, the tops and outer sides of your thighs, your buttocks, and your upper arms. But the all-around winner is the abdomen, which usually has the most ample folds of fat and absorbs insulin faster and more consistently than other areas do.

As a rule, you shouldn't inject in the same site from one shot to the next. This can make the skin harden, create thick lumps,

SHOTS MADE SIMPLE

Giving shots may seem like something only someone in a white coat should do, but you're perfectly qualified to handle it on your own. The following guide covers the steps involved in administering a single dose of insulin. (Mixing doses is slightly more complicated but involves the same basic techniques.) First, some prep: Wash your hands with soap and water and check the bottle to make sure you're using the right insulin if you take different kinds at different times of day. Got your insulin, syringe, and some alcohol wipes? You're good to go.

❶ Gently roll the bottle between your palms (shaking it can make the insulin less potent). Check its appearance. Except for regular insulin, which is clear, the contents should look uniformly cloudy. Don't use it if it's clumped or settled at the bottom or if the bottle has a frosty look.

❷ After wiping the stopper with an alcohol wipe, take the cover off the syringe and pull the plunger back until it reaches the dose you need, as marked by the lines printed on the side.

❸ Stick the needle through the stopper and press the plunger down so all the air in the syringe goes into the bottle.

or cause small indentations to form. But neither do you want to move to a new part of the body with each shot, since insulin is absorbed more slowly in some areas than others, which would make it tougher to keep the effects of your injections consistent. Solution: Inject in the same general area, but place consecutive shots about an inch away from each other, rotating the sites as you go. If you're injecting at several different times of day, you might want to take, say, your morning shots in one area of the body and your evening shots in another, but still rotate the shots at those times within their designated areas.

Minimizing the Pain

Fine, sharp needles go a long way toward keeping shots prick-free, but you can take additional steps to minimize the pain:

➲ Relax. Tense muscles can promote tightness that makes it harder for the needle to penetrate your skin.

➲ Clean the injection site ahead of time with plain soap and water. If you use alcohol as a disinfectant, wait until it dries before going ahead with your injection, or the needle may push alcohol into the skin, causing stinging.

CAUTION

When giving yourself shots in the abdomen, avoid injecting in the area two inches around the navel, where tougher tissue can make insulin absorption inconsistent. You should also avoid injecting into moles, scar tissue, or hard muscles like the shoulders.

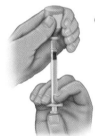

❹ Turn the bottle and syringe upside down so the tip of the needle is submerged in insulin. Now pull the plunger back out again, drawing insulin from the bottle until you reach your dose mark.

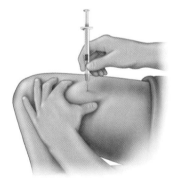

❻ After cleaning the injection site, pinch a fold of skin and push the needle in at a 90-degree angle. If you're thin, think about using a short needle or inserting it at a 45-degree angle to avoid injecting into muscle. Push the plunger down; release the skin and pull the needle out, pressing a cotton swab near the needle as you pull. Keep pressing (but don't rub) with the swab for a few seconds.

❺ If you see any air bubbles (which dilute the insulin's strength), push the plunger back in and draw the insulin again. Repeat this process until you've got the right dose and no bubbles.

⮞ Insert the needle quickly: As with tearing a bandage off sensitive skin, slowness and hesitation make it hurt more.

⮞ Keep the angle of the needle steady as it goes in and out so it's not swiveling around under your skin.

⮞ Choose a fresh site with each injection so you're not putting the needle into tissue that's still sensitive from your last shot.

⮞ Avoid giving shots in the inner thigh, where rubbing from leg movement can cause soreness at the injection site.

Injection Alternatives

Needles are the tried-and-true way to deliver insulin. They're reliable, consistent, and relatively easy to use. Still, if you're looking for options, you'll find plenty of them in a range of newer devices. Are these gadgets right for you? The only way to know is to find out more.

First, think about what you believe are the main drawbacks of needle-and-syringe delivery. Do you hate needles? Do you feel it's inconvenient to stop what you're doing to give yourself a shot? Do you feel there's just too much paraphernalia to drag around with you? You'll find alternative delivery systems to address all of these issues.

Insulin Pumps

What if there was a way to deliver insulin in a slow and steady trickle all day like a real pancreas does? That's the idea behind electronic insulin pumps. These wearable devices hold a one- or two-day supply of short-acting insulin that's dispensed continuously for basal coverage while providing a preprogrammed spurt of insulin at the touch of a button before meals. Pumps allow close control of blood sugar without the need for a lot of injections. Every two or three days, you need to change the site of the catheter that connects the pump to your body, which involves inserting a small needle just under the skin.

Insulin pumps are becoming more and more popular among people with type 1 diabetes (for whom they're mainly intended) because the instant adjustments allow a great deal of flexibility, they provide excellent glucose control, and their precise delivery

WHAT THE STUDIES SHOW

Automatic insulin pumps would seem ideal for children, but doctors tend to worry that kids aren't responsible enough to do extra blood testing and carefully program their doses to match their meals. Yet a 2002 study at Strong Children's Hospital, in Rochester, New York, found that, with only a couple of exceptions, 53 children under age 13 were safely able to achieve better glucose control with less hypoglycemia using pumps than they did with injections.

often lets you use less insulin than with injections. What's more, new water-resistant pumps can be worn almost anytime, anywhere—even when swimming. Pumps can also be quickly disconnected for, say, sexual activity. Fail-safe controls keep the unit from giving you an insulin overdose, beep if flow shuts down due to a clog, and signal when the batteries are running low.

For all their advantages, though, pumps aren't perfect. For one thing, they're pricey, costing between $3,000 and $5,000, and insurance doesn't always pick up the full tab. Some doctors are finding that the new insulin glargine, with its rapid onset and steady action, can control basal glucose almost as well as a pump, at less cost. Problems like clogs and infections at the injection site can sometimes interfere with your insulin delivery, although patient education and practice can minimize these problems—as can more frequent self-monitoring with blood tests, which you'll find are still necessary. Talk to your doctor to determine whether or not an insulin pump is a good idea for you.

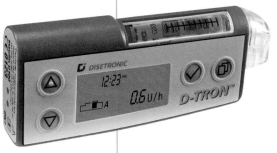

Three More Options

If you conclude that a pump's not right for you, there are more alternatives for you to consider.

Insulin Infusers. Infusers are like an insulin pump—without the pump. What's left is a catheter that remains in place at the injection site (usually the abdomen). You still need a needle to insert the catheter, but once the catheter's in place, you can leave it there for two or three days and administer insulin with a syringe through a self-sealing port. As with pumps, infections develop more easily at the injection site with this method, so you'll have to be diligent about keeping paraphernalia sterile, especially when you insert the catheter.

Pen Injectors. These devices don't eliminate needles, but they make injections more convenient by prepacking the insulin, needle, and syringe into one small unit that looks like a fountain pen. In this case, the "ink" cartridge is a vial that contains insulin, which you inject using a needle at the pen's tip—no insulin bottle or syringe-filling procedure necessary.

TALKING GARBAGE

To safely dispose of needles, syringes, and lancets (sometimes called "sharps"), collect them in a puncture-resistant container with a tightly fitting top, such as a coffee can or—even better—a plastic soda bottle. (Don't use glass containers, which can break.) Or you can purchase an FDA-approved sharps container like the one below, which is sold at many pharmacies. Keep the container handy so you can drop sharps into it immediately after use, then put it away well out of reach of children. Once the container is full,

put on the lid and seal it with heavy-duty tape. Check with your local municipal authorities on how to get rid of medical waste: You may be able to put it out with the trash, but some communities arrange for special pick-ups or provide drop-off sites.

When it's time to take your shot, you uncap the pen, choose your dose by turning a dial that clicks into place (the pen holds multiple doses), then press a button to inject the insulin. The nondisposable pens generally cost $40 to $60.

Jet Injectors. If you don't want to use needles at all, you might try a jet injector. These devices use a powerful burst of air to shoot a fine spray of insulin directly into your skin. Jet injections are not entirely pain-free: You'll feel a nip from the pressurized blast, and some people find that the jets cause bruising. But they can be a good option for children or anybody who'd rather not stick themselves with needles. Like pen injectors, jets can carry multiple doses at a time, and you can choose the amount of insulin you want by turning a dial. Jet injectors cost around $1,000, so price may be a barrier. Some units require thorough cleaning every two weeks by taking the unit apart and boiling the components or using germ-killing cleaners. If you're considering a jet injector, ask your doctor if you can arrange to test one before buying.

Should You Consider Surgery?

Going under the knife is always a big decision because it poses so many risks—of complications during the procedure, problems with anesthesia, and post-op pain and disability, to name a few. But what if an operation could dramatically improve your blood-sugar control and reduce your diabetes-related risks? Surgery may indeed offer solutions for some people.

Diabetes isn't like heart disease or cancer, in which the problem to be attacked is often clearly visible as, say, a clogged artery or a tumor. How do you surgically correct an imbalance that exists at the molecular level within the blood flowing throughout your entire body? New techniques are on the horizon, but at the moment, there are two ways.

For Type 1: Pancreas Transplants

The most obvious surgical solution to diabetes is to get a new pancreas, an option that's mainly considered for type 1 patients because they can't produce any insulin naturally. A pancreas transplant provides a replacement source of insulin, with the donated organ (or part of one) typically installed in the pelvis just above the bladder. The old pancreas is usually not removed because it can still make digestive enzymes.

When successful, a pancreas transplant can eliminate the need for supplemental insulin, bringing glucose under normal control. Furthermore, there's evidence that the progression of complications such as diabetic retinopathy may be slowed and perhaps even arrested thanks to the new pancreas. But—and you knew this was coming—the procedure can have drawbacks.

Beyond the very real difficulty of finding donors, the body's immune system is naturally inclined to reject foreign tissue and thus wants to attack the new pancreas. Fending off this attack requires taking potent immunosuppressant drugs (such as cyclosporine or corticosteroids), which make you more vulnerable to infection from viruses and bacteria and less able to fight other diseases, including cancer.

Usually, pancreas and kidney transplants (necessary because of kidney failure from damage caused by high blood sugar) are done at the same time, and about 80 percent of people who have such double operations are free of insulin treatment after a year. But as many as 15 percent of patients don't survive more than five years after the surgery (partly because they are quite sick to begin with). When successful, however, the improved blood-sugar control appears to protect the newly transplanted kidney from the recurrence of diabetic kidney failure.

For Type 2: Weight-Loss Surgery

Because obesity is so closely tied to diabetes and its cardiovascular complications (especially in people with type 2), some doctors think weight-loss surgery offers a quick way to wipe out a number of big health problems in one fell swoop. Other doctors are more cautious, saying it's unwise to undergo major elective surgery when you can choose far less drastic options.

The goal of weight-loss surgery is to reduce the amount of food the stomach can hold. The most common way to do this is with gastric bypass surgery, usually by means of an operation called vertical banded gastroplasty. In this procedure, a special band and staples crimp the upper portion of the stomach into a small pouch. The contents of this pouch are rerouted, through a narrow outlet, to the small intestine, allowing the digestive system to handle only an ounce or two of food at once. (Eventually, as the pouch stretches, it can handle about four ounces.) Often the surgery is combined with a bypass that diverts the stomach contents around the upper part of the small intestine, where much of the breakdown and absorption of food normally takes place. Although bile and secretions from the pancreas work to break food down further along the small intestine's pipeline, food is incompletely digested, so fewer calories are absorbed into the body.

Results can be dramatic. You'll typically trim two-thirds of your excess body weight within two years. But the operation forces you to eat slowly and in tiny amounts; nausea, vomiting, diarrhea, and sweating often result if you eat too much or too fast. The post-operative complication rate—usually stemming from wound infections and abdominal hernia—stands at a high 20 to 40 percent.

Still, weight-loss surgery is becoming more popular, with the number of operations today more than three times what they were just a few years ago. And a new technique called laparo-scopic banding now eliminates the use of staples, replaces major incisions with small "keyhole" openings in the body, and allows the crimp on the stomach to be adjusted or removed altogether. While some doctors find the technique less reliable than traditional surgery, a study published in early 2002 found that weight loss with the new procedure led to remission of diabetes in 64 percent of patients.

Is weight-loss surgery for you? Ask your doctor about the medical guidelines for who's a good candidate. (For example, you must have a body mass index above 40.) Be clear about what eating will be like afterward—and remember the other options you have with diet, exercise, and drugs.

PUMPING UP CONTROL

Wearing an insulin pump is an excellent way to control blood sugar—even if it's not the most attractive fashion accessory, according to Stephanie Peter, 24. "I heard about the pump back in high school and gave some thought to getting one in college—but decided I didn't want that thing on me," says Peter, of Quincy, Illinois. She changed her mind when she began working full-time.

Peter had tried various insulin regimens since age 10, when she was diagnosed with type 1 diabetes. "I had the classic symptoms—weight loss, bed-wetting, constant thirst. My dad found half-filled cups of water all around our home," she recalls.

During her college years, while on fast-acting Humalog and long-acting ultralente, Peter found it particularly difficult to keep her blood sugar in check. "I'd begun working out, and I needed to adjust the ultralente at night if I planned to exercise the next day," she says. But she didn't always know when she'd be able to fit in that workout—and if she couldn't fit it in after all, her blood-sugar would end up too high. On the flip side, an unplanned exercise session might lower her blood sugar too much. "I often had to eat even when I wasn't hungry or didn't want to take the time, and it became inconvenient," she says.

Still, she couldn't bring herself to plug in a programmable system. "I wanted to wear formal dresses, not a pump," she says. "I had no problem giving myself up to six shots a day—it was just like brushing my teeth."

Then Peter began an internship, and the idea of a pump took on new appeal. "With work, my life became more scheduled, but also more hectic. Carrying needles around became a pain," she says. "I knew other people had had good luck with the insulin pump, so I decided to try it out for a couple of days." More than a year later, she's still wearing it.

The pump replaces most shots, but not monitoring, adds Peter. "You don't put it on and forget it," she says. "It takes a lot of monitoring, and you have to be motivated." For example, she's noticed that her sugar tends to be high in the afternoon, but she can easily correct for it by pumping extra insulin.

Meanwhile, Peter has managed to fit the pump into her wardrobe—in fact, a seamstress sewed a special pocket for it in a bridesmaid's dress she wore recently. "When I buy clothes, I think, Where will the pump fit? What sort of bra do I need? It's an issue, and it's still my one complaint," she says. "But it's really not obvious under shirts, and when people do notice it, they think it's pretty cool."

7

Preventing
Complications

By itself, high blood sugar doesn't seem that bad. After all, you can have it for years without even knowing it. The problem is the havoc it wreaks on your eyes, kidneys, nerves, heart, arteries, feet—you name it. Controlling blood sugar is the critical first step to keeping diabetes-related complications at bay. But other simple strategies, such as taking a daily aspirin, having regular eye check-ups, and wearing comfortable shoes, can go a long way toward preserving your health.

To manage diabetes successfully, it helps to be a visionary—someone who can see how the actions you take (or don't take) today will affect you in the future. That's because, ultimately, diabetes makes you look ahead. If you don't control your disease, you can count on serious health problems down the road. But if you take charge today, you can minimize—or completely prevent—complications tomorrow.

For many people with diabetes, long-term complications have already set in. Even though it can take as long as 10 to 15 years for serious damage to occur, cases of type 2 often develop silently over long periods, and many people who have just been diagnosed find they already have related health problems.

No matter what your current situation, it's never too late to take steps that will keep you healthier in the days, months, and years ahead. And if you have the benefit of an early diagnosis, the chances are good that you can avoid the worst effects of diabetes, which include:

- higher cardiovascular risks
- kidney disease
- eye disease
- nerve disease
- foot damage
- related complications, such as sexual dysfunction, gastrointestinal problems, and infections.

Why Complications?

It seems strange that one disease can cause so many other problems throughout the body. After all, kidney disease by itself doesn't cause heart disease, and eye damage doesn't promote nerve damage. Why do these seemingly unrelated problems appear together when you have diabetes? The answer is that they're not unrelated but linked by high blood sugar.

You know from handling sweet foods in your own kitchen that when sugar is more concentrated, it becomes stickier. The same is basically true in your blood. Excess glucose can stick to cells in the blood, making it more difficult for red blood cells to deliver oxygen or white blood cells to fight infection. Sticky glucose can also make it harder for blood to flow through blood vessels, impeding circulation to important areas like the feet and organs like the kidneys and eyes. When glucose clings to fatty substances in the blood, they may be more likely to adhere to blood-vessel walls, gumming them up and leading to clogs that cause heart attacks or stroke.

Because high blood sugar is the common culprit in diabetes complications, the single most important thing you can do to bring down your risks for all of them is to get your blood sugar under the best control you can. Recent studies show what a difference good glucose control can make.

▶ People with type 1 diabetes who maintain tight blood-sugar control can cut their overall risk of complications by half, according to the Diabetes Control and Complications Trial, or DCCT (1993). In that study, good blood-sugar control cut risk of eye disease by 76 percent, nerve damage by 60 percent, and kidney damage by 35 to 56 percent.

▶ People with type 2 diabetes who bring blood sugar down gain a 35 percent reduction in risk of complications with every percentage-point drop in their hemoglobin A1c test results, according to the 20-year United Kingdom Prospective Diabetes Study (1998).

▶ People with impaired glucose tolerance who improved their blood-sugar profile by losing weight with diet and exercise cut their risk of ever developing diabetes (and its complications) by 58 percent, according to the Diabetes Prevention Program (2002).

This mounting evidence takes the "Why complications?" question in a different direction—why suffer from them at all when it may be in your power not to?

Cutting Cardiovascular Risks

Cardiovascular disease and diabetes often appear together. It isn't entirely clear how the two diseases affect each other, but the most pertinent facts are clear enough: If you have diabetes, you're two to four times more likely than the general population to have heart disease. In fact, heart attacks are what ultimately kill 80 percent of people with diabetes.

The risks are so high that, according to the American Diabetes Association (ADA), having diabetes puts you in the same danger zone as a person who has already had a heart attack—and is thus likely to have another. Heart attack is just one of several problems to watch out for when you have cardiovascular disease. Most of them come down to two basic conditions, both of which you can take steps to control.

Assessing Atherosclerosis

Cardiovascular is an umbrella term that includes both the heart (the *cardio* part) and the blood vessels (the *vascular* part). In a healthy person, a strong heart sends blood through the body via a network of smooth and elastic blood vessels. But problems arise when blood vessels become stiff, narrowed, or clogged—a condition known as atherosclerosis.

Atherosclerosis can occur in a number of ways related to diabetes. High blood sugar can slow blood circulation and promote the formation of clots. Being overweight (especially if you carry fat mostly in the abdomen) and having high levels of such blood fats as cholesterol and triglycerides (common with diabetes) can lead to obstructions in blood vessels. Depending on where they occur, these slowdowns in blood flow can trigger a number of different problems.

▶ When arteries that feed the heart become obstructed, the heart can't pump as efficiently as it should. Initially, this can cause chest pain from angina, a condition in which heart tissue is damaged from lack of nutrients. If a coronary artery becomes completely blocked, the result is a heart attack.

▶ If blood flow slows down in the arteries that feed the brain, lack of oxygen can cause what's known as cerebrovascular disease, in which areas of the brain become impaired. Often, the condition starts with temporary loss of brain function that can produce symptoms like slurred speech, weakness, and numbness. A total blockage can cause a stroke.

▶ When blood flow to the arteries feeding the legs is impeded, a condition known as peripheral vascular disease develops. A partial blockage can cause temporary pain (called claudication) in the thighs, calves, or buttocks. A total blockage can cause gangrene, although this doesn't happen often, because blood to the legs can usually bypass the clog using other arteries. Still, poor leg circulation, often combined with nerve damage, can lead to serious problems in the feet.

High Blood Pressure Havoc

High blood pressure can build up silently, just as diabetes can, and the two diseases often develop in tandem. If you have diabetes, you're twice as likely to have high blood pressure than the average person is, and about 60 percent of people with type 2 diabetes do. Controlling high blood pressure is critical if you have diabetes because the damage it causes contributes not only to atherosclerosis but also to kidney and eye disease. All told, it has a hand in 35 to 75 percent of all complications that go along with diabetes.

You need a certain amount of blood pressure (the force that blood exerts against artery walls) for good circulation. But too much gradually weakens the heart by making it work harder and damages the lining of blood-vessel walls, making it easier for atherosclerosis to set in. High blood pressure can also weaken arteries in the brain and cause them to balloon, a condition called an aneurysm. The bursting of an aneurysm is potentially fatal.

According to the ADA, you should strive to keep your blood pressure down to at least 130/80 mm Hg if you have diabetes—and lower than that is even better.

THE RACE FACTOR

Already at higher risk for diabetes, African Americans are also at higher risk for hypertension than other ethnic groups, particularly Caucasians. One reason may be that 32 percent of blacks report getting no off-the-job physical activity in a given week, compared with 18 percent of whites. But one recent study of data from the National Health and Nutrition Examination Survey finds that even blacks who exercise are more likely to have high blood pressure than whites who do the same amount of working out. Researchers suggest that other, unknown factors may be at work. One theory: African Americans may be less able to properly excrete salt from the body.

Preventing Cardiovascular Disease

Some of the steps you're already taking to control diabetes can also work wonders against heart and vascular problems. But you and your doctor may want to try other options as well—including drugs that attack a number of diabetes-related problems at once. Here are some of the most important steps to consider:

⭢ **Keep up the good work.** By exercising regularly and following your meal plan, you stand to lower your risk of cardiovascular complications. For example, eating more carbohydrates and fiber while consuming less saturated fat can reduce cholesterol in the blood and help you lose excess weight—a major contributor to high blood pressure. At the same time, exercise strengthens the heart, keeps blood vessels supple, and appears to lower blood pressure even if you're not dropping pounds.

➲ **But go a little further.** You may need to take your diet one step beyond what you're already doing by eating less salt. Over the years, researchers have debated whether salt really affects

COLLATERAL DAMAGE

Over time, poorly controlled diabetes can wreak havoc throughout the body. But keeping your blood sugar in line will significantly reduce your risks. What's more, there are other steps you can take to minimize the damage.

SITE	DAMAGE	PREVENTION
Blood vessels	High blood sugar slows circulation, promotes high levels of such blood fats as cholesterol, and encourages the formation of blood clots. Potential result: blockages that can cause heart attack and stroke.	■ Lower blood pressure with diet and exercise. ■ Quit smoking. ■ Take aspirin. ■ Consider ACE inhibitors. ■ Eat heart-healthy foods like fish, tea, and antioxidant-rich fruits and vegetables.
Kidneys	Blood sugar gums up delicate capillaries that filter wastes. Kidneys work harder but less efficiently, gradually losing function and ultimately failing.	■ Get tested regularly for signs of damage. ■ Bring down high blood pressure. ■ Drink cranberry juice to discourage urinary tract infections. ■ Consider eating less protein.
Eyes	High blood sugar weakens small blood vessels and makes them rupture. New blood vessels proliferate out of control, causing eye damage that can lead to vision loss or blindness.	■ Get regular checkups from an ophthalmologist. ■ Lower your blood pressure. ■ Consider laser surgery if necessary.
Nerves	Blood sugar may block nerve signals or interfere with normal nourishment of nerves. The range of effects can include pain, lack of sensation in the body's peripheries, muscle weakness, and loss of control over automatic functions like heartbeat, digestion, and sexual response.	■ Report symptoms to your doctor immediately. ■ Get more nerve-friendly B vitamins in such foods as potatoes, fish, and meat. ■ Try over-the-counter analgesics for pain. ■ Change your diet to make digestion easier. ■ Ask about antidepressants to counter pain, and other drugs to treat specific symptoms.
Feet	Combination of poor circulation and nerve damage can make feet prone to injuries that heal slowly and can quickly become infected.	■ Wear good shoes everywhere. ■ Inspect feet daily. ■ Keep feet clean and dry. ■ Change socks frequently. ■ Tell your doctor about any changes.

blood pressure. But one of the most conclusive studies to date—the 2001 Dietary Approaches to Stopping Hypertension, or DASH II, study—showed that eating less than one teaspoon of salt a day could lower your stroke risk by 42 percent and your heart-disease risk by more than 20 percent. Americans on average get 8 to 10 times more salt than they need. You can significantly cut your consumption by eating fewer processed foods and more naturally low-salt whole foods like fruits and vegetables.

⊃ **Don't smoke.** There are plenty of reasons to give up smoking, but start with the fact that it doubles your risk of having a heart attack. In fact, smoking speeds up or exacerbates just about every process that contributes to cardiovascular disease: It reduces blood flow through the arteries by making them even stiffer and narrower, raises blood pressure, contributes to the formation of plaques that can lead to clogs, makes it easier for blood to clot around obstructions, and worsens pain from peripheral vascular disease.

⊃ **Ask about aspirin.** This anti-inflammatory has proven to be a power hitter in the battle against cardiovascular disease. In addition to relieving pain, aspirin makes the clot-forming particles in blood, called platelets, less able to stick together. As a result, taking aspirin every day can cut your risk of a heart attack by a whopping 60 percent. One recent study finds that taking one at bedtime can also reduce high blood pressure.

Check with your doctor about whether you should take low-dose aspirin (81 mg) or full-strength (325 mg)—or if aspirin is even appropriate for you. Many people find that it irritates or causes bleeding in the stomach, though taking coated tablets that dissolve in the small intestine can help you avoid these problems. Still, you should avoid aspirin if you have a stomach ulcer or liver disease. And talk to your doctor about how aspirin affects the performance of other medications you may be taking—including blood thinners and drugs for hypertension.

⊃ **Check your ACE in the hole.** You can choose from an array of drugs that fight high blood pressure, but one class of medications appears to have special benefits to people with diabetes. Called ACE (angiotensin-converting enzyme) inhibitors, they work by blocking a process in which one hormone turns into

another that constricts blood vessels. ACE inhibitors are popular for bringing down blood pressure because, compared with other blood-pressure medications, they have few side effects other than causing a persistent dry cough in a few patients. (Newer drugs called angiotensin II receptor blockers eliminate that problem). The bonus: Research shows that ACE inhibitors lower the risk of cardiovascular problems in people with diabetes even if they don't have high blood pressure. What's more, a study published in 2000 found that people taking the ACE inhibitor ramipril were 30 percent less likely to develop diabetes, suggesting that the drug improves insulin sensitivity.

↪ **Seek help from statins.** People with diabetes often have high cholesterol, a risk factor for heart attacks. But many of them aren't reaping the benefit of cholesterol-lowering drugs called statins. If you thought you weren't a candidate for statins, think again. The National Cholesterol Education Program recently revised its cholesterol guidelines, so talk to your doctor.

↪ **Turn to tea.** Certain foods appear to have an especially powerful protective effect against cardiovascular damage. One of these is tea, which numerous studies have linked with better heart health. In one of the most recent studies, heavy tea drinkers (who averaged two or more cups a day) had a 44 percent lower death rate after a heart attack than people who didn't drink tea;

SHOULD YOU TAKE WEIGHT-LOSS DRUGS?

Slimming down has the double benefit of reducing your risk of cardiovascular disease and controlling high blood sugar, which makes weight-loss drugs sound like an appealing option for people with diabetes.

While it's not possible to lose pounds just by popping a pill (you still have to exercise and eat a low-fat diet), two weight-loss drugs can help if diet and exercise aren't enough. A recent German study even found that one of them, orlistat (Xenical), lowered blood sugar after eating, reducing the need for glucose-controlling medication.

Still, doctors advise approaching diet pills with caution. Orlistat, which works by blocking fat absorption in the intestines, can cause a range of unpleasant gastrointestinal side effects, including having to defecate more often, fecal incontinence, and oily stools. The other common weight-loss drug, an appetite suppressant called sibutramine (Meridia), often causes headaches, dry mouth, and constipation. More important, it raises blood pressure in some people and shouldn't be used if you have hypertension. Other weight-loss drugs have been taken off the market because of concerns that they may cause heart-valve abnormalities. Check with your doctor to see if weight-loss drugs are appropriate for you.

moderate tea drinkers had a 28 percent lower death rate. Tea's protective effect is thought to come from its bounty of flavonoids, antioxidant compounds found in both black and green tea that appear to prevent cholesterol from clogging arteries, discourage blood from clotting, and keep blood vessels supple.

➲ **Get your fill of fish.** Another food with potent heart-protecting power is fish—or, more specifically, oils they contain known as omega-3 fatty acids. These oils can make blood less prone to clotting, lower triglyceride levels, and reduce blood-vessel inflammation, which can promote plaque buildup. In one study published in 2002, women who ate five or more servings of fish per week reduced their risk of coronary artery disease by more than a third, and their risk of having a heart attack by half over a 16-year period. Another study published at the same time found that men without heart disease who ate several servings of fish per week were 81 percent less likely to die suddenly. Fish that are particularly rich in omega-3s include cold-water varieties like salmon, trout, mackerel, and tuna.

➲ **Aim for antioxidants.** Antioxidant nutrients like vitamins C and E counteract a process called oxidation, in which unstable molecules produced by the body's use of oxygen damage healthy tissue. Among their benefits, antioxidants make cholesterol less likely to stick to artery walls. Vitamin C is found in such foods as citrus fruits, red and green bell peppers, broccoli, and tomatoes. You can get vitamin E in peanuts, sunflower seeds, wheat germ, and vegetable oils.

➲ **Supplement with folic acid.** This B vitamin has been shown to lower levels of homocysteine, a substance linked to cardiovascular disease risk. A multivitamin should do the trick.

HEEDING THE WARNING SIGNS

Cardiovascular emergencies can sneak up on you suddenly, though there's often time to react effectively if you pay attention to warning signals. Call your doctor immediately if you experience any of the following symptoms:

AILMENT	SYMPTOMS
Heart attack	■ Tightness or pain in your chest ■ Pain or discomfort that radiates from the chest to the neck, shoulders, or arms, especially on the left side where your heart is ■ Dizziness, lightheadedness, sweating, nausea, or shortness of breath (Don't assume these are signs of hypoglycemia if you're also experiencing pain.)
Stroke	■ Weakness or numbness of the face, arm, or leg, especially on one side of the body ■ Difficulty speaking or understanding others ■ Mental confusion ■ Vision problems ■ Difficulty walking or keeping your balance ■ Severe headache
Aneurysm	■ Severe headache, back pain, or abdominal pain that won't go away ■ Dizziness ■ Blurred vision ■ Nosebleeds

Caring for Your Kidneys

The first thing to appreciate about your kidneys is that you have two of them, nestled on either side of your spine toward the back of your torso just above your waist. Two is really more than you need—people can survive with only one (assuming it's healthy). But it's a sign of how important the kidneys are that the body builds in such redundancy.

The kidneys are the body's sewage plant, where blood flows to be filtered through a complex of tiny blood vessels called capillaries. Cleansed blood is sent back into circulation while wastes and toxins are taken out and sent south to the bladder for excretion in urine. The kidneys are hardworking and efficient, and they tend to keep quiet even when their job becomes difficult—which is what happens when persistent blood-sugar overloads foul the delicate capillaries and structures that filter your blood.

It takes years of blood-sugar abuse to wreck the kidneys, but once the kidneys are damaged, there's no repairing them. Total loss of renal function ultimately requires dialysis, in which you're hooked up to a blood-cleansing machine for two to four hours a few times a week. Another option is a kidney transplant.

The Kidney-Disease Countdown

Between 20 percent and 40 percent of people with diabetes develop kidney disease, also known as nephropathy. In fact, diabetes is the leading cause of kidney failure in the United States. Still, the remarkable results from the Diabetes Control and Complications Trial make it clear that you can avoid kidney disease, especially if you're alert to what happens as it progresses—and you act early. You can expect uncontrolled kidney damage to move ahead in several stages.

▶ First, the kidneys start filtering waste faster in an attempt to clear blood of excess sugar, boosting what's known as the glomerular filtration rate, or GFR. Some of the structures inside the kidneys begin getting bigger, intruding on space normally used by blood-filtering capillaries, making them less efficient and causing the kidneys to work harder.

▶ After a year or so, the kidneys start becoming less able to filter waste or keep nutrients that should stay in the body from being expelled. Small amounts of a protein known as albumin may become detectable in the urine, a condition known as microalbuminuria.

▶ As the kidneys become more damaged, you lose more albumin, whose job is to keep water within the bloodstream. The deficit causes water to build up in the body's tissues, causing such classic symptoms of kidney disease as puffiness around the eyes and swelling of the hands and feet. At the same time, the liver starts to pump out cholesterol and other fats that are involved with manufacturing albumin, boosting your cardiovascular risks. If you have type 2 diabetes, there may still be time to ward off kidney failure at this stage (known as nephrotic syndrome), but it may be too late if you have type 1.

THE BLOOD-CLEANSING KIDNEYS

The kidneys produce and eliminate urine through a complex system of some 2 million tiny filters called nephrons. At the top of each nephron, in the Bowman's capsule, is the glomerulus, a microscopic cluster of capillaries. Blood flows at high pressure through the glomerulus, where urea, toxins, and other wastes are filtered out and ultimately expelled through the urine. The purified fluid is returned to the blood via the renal vein. Over time, high blood sugar destroys the nephrons.

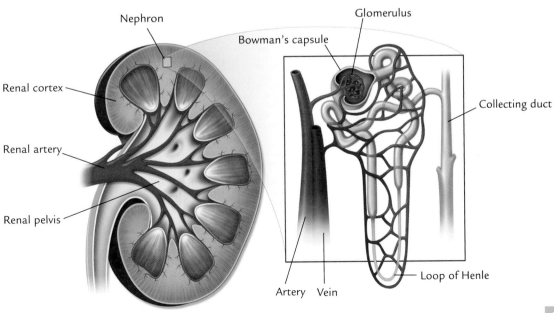

Nephron
Glomerulus
Bowman's capsule
Renal cortex
Collecting duct
Renal artery
Renal pelvis
Loop of Henle
Artery   Vein

▶ The last two stages are in the realm of kidney failure, in which the body becomes increasingly less able to filter waste. In the first stage of kidney failure, called renal insufficiency, treatment may still help, but as damage gets worse, you enter end-stage renal failure, when even good blood-sugar control probably can't stave off the inevitable: dialysis or a transplant.

Kicking Kidney Complications

Closely controlling blood sugar is the single most important way to keep kidney disease at bay. But managing high blood pressure, which can narrow arteries leading to the kidneys and damage the delicate blood vessels inside them, also plays a big role. That means there are plenty of steps you can take to reduce your risk or slow the progress of kidney disease. Some of these cut your chances of developing other complications as well.

➲ **Test regularly.** Hallmark symptoms, such as swelling, fatigue, and pain in the lower back, don't usually show up until a lot of kidney tissue has already been damaged—perhaps as much as 80 percent. But it's possible to detect the early signs of kidney disease well before that with tests. One of the most sensitive is a test for microalbuminuria, which the American Diabetes Association recommends you get at least once a year. Your doctor may also suggest that you be tested for creatinine, a waste product of muscles that a healthy kidney will clear from the blood but a damaged one will leave behind in detectable amounts.

➲ **Treat high blood pressure.** Taking ACE inhibitors to control hypertension benefits the kidneys by relieving pressure that can damage delicate filtering structures and keeping blood vessels flexible. In fact, some studies find that taking ACE inhibitors cuts deaths from diabetic kidney disease in half. Even in people who don't have high blood pressure but have signs of kidney damage, research suggests that ACE inhibitors are beneficial. Anything else you do to bring down blood pressure—especially not smoking—will also benefit your kidneys.

➲ **Cut back on protein.** Not everyone agrees that eating less protein will help stave off kidney disease, especially in its early stages. But once it has set in, the ADA recommends that protein should account for no more than about 10 percent of your calorie intake. Most Americans eat far more protein than they need, leaving the kidneys to excrete the excess—a burden that may accelerate damage. Several small studies suggest that restricting protein is especially helpful if kidney disease progresses even though blood sugar and blood pressure are under control.

→ **Protect against infection.** Feeling a burning sensation when you urinate, constantly having to go, and cloudy or bloody urine are signs of a urinary tract infection (UTI), which should be treated with antibiotics. UTIs are common in people with diabetes, partly because damage to nerves that control the bladder can keep you from voiding properly, leaving waste to fester in the body. That's bad news for the kidneys, which can be further damaged by the ravages of bacteria. Besides being alert for symptoms, try making cranberry juice a regular part of your diet: Studies find it helps prevent UTIs, possibly by making it more difficult for bacteria to adhere to tissue inside the urinary tract.

→ **Mind your meds.** A wide range of drugs, prescription and over-the-counter, can be hard on the kidneys. Among them are ibuprofen (such as Advil and Motrin) and naproxen (Aleve), along with more potent anti-inflammatories available by prescription. Other prescription drugs that can make kidney damage worse include certain antibiotics and lithium. Be sure to check with your doctor whenever you get a new prescription to see if there are any warnings about taking it if you have kidney disease.

Being Wise with Your Eyes

Like the kidneys, the eyes are nourished by small blood vessels that can easily be damaged when you have diabetes. Left alone, the damage can lead to vision loss, and diabetes remains the leading cause of blindness in adults. But the good news is that most eye problems can be treated if caught early—and it may be possible to see your way clear of them altogether.

Again, close blood-sugar control makes a big difference. In the Diabetes Control and Complications Trial, risk reduction from good blood-glucose control was larger for eye disease (76 per-

cent) than for any other complication. Still, you can't afford to be complacent about the possibility of eye damage, especially because you typically won't notice it in its earliest stages.

Most eye damage from diabetes takes place in the retina, the light-sensitive area at the back of the eye that registers visual signals and sends them to the brain through the optic nerve. High blood sugar (especially when combined with high blood pressure) can weaken small blood vessels that supply the eyes with oxygen and nutrients, causing them to puff up and rupture like balloons—a condition known as nonproliferative retinopathy. In some cases, leakage and lack of nourishment can directly damage the retina and make your vision blurry, but you may not notice anything at all.

If the damage progresses, you can develop a more severe condition called proliferative retinopathy, in which more blood vessels start to sprout in the retina to make up for blood delivery lost through burst vessels. This only compounds the problem by leading to more ruptures. These can block light to the retina and cause hemorrhages and pressure inside the eyes, which contributes to scar tissue that can eventually cause the retina to start tearing away from the eye. Retinopathy can also cause macular edema. In this condition, the central area of the retina (called the macula), which allows you to see sharp detail and color, swells, causing loss of fine vision.

How to Stay a Visionary

The key to keeping your sight clear is to keep your eyes peeled for symptoms that point to a problem.

➲ **Be alert to changes.** It's easy to dismiss subtle changes in your vision as minor annoyances, but when you have diabetes, you can't assume you need a new eyeglass prescription or that your eyes are just getting "old." Granted, those may be possibilities—and high or low fluctuations in blood sugar can temporarily affect your vision as well. But you should still call your primary-care physician or an ophthalmologist right away if:

▶ Your eyesight seems blurry

▶ You experience double vision

▶ Your vision becomes distorted or straight lines, such as telephone poles, look warped

▶ Spots or lines seem to float in front of your eyes

- ▶ Your field of vision seems narrower
- ▶ You have more difficulty seeing clearly in dim light
- ▶ It seems as though a window shade has been drawn over your field of vision
- ▶ You feel pressure or pain in your eyes
- ▶ You have trouble perceiving colors, especially blue and yellow, or making distinctions between similar colors

⟳ **Keep regular watch.** You may not be able to see or feel the earliest signs of retinopathy, but a doctor can easily pick them up during an eye exam, so it's important to schedule regular vision checks. Don't settle for the eye chart on the wall: Go to an oph-thalmologist, who will give you a comprehensive exam that includes dilating your pupils to look directly at the retina. The American Diabetes Association recommends that people with type 1 diabetes get an eye exam within three to five years of the

HOW DIABETES AFFECTS THE EYES

L ining the interior of the eye is a the retina, a delicate 10-layer membrane packed with nerve fibers and photoreceptors. Diabetic retinopathy occurs when uncontrolled high blood sugar damages or blocks the tiny blood vessels (capillaries) throughout the retina, cutting off the blood supply to small patches of retinal tissue. The damaged blood vessels also tend to leak, producing swelling within the retina. As retinal damage progresses, new blood vessels sprout, and vision may become increasingly blurred. About 25 percent of people with diabetes have some degree of retinopathy.

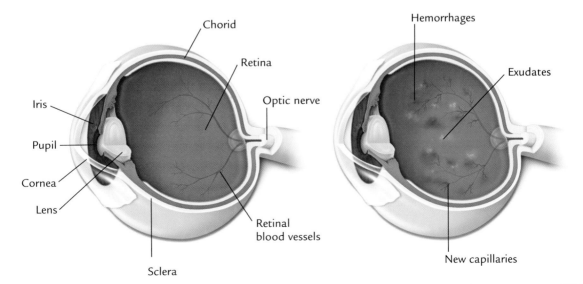

Chorid
Retina
Optic nerve
Iris
Pupil
Cornea
Lens
Retinal blood vessels
Sclera

Hemorrhages
Exudates
New capillaries

WHAT THE STUDIES SHOW

Aspirin helps protect your heart, but there's evidence that it can help protect your eyes, too. A study at the Schepens Eye Research Institute in Boston found that diabetes patients had a fourfold increase in tiny blood clots in the capillaries that nourish the retina. These clots may eventually starve the retina of oxygen and nutrients and trigger the growth of new, abnormal blood vessels. Aspirin may protect the capillaries from clots and help stave off retinopathy, say the researchers.

onset of the disease and that people with type 2 have an exam immediately after diagnosis. After that, everyone with diabetes should have their eyes checked once a year.

➲ **Get help for hypertension.** Easing your blood pressure can reduce your risk of retinopathy or slow its progression. Ask your doctor if, in addition to changing your diet, getting more exercise, and not smoking, you should take medication.

➲ **Evaluate your exercise.** Once you learn you have retinopathy, check in with your doctor to take another look at your exercise program. Certain forms of exercise can be jarring to the delicate structures within the eye or may increase the amount of pressure inside the eye and thus lead to more retinal bleeding.

➲ **Consider surgery.** The best way to prevent further damage from retinopathy may be to fix the harm that's already been done. Using a type of laser surgery called photocoagulation, an ophthalmologist aims a thin beam of laser light at the retina to destroy ruptured blood vessels, seal areas that are leaking, and prevent new vessels from forming. In some cases, laser surgery can slow the rate of vision loss by 90 percent or more. Another form of surgery, called cryotherapy, destroys abnormal blood vessels by freezing them with a probe—a technique that's especially useful in areas a laser can't reach or for people who still have proliferative retinopathy after laser surgery. In a third operation, called a vitrectomy, the eye's jellylike core (the vitreous humor) is taken out so that doctors can remove scar tissue from inside the eye and repair the retina if it has started to detach.

Nipping Nerve Damage in the Bud

Diabetes can literally be unnerving. It's no joke: Nerve damage may be one of the most far-reaching complications of the disease because the nervous system controls or contributes to so much—everything from your sense of touch (and pain) to muscle movement, digestion, and sexual function, just to name a few. Fortunately, you probably have time to prevent nerve damage, which usually develops after you've had diabetes for 10 to 15 years.

Doctors don't entirely understand how diabetes causes nerve damage, but likely possibilities are that high blood sugar upsets the balance of chemicals that allow nerves to transmit electrical impulses, deprives nerves of oxygen by impeding circulation, and damages the nerves' protective coating (called the myelin sheath). You can breathe a sigh of relief that diabetes doesn't seem to affect the brain and spinal cord—the components of the central nervous system. Still, the rest of the body's nerves, which carry electrical impulses through what amounts to an intricate network of "wires," are vulnerable to diabetes-related signal slowdowns, miscommunication, or interruptions.

There are three major types of nerve damage, or neuropathy, each of which can affect the body in many different ways. If you develop neuropathy, your doctor will determine which kind it is mostly by your symptoms and where they occur.

Polyneuropathy: On the Fringes. The most common type of nerve damage affects multiple nerves throughout the body (*poly* means "many"), but it mainly hits the long nerves of the peripheral nervous system that run through the arms and legs. You'll often hear this kind of nerve damage referred to as distal symmetric neuropathy because it strikes areas away from the central nervous system (*distal* refers to distance from the center) and tends to cause symptoms on both sides of the body (symmetric). Polyneuropathy generally doesn't affect movement; it instead disrupts sensation, often causing pain, cramps, or tingling in the hands or feet and, later, numbness.

Focal Neuropathy: In the Spotlight. Far less common, focal neuropathy concentrates on a single nerve, or set of nerves, and often affects only one area of the body—which is why it's sometimes called mononeuropathy (*mono* means "one"). Unlike polyneuropathy, which tends to develop gradually over time, it pops up suddenly, often causing numbness or pain, or weakness in the muscles, depending on which nerves are affected. Although it can crop up anywhere, focal neuropathy often causes Bell's

TESTS OF NERVES

While it's up to you to sound the neuropathy alarm, if you suspect you have nerve damage, your doctor can confirm and fine-tune the diagnosis with subtle tests. In one, she may hold a tuning fork against body parts, such as your foot, to find out whether you can detect its vibration. Similarly, she may touch you with a hairlike fine wire to gauge your response to delicate stimuli or apply heat or cold to make sure you could tell if you were being harmed by, say, scalding bathwater. If any of these tests indicate that you have nerve damage, your primary-care physician will probably send you to a neurologist to learn the extent of the damage.

palsy, in which nerves lose control over muscles in the face, causing your features to droop. Focal neuropathy can make your eyes cross if it affects muscles that control eye movement, and it can cause carpal tunnel syndrome, in which compressed nerves in the wrist produce pain or weakness in the hand and forearm.

Autonomic Neuropathy: Control Issues. The autonomic nervous system governs the body functions that you don't normally have to think about much, such as heartbeat, digestion, sweating, and bladder control—but that become more top-of-mind if nerves are damaged. Among the problems that can result from autonomic neuropathy are:

▶ Cardiovascular glitches, such as irregular heartbeat and a condition called orthostatic hypotension, in which your blood pressure fails to quickly adjust when you stand up, making you feel faint or dizzy. Deadened nerves can also fail to pick up pain from a heart attack.

▶ A condition known as gastroparesis, in which muscles of the gastrointestinal tract become slow and inefficient. Sluggish digestion not only causes GI problems like nausea, vomiting, bloating, diarrhea, constipation, and loss of appetite, but it makes blood-sugar patterns more difficult to predict and counter with insulin.

▶ Poor bladder function, in which nerves may have trouble telling when the bladder is full and don't empty the bladder completely when you void. One result is higher risk of urinary tract infections, which in turn can accelerate kidney damage.

▶ Sexual dysfunction, in which men find it difficult to get or maintain an erection and women experience vaginal dryness or tepid sexual response. Usually, however, sex drive is unaffected in both sexes.

▶ Dulled response to nervous symptoms of hypoglycemia, such as shakiness, sweating, and anxiety, a dangerous condition known as hypoglycemia unawares.

▶ Profuse sweating and poor regulation of body temperature.

Keeping the Verve in Nerves

In the case of nerve damage, closely controlling blood sugar—your top priority—can reduce your risks by as much as 60 percent. Once neuropathy develops, treatments vary depending on how the nerve damage is affecting your body. Among the steps you can take to minimize damage and discomfort:

⮑ **Get in touch with your feelings.** As with most diabetes complications, the sooner you pick up on nerve damage, the more you can do to keep it from escalating. Don't dismiss sensations or difficulties that disappear: In many cases, symptoms come and go or swing from mild to severe. Tell your doctor immediately if you experience:

▶ Tingling, numbness, burning, or prickly pain in your arms, legs, hands, or feet. Stay alert: The sensations can be very subtle at first. Try to be especially aware of unusual sensations in the feet, which are often affected first, or at night, when symptoms are usually worse

▶ Sensitivity to touch—even the light brushing of your sheets against you when you're in bed

▶ Leg cramps that may come and go, especially at night

▶ Difficulty sensing the position of your feet or toes, or a sense that you can't keep your balance

▶ Calluses or sores on your feet

⮑ **Adjust your diet.** Check with your dietitian to see if changes in the foods you eat might help keep some symptoms of neuropathy in check. If you're suffering from gastroparesis, try eating smaller, more frequent meals or consuming softer foods to ease digestion. Ask if you should eat less fiber, which is good for blood-sugar control for the same reason it may be bad for gastroparesis: It slows digestion. If you feel lightheaded when you stand, ask if you should consume more salt to help stabilize your blood pressure. Check with your doctor first though, especially if you may also be at risk for hypertension.

⮑ **Boost your B's.** In some cases, neuropathy is fostered by a deficiency in the vitamins B_6 and B_{12}, both of which are involved in the function of the nervous system. You can get vitamin B_6 from avocados, bananas, poultry, pork, potatoes, and fish like tuna, while B_{12} is found in chicken, beef, and a wide variety of seafood, including oysters, sardines, and other fish. Ask your dietitian or doctor if you should take supplements.

⮑ **Supplement your nerve health.** See page 200 to learn about alpha-lipoic acid, an antioxidant supplement that can help protect the nerves and ease the pain of neuropathy.

➲ **Reach for relief.** Try to temper the pain of polyneuropathy with over-the-counter pain relievers—especially aspirin, since it also carries the bonus of cardiovascular benefits. (If you're already taking small doses of aspirin daily, ask your doctor how to adjust the amount.) You may also find relief from topical creams containing capsaicin, a compound found in hot peppers that alleviates pain by interfering with signals that nerve cells send to the brain. When using these creams, be extremely careful to keep them away from the eyes and other sensitive areas.

➲ **Ask about medication.** Drugs are available to help control many of the specific conditions that can result from neuropathy. Sildenafil (Viagra) for sexual dysfunction is just one example. There are also drugs that help you empty your bladder, ward off episodes of low blood pressure, and treat gastroparesis. You might also benefit from taking a tricyclic antidepressant, such as amitryptyline (Elavil), nortriptyline (Pamelor), desipramine (Norpramin), or trazodone (Desyrel)—not because you've got the blues but because they've been found to take the edge off neuropathy pain. Give these drugs time to work; it often takes several weeks for them to become effective. Your doctor might also recommend an anticonvulsant drug, such as phenytoin (Dilantin), carbamazeprine (Tegretol), or gabapentin (Neutronin), which can reduce pain from nerve damage.

Sidestepping Foot Problems

The feet can take a beating when you have diabetes. Poor circulation from damaged blood vessels slows healing and makes feet more prone to infection, while nerve damage can dull sensation and leave you oblivious to injuries that can quickly get out of control.

In the grand scheme of things, foot hassles seem almost comically mundane. But you can't dismiss broken skin, corns, calluses, bunions, ingrown toenails, and other problems as minor irritations when you have diabetes. Left untreated for long, such conditions can put you at risk of actually losing a foot—or even a leg—to gangrene (tissue death). In fact, about 15 percent of people with diabetes in the United States eventually develop foot problems that threaten a limb, and more than 50,000 must undergo amputations every year.

It all begins with some form of injury that abrades or breaks the skin, the protective barrier that keeps germs out of your body. Perhaps your shoes don't fit quite right or you stepped on a stone. Once the damaged area becomes infected, healing may prove difficult, especially if you keep walking on it or aren't aware that it's there, and an open sore, or ulcer, can quickly develop. This is serious business—and a reason to call your doctor. Infection from uncontrolled ulcers can burrow deeper into your skin and eventually reach the bone, putting the entire foot or leg at risk. When you've had diabetes for a long time, feet may also become vulnerable to a condition called Charcot's foot, in which numbness and poor reflexes from neuropathy cause missteps that over time destroy joints in the foot.

Fortunately, paying a little extra attention to your feet can go a long way toward keeping them healthy. Here are some of the most important steps you can take.

➲ **Always wear shoes.** Think of your shoes as bodyguards for the feet, protecting them from blows, scrapes, or sharp objects, not to mention keeping them warm and dry. You'll significantly improve this protection if you avoid going barefoot (even at the beach, where sand can cause abrasions and debris can puncture the skin) or wearing open shoes, such as flip-flops, sandals, or clogs. Don't even take your shoes off when you're indoors, where something as minor as stubbing your toe on the coffee table can lead to a foot ulcer.

➲ **Do a daily check.** Give your feet an exam once a day, perhaps at bedtime, going over them with both your eyes and your hands. Let your doctor know if you find evidence of any problems. Besides blisters, cuts, bruises, cracking, peeling, or other obvious signs of damage, look for areas that are shaded differently (either paler or redder), which could indicate persistent pressure from shoes. Feel for areas of coldness, which could be a sign of poor circulation, or warmness, which might be evidence of an infection, along with redness or swelling. If you have trouble seeing the bottoms of your feet, place a mirror on the floor and look at the reflection. If you have poor vision, ask a partner to inspect your feet for you.

◯ **Wash and dry.** Keep your feet clean by washing them every day with lukewarm water and soap. (Avoid hot water, which, if you have neuropathy, may scald you without your knowing it.) Avoid soaking your feet, though, which will soften skin and make you more vulnerable to infection. Dry feet by blotting (not rubbing), making sure you get in between the toes to discourage fungal infections. Use a moisturizing cream to prevent dryness and cracking, but don't put it between your toes, where it may encourage skin to wear away.

◯ **Clip with care.** Keep your toenails neatly trimmed, cutting them straight across to prevent ingrown nails and filing rough edges to avoid damaging adjacent toes. Some doctors advise against using nail clippers out of fear that you'll accidentally cut

TAKE-CHARGE TIPS

Finding shoes that fit is important for anybody, but doubly so for people with diabetes. Your podiatrist can help if you have trouble finding the right footwear, but you should be able to score comfortable shoes off the rack if you heed these tips:

◯ **Follow three fit factors.** Don't settle for any shoe that doesn't meet all three criteria for a good fit:

The tip of the shoe should extend about the width of your thumb beyond your longest toe.

The ball of your foot should fit comfortably—without cramping the toes—into the widest part of the shoe.

The heel should fit snugly without slipping when you walk.

◯ **Measure every time.** Don't just tell the salesperson your size—get a new measurement. Changes in weight, blood circulation, and foot structure can make your foot a different size or shape than it was.

◯ **Try on both shoes.** It's likely that one of your feet is slightly larger than the other, so make sure shoes fit both feet. If necessary, buy for your larger foot and see your podiatrist about padding the other shoe.

◯ **Don't assume it will stretch.** Shoes may mold better to your feet the longer you wear them, but don't let a salesperson tell you the basic fit will improve with time. The shoe should fit—now.

◯ **Buy late in the day.** Feet swell by as much as 5 percent over the course of the day, so shopping in the P.M. hours will ensure that feet aren't cramped when you put new shoes on in the morning.

◯ **Ask about returns.** If you've lost sensation in your feet, you can't trust how shoes feel in the store. Bring them home and wear them around the house for half an hour, then check your feet. If you see areas of redness, which indicate pressure from a poor fit, bring the shoes back.

the skin next to the nail. If you're concerned, consider using a file or an emery board to shave nails down (go no shorter than the ends of your toes) or having a partner help.

⊃ **Get a clean start.** Begin each day by putting on a fresh pair of socks made of a breathable material like cotton, cotton blend, or wool, which wicks moisture away from skin and helps keep your feet dry. Make sure socks fit well without bunching up, and don't wear socks with seams that will rub your feet, potentially causing pressure sores. If your feet tend to sweat a lot, change your socks throughout the day as needed.

⊃ **Wear good shoes.** Footwear should provide both comfort and protection. Leather uppers are best because they conform to the shape of your foot and breathe so that feet perspire less. Opt for low heels for stability and soles made of crepe or foam rubber for excellent cushioning. It's a good idea to have at least two pairs of shoes that you wear regularly so you can alternate from one day to the next, giving shoes time to air out between each wearing. New shoes should never be worn for more than a few hours at a time. When you put on your shoes, shake them out and feel inside to make sure there's no debris that could cause pressure or irritation.

⊃ **Touch base with your doctor**. A foot exam should be a routine part of every doctor's visit, just like taking your blood pressure. Feet should be checked at least once a year—more often if you have signs of neuropathy or poor circulation or you've already had foot ulcers. (Bring your most-worn pair of shoes to the appointment so your doctor can check wear patterns.) But don't wait for your annual physical if you notice any changes in your feet. Not every minor cut demands a physician's attention, but call your doctor if you develop an infection or sore, your foot is punctured by a sharp object, a toe becomes red and tender, or you notice any change in sensation, such as numbness, pain, or tingling. Do not use acid treatments or over-the-counter wart or corn removers, and never try to perform do-it-yourself "bathroom surgery" to treat problems like warts, corns, calluses, or ingrown toenails.

8

Alternative Therapies

You're following a meal plan, watching your weight, getting exercise, and possibly taking drugs or insulin for your diabetes. Can anything else help? Maybe. Certain herbs and other supplements show promise for bringing down blood sugar and protecting the eyes, nerves, kidneys, and heart. Other alternative therapies, such as biofeedback and acupuncture, may help reduce stress and relieve nerve pain. Should you try them? Weigh the research, consider the potential side effects, consult your doctor—then make the decision for yourself.

The wonders of modern medicine have given us such powerful drugs as Glucophage to keep blood sugar in check and statins to lower the risk of heart-related complications. But what about the world of not-so-modern medicine? For thousands of years healers relied on natural therapies, many of them herb-based, to treat conditions like diabetes. Can any of them help you?

More and more patients—and even many doctors—are starting to ask that question as interest in so-called alternative medicine continues to grow. According to one recent study, visits to regular doctors remained stable through the late 1990s, but visits to alternative therapists jumped by 47 percent. Perhaps more surprising, surveys also find that as many as 60 percent of physicians have recommended alternative therapies to patients—a reflection of the fact that more than 75 U.S. medical schools now provide training in various types of alternative medicine. To learn more about these hugely popular but poorly understood therapies, the National Institutes of Health established in 1993 an Office of Alternative Medicine, which has lent an air of credibility—and, in some cases, scientific validation— to alternative medicine in the United States.

What Is Alternative Medicine?

In many ways, what you define as "alternative" depends on your culture. Many alternative therapies come from Eastern regions, such as Asia and India, where healing traditions tend to be less scientific than they are in the West. But not all Western countries view medicine the same way, either. Germany, for example, has a long history of incorporating herbal therapies into conventional medicine and conducting research into their benefits. In the United States, herbal supplements, while growing in popularity, are less a part of mainstream medicine largely because they're not studied as vigorously as drugs are.

American doctors sometimes refer to nontraditional treatments as "CAM"—for complementary and alternative medicine. "Complementary" emphasizes the fact that alternative therapies may sometimes be useful as an adjunct to traditional medical care but should never be seen as a substitute—as many alternative practitioners will be the first to tell you. In fact, you should be sure to ask your doctor about any supplement or alternative treatment you want to try, or at least inform your medical team what you're using. Many alternative treatments, especially herbs, can interfere with other medications and may affect how your doctor advises you to treat your diabetes.

How to Judge Alternative Therapies

One way to summarize the difference between alternative and conventional medicine is that the former is more art and the latter is more science. That balance is beginning to shift as more research is done into the potential benefits of alternative therapies. But one of the main drawbacks of CAM is that in many cases, the scientific evidence that a therapy works is sketchy, and safety risks are often not well understood.

That doesn't necessarily mean alternative medicine is automatically worthless or dangerous. But it does give you reason to approach it with an open mind—including a healthy openness to skepticism. Marketing and promotional material (along with much of the information published in books or on websites promoting alternative medicine) makes supplements and other products sound good. But you can't put a lot of stock in the ways manufacturers typically get their point across:

Unquestioning faith. In many cases, labels and advertising will simply state what a product is used for as if there is no doubt that it will work.

Vague research. In other cases, "research" or "studies" are cited with no further details about who conducted it.

Testimonials. A favorite "proof" that a therapy works is to quote somebody (preferably a celebrity) who says it was good for him or her. But from a scientific perspective, anecdotes are the least convincing form of evidence.

History. The fact that a therapy has been used for hundreds or even thousands of years is often held out as evidence of effectiveness, but tradition is not necessarily proof.

DID YOU KNOW

The word *drug* comes from the French term *drogue*, meaning "herb"—an indication that herbal remedies are not as far removed from conventional medicines as you might think. In addition to aspirin, many mainstream drugs have been developed from substances found in plants, including morphine and quinine.

The Standards for Studies

Why is the research thin on alternative remedies? Partly, it's a matter of money. No one can patent a natural product like an herb, and pharmaceutical companies, which fund much of the research into conventional medicines, generally aren't willing to sink development dollars into products on which they have no exclusive claim.

So how can you tell if an alternative treatment will work for you? The only real answer—as is true for many drugs as well—is to try it and see, if your doctor approves. But before you do, it's wise to gather as much information about the therapy as you can and consider the research that's been done on it.

When evaluating research, you can get a sense of its value by looking at the criteria that researchers themselves use. In the world of medical science, the best studies are those that are:

Big. Your diabetes isn't exactly the same as the next person's, so if you and someone else both take the same supplement, you can expect slightly different results. In many cases, even the best conventional drugs don't work for some people. In other cases, a person's health may improve for reasons that have nothing to do with the treatment being tested. Getting reliable findings therefore depends to some degree on conducting tests that involve as many people as possible. Most studies of alternative therapies, however, are small.

Human. Scientists often start with lab tests to determine a substance's chemical properties and effects. These experiments are a good start, but they can't reliably predict what will happen in the human body. Animal tests are more informative, and most telling are tests done on people.

Controlled. The least reliable experiments are those in which people are simply given the therapy and asked if it makes them feel better. In many cases, people will say yes even when the treatment is known to have no medical benefit—a phenomenon known as the placebo effect. Better experiments are controlled, meaning that one group of people gets the real treatment while a second group gets a fake one so that results can be compared and the possible impact of the placebo effect can be factored in.

Double-blind. To further guard against the placebo effect, it's best that study subjects don't know which treatment they're getting. To make absolutely sure that subjects are kept in the dark—that they won't get an inkling from the researchers, through body language or other subtle clues, of whether they're getting the real medicine or not—the people administering the treatments shouldn't know who's getting what, either.

Peer-reviewed. At the top of the heap are studies that not only meet all the above criteria but also have been assessed as valid by other experts in the field before being published in what's known as a peer-reviewed journal.

The Natural Medicine Cabinet

Some of the most popular alternative therapies for combating diabetes or its complications are herbal and plant-based supplements that you can find at health-food stores and many pharmacies and supermarkets. Do they work? For the most part, the jury is still out, but research so far suggests that a few may hold real promise.

Whether to use herbal remedies is a personal decision you'll need to make with the help of your doctor. Certainly, you should approach them with caution. Don't simply assume that "herbal" means "safe," because, in most cases, thorough research on long-term effects has not been done. The fact is, many medicinal herbs do have effects on the body—which is reason for both hope and concern. The information presented below is not an endorsement of these therapies, but it can start you thinking about whether certain supplements may be useful to you.

Gunning for Glucose Control

The major goal of herbal therapies for diabetes is the same as for drugs and insulin: to bring down high blood sugar. Here's where it's important to remember that these therapies are complementary: Even if they work, you should never take them as a substitute for your insulin or regular medication, though they might be useful in lowering the doses you require.

It's extremely important that you monitor your blood sugar closely if you take these remedies, for two reasons. First, you won't know how effective they are unless you measure their impact on your glucose. Second, if they're able to bring blood sugar down, you need to be on the alert for an increased possibility of hypoglycemia. Among the herbs that show the most promise for lowering blood sugar are:

Gymnema. Known botanically as *Gymnema sylvestre,* this plant is native to Africa and India, where its Hindi name translates as "sugar destroyer." The name aptly describes what it does to the sense of taste. Placed on the tongue, it impairs the ability to distinguish sweetness and bitterness—perhaps one reason it's been used to treat diabetes in India for more than 2,000 years.

Although herbalists generally regard gymnema as the most powerful herb for blood-sugar control, it hasn't been studied in experiments that are both controlled and double-blind. Nonetheless, the research that has been done suggests that the herb has promise. In one of the best controlled (but not blind) studies, insulin requirements were cut in half for 27 people with type 1 diabetes who took a 400-milligram extract of gymnema for 6 to 30 months, while the insulin needs of the control group didn't change.

It's thought that gymnema might work by boosting the activity of enzymes that help cells use glucose or by stimulating insulin-producing beta cells in the pancreas. Safety studies haven't been done (be especially cautious if you're pregnant or nursing or have liver or kidney disease), but the herb is not known to cause serious side effects.

Fenugreek. Better known today as a spice hailing from the Mediterranean and Near East than as a medicine, fenugreek has nevertheless been put to a variety of uses over the centuries. For example, records dating back to 1500 B.C. indicate that it was used to induce childbirth in ancient Egypt. In Europe, the German Commission E, which regulates herbal medicine, has approved it for use in an inflammation-fighting poultice.

Numerous animal trials and a few small studies conducted with a total of about 100 people have suggested that fenugreek seeds can lower blood glucose. In one of the largest (though not double-blind) studies, 60 people with type 2 diabetes who took 25 grams of fenugreek daily showed significant improvement in their overall blood-sugar control, post-eating glucose levels, urine glucose, and cholesterol levels.

The reason for these benefits may not be all that mysterious. Fenugreek is a legume—a relative of chickpeas, lentils, peanuts, and green peas—and is rich in fiber, which naturally slows digestion and the absorption of glucose. But lab research also indicates that fenugreek contains an amino acid shown to boost the release of insulin.

Don't take fenugreek supplements if you're pregnant or have liver or kidney disease, and don't ingest it within two hours of taking an oral diabetes medication because it may interfere with the body's absorption of the drug. Also be cautious if you're taking blood thinners, with which fenugreek may interact.

Bitter melon. Also known as bitter gourd, balsam pear, karella, or (scientifically) *Momordica charantia,* bitter melon is a dietary staple in Asia and India. Actually a vegetable, it has long been a folk remedy for diabetes in the East, and a number of studies in people (none of them double-blind) suggest it may indeed have some benefits. In one uncontrolled study of 18 people who had recently been diagnosed with type 2 diabetes, 73 percent of those who drank about a half cup of bitter-melon juice (which lives up to its unpalatable name) saw significant drops in blood-sugar levels. In another study, five people who took 15 grams of bitter melon in powdered form (available in capsules) brought their blood sugar down by 25 percent in three weeks.

Bitter melon is thought to help cells use glucose through such active ingredients as plant insulin, which is chemically similar to the insulin from cows that is often used to treat type 1 diabetes. Other substances in bitter melon are thought to block sugar absorption in the intestine.

In addition to having a terrible taste, bitter melon can cause side effects like gastrointestinal distress and headaches, and it shouldn't be taken during pregnancy.

Ginseng. In Chinese, *gin* means "man" and *seng* means "essence"—perhaps not only because the ginseng root's shape sometimes resembles a human figure but also because the root supposedly can treat just about everything. In fact, ginseng's genus name, Panax, comes from two Greek words for "cure" and "all."

Ginseng is said to have whole-body effects that make it broadly useful for building resistance to disease, recovering from illness, combating the physical effects of stress, and even promoting longer life (not to mention boosting your sex drive).

Can you take seriously something that sounds too good to be true? Some of the research into ginseng's effects on diabetes, while far from conclusive, is unusually strong and has appeared in respected peer-reviewed journals. In one University of Illinois study, published in a 2002 issue of the journal *Diabetes,* over-weight mice with type 2 diabetes who were injected with an extract of Asian ginseng (one of two types of ginseng) normal-ized their blood sugar, dropped 10 percent of their body weight, and lowered their cholesterol by about a third.

A University of Toronto study published in the *Annals of Internal Medicine* two years earlier found that 10 people who took three grams of American ginseng (the other type) 40 min-utes before eating reduced their post-meal glucose levels by about 20 percent compared with a control group. An earlier study reported in *Diabetes Care* found that taking ginseng low-ered hemoglobin A1c numbers in people with type 2.

It's not clear how ginseng works, but slowing carbohydrate absorption, boosting glucose uptake, and improving insulin secretion have all been suggested. So has the idea that ginseng, which can cause excitability, simply makes people more active. Other possible side effects include headache, increased blood pressure, and insomnia. Ginseng can interfere with certain heart drugs and the blood thinner warfarin. When buying ginseng, steer clear of Siberian ginseng, which is completely unrelated to the "true" ginsengs and is probably inferior. Also be warned that ginseng is expensive to cultivate, so it's often adulterated with other substances, such as caffeine.

Other Potential Blood-Sugar Busters

A number of other plant-based supplements have been suggest-ed as blood-sugar busters, based on preliminary research that's even thinner than that for the supplements discussed above. Among these potential prospects are:

Aloe vera. It's a desert plant most famous for the soothing qualities of gel extracted from its leaves, but taking it internally may lower blood sugar, according to a handful of trials done mostly in Britain. In one study, five type 2 patients who took half a teaspoon of aloe vera a day for 4 to 14 weeks dropped their fasting blood-glucose results from an average of 273 to 151 mg/dl.

Bilberry. Related to the blueberry and grown in Europe and Canada, bilberry is a folk remedy for diabetes, though no human studies have been done on its blood-sugar effects. In animals, it's been shown to lower blood glucose by 26 percent and triglycerides by 39 percent, potentially making it even more beneficial if you have heart disease. The safety of the extract hasn't been established (high doses may interact with blood thinners), but it's fine to eat as a fruit.

Cilantro. This popular herb is used in traditional Chinese medicine for a variety of purposes, but an animal study published in a British nutritional-science journal found that it lowered blood sugar when introduced into the diet and drinking water of mice with diabetes.

Prickly pear. Also known as nopal, this cactus is a Mexican folk remedy for diabetes and has been studied in a number of small, uncontrolled trials. In two of them, people with type 2 diabetes who consumed 500 grams of nopal (a sizable amount, equal to about a pound) saw their blood sugar drop significantly within a few hours. One suspected mode of action is prickly pear's high fiber content. Perhaps not surprisingly, possible side effects include gastrointestinal distress.

Pterocarpus marsupium. The bark of this tree from India contains a compound, called epicatechin, that some studies have found improves the function of insulin-producing beta cells in the pancreas. In one study from India of 97 people with type 2 diabetes, 69 percent of those taking two to four grams of the herb daily achieved good glucose control within 12 weeks.

Nerves: A Touchy Subject

Some natural remedies for people with diabetes don't lower blood sugar, but they may prove useful for reducing the impact of certain complications, such as neuropathy. That's not easy to prove, though, because nerve damage occurs slowly, over the long haul, while studies of natural remedies tend to be short-term. But at least two supplements seem to show some promise in negating neuropathy.

DID YOU KNOW

Ginseng is traditionally consumed in teas. Look for tea bags containing the powdered root. Such teas are sometimes labeled "red ginseng." This ginseng has been steamed and dried, a process that turns it red. "White" ginseng is simply the dried root.

Alpha-lipoic acid. Sometimes called ALA for short, alpha-lipoic acid is a powerful antioxidant that works to protect cells against the damaging effects of molecules known as free radicals. These chemical scourges are thought to contribute to neuropathy brought on by diabetes, and numerous studies suggest that ALA can stave off damage to nerves caused by free radicals. ALA may also reduce harmful swelling of nerves by blocking an enzyme that causes a glucose by-product (called sorbitol) to build up inside nerve cells.

The body produces small amounts of ALA on its own, and you get a certain amount from such foods as meat and spinach. But neither of these sources provides enough to exert a therapeutic effect—especially since people with diabetes may be prone to low levels of ALA.

What are the effects of ALA? A number of high-quality studies around the world have addressed that question, and the answers, while not yet conclusive, are intriguing. For example, a Mayo Clinic study has shown that three months of ALA supplementation significantly improved the ability of nerves to conduct signals in people with diabetes. And a university study of more than 300 people with diabetes in Germany found that patients taking 600 milligrams of ALA for three weeks experienced less pain and other symptoms of polyneuropathy.

Yet results have been mixed in some of the largest trials, done in Germany in a series of studies called ALADIN—for Alpha-Lipoic Acid in Diabetic Neuropathy. In one double-blind trial involving 328 people with type 2 diabetes, those who received daily ALA injections for three weeks felt significantly less pain from neuropathy than those receiving a placebo. But a larger follow-up study found little difference in symptoms between people treated with ALA injections and pills for nine months and those not receiving the real medication.

Beyond the issue of effectiveness is the question of safety. The safety of ALA hasn't been formally established, but the substance has been used to treat diabetes in Germany for more than 30 years without reports of serious side effects. Still, animal studies suggest it's toxic to rats deficient in thiamin, so some natural therapists suggest taking a supplement of this B vitamin when using ALA.

Gamma-linolenic acid. Though the name sounds a bit similar to ALA, gamma linolenic acid (GLA) is an essential fatty acid whose most concentrated source in nature is the oil from a wildflower called evening primrose (so called because its yellow petals open at dusk). Normally, the body makes all the GLA it needs from other types of fat, but some research indicates this process may be impaired in people with diabetes, suggesting that supplements may be a good idea. You need GLA because the body converts it to prostaglandins—hormonelike substances that regulate a variety of functions, including inflammation, dilation of blood vessels, and hormone activity. Getting more GLA is thought to help prevent neuropathy in part by boosting the flow of nutrients and oxygen to nerves.

At least one good-size, controlled, double-blind, peer-reviewed study backs up such claims. This investigation, which involved 111 people with neuropathy, found that those who took 480 milligrams of GLA daily scored significantly better on 13 out of 16 tests for nerve damage after a year than people who received a placebo. Another double-blind study, though much smaller (22 people), produced similar results with a smaller dose of GLA, contained in about 4 grams of evening primrose oil.

Because evening primrose oil has been studied as a treatment for a variety of problems (including eczema and rheumatoid arthritis) and is widely used in Europe, it has a fairly long safety record and is not known to cause serious side effects. However, small numbers of people may experience headache or gastrointestinal distress.

Natural Eye Protection

Can natural therapies protect eyes from the weakening and bursting of blood vessels that occur with retinopathy? Certain supplements may be helpful, though the evidence for them is not as strong as for some of the therapies recommended for other aspects of diabetes.

L-carnitine. L-carnitine is a type of amino acid—small units of organic material that link together to form proteins. A form of L-carnitine called acetyl-L-carnitine, or ALC, is known to have a potent antioxidant effect and has been proposed as a treatment for both diabetic retinopathy and diabetic nerve disease. You can get L-carnitine from high-protein foods, such as beef and lamb, along with dairy products, but at least one European study suggests that people with diabetes may be naturally deficient in the amino acid.

Will L-carnitine prevent eye damage? Most of the evidence that hints at a benefit comes from animal research. One study, published in the journal *Diabetes*, found that rats given ALC reversed abnormal results on a test that measures retinal function, while rats in a control group showed no improvement. Similar results were produced in a European study using another form of L-carnitine, called propionyl-L-carnitine.

Other studies have suggested that acetyl-L-carnitine may help protect the heart by reducing the risk of angina, in addition to lowering blood sugar and reducing pain from intermit-

HOW MUCH SHOULD YOU TAKE?

Even though they may have medicinal effects, natural supplements aren't prescribed like drugs, which have dosage guidelines based on research into effectiveness and safety. Still, in many (but not all) cases, studies suggest therapeutic supplement doses that, as far as is known, are non-toxic. You should check with your doctor for advice on dosages that might be right for you, but the following are typical.

SUPPLEMENT	USE	TYPICAL DOSE
Alpha-lipoic acid	Reducing nerve damage	100 – 800 mg daily
Bilberry	Lowering blood sugar and preventing retinopathy	40 – 160 mg three times daily
Bitter melon	Lowering blood sugar	5 – 30 g three times daily
Fenugreek	Lowering blood sugar	25 – 50 g daily
Garlic	Preventing cardiovascular disease	400 – 600 mg daily
Gamma-linolenic acid	Reducing nerve damage and preventing heart disease	200 – 600 mg daily
Ginseng	Lowering blood sugar	100 – 250 mg twice daily
Gymnema	Lowering blood sugar	400 – 600 mg daily
L-carnitine	Protecting vision and preventing cardiovascular disease	500 – 1,000 mg daily
OPCs	Preventing cardiovascular disease	200 mg daily (grapeseed extract)

tent claudication in the legs. It's also used to treat conditions unrelated to diabetes, such as muscular dystrophy. Wide use of L-carnitine hasn't revealed any problems with toxicity, but its safety hasn't been well studied.

Bilberry. In addition to its reputed ability to lower blood sugar, bilberry is used to treat a variety of eye problems, including diabetic retinopathy. Evidence that bilberry improves vision is partly anecdotal: For example, during World War II, Royal Air Force bomber pilots claimed they could see better on night raids after eating bilberry. But there's reason to believe its benefits might be real. Bilberry is rich in flavonoids—vitaminlike antioxidant plant substances, some of which are known to strengthen tiny blood vessels like those that nourish the retina. Bilberry is particularly packed with flavonoids known as anthocyanosides, which have been shown both to make blood vessels less leaky and fragile and to shore up connective tissue like that of the retina.

One small, controlled, double-blind study of 14 people with retinal damage from diabetes or high blood pressure found that bilberry produced significant improvements in blood vessels in the eye. But little other controlled research has been done to show how well bilberry works. Still, it may be worth trying, with the approval of your doctor or dietitian. Bilberry supplements generally aren't known to have ill effects, and the fruit is certainly safe—as are other foods containing anthocyanosides, such as blueberries, blackberries, and grapes.

Help for the Heart and Kidneys

Complications of diabetes are often interrelated, and that's certainly true of heart and kidney disease. For example, kidney disease can raise blood levels of cholesterol and triglycerides, which not only boosts your risk of cardiovascular disease but also further accelerates kidney damage. A number of supplements may run interference against this vicious cycle.

OPCs. If you pay attention to scientific names, you might guess that OPC supplements—short for oligomeric proanthocyanidin complexes (also sometimes referred to as PCOs)— share common ground with the flavonoids in bilberry. The two, in fact, are closely related and seem to have similar effects. OPCs, found primarily in grapeseed extract, are powerful antioxidants and appear to strengthen blood-vessel walls, making them less leaky—important for protecting the delicate capillaries that filter wastes in the kidneys.

Little controlled research has been done to show how well OPCs might protect the kidneys. In one study from France (where grapeseed extract was first popularized), people with diabetes or high blood pressure who took 150 milligrams of OPCs daily were able to decrease the leakiness and fragility of blood vessels in the kidneys. However, these results are highly preliminary. Still, tests have been done on OPC safety, and it's come up clean, aside from occasional allergic reactions and mild gastrointestinal problems. One caveat: High doses may interfere with blood thinners, such as warfarin (Coumadin) or aspirin.

Garlic. The ancient Greeks said that this pungent herb could clear the arteries—and modern research suggests that that may

be only the beginning. Dozens of studies since the 1980s have looked at garlic's effects on a variety of cardiovascular risks, and, while not always consistent, results have generally been positive. Fortunately for you and the person standing next to you, garlic in the powdered, capsule form used in many studies won't give you garlic breath.

Many of these studies, when taken together, suggest that garlic can lower cholesterol by 9 to 12 percent, bring down blood pressure by 5 to 10 percent, prevent blood from clotting around artery obstructions, make blood vessels more pliable, and lower your overall risk of heart attack. The research isn't perfect, though. For example, in one study where garlic was shown to be just as effective as a prescription cholesterol-lowering medication, participants all made changes in their diets that could have affected the results. Still, the balance of evidence suggests that garlic has real benefits for the heart and blood vessels.

Garlic may thin the blood, so check with your doctor before taking garlic supplements if you're also taking aspirin or other blood-thinning drugs or other supplements with blood-thinning effects, such as ginkgo or high doses of vitamin E.

L-carnitine. In addition to its possible benefits for the eyes, this amino acid has been shown in controlled studies to reduce death rates in people who have had a heart attack, relieve symptoms of intermittent claudication in the legs, and improve heart function in people with angina. In one study, for example, people who took four grams of L-carnitine a day after experiencing a heart attack had a death rate of 1.2 percent over the course of a year, while those who took a dummy pill had a death rate of 12.5 percent. The people taking the L-carnitine also had better blood pressure, lipid profiles, and heart rates. Paradoxically, the best dietary sources of L-carnitine—namely beef, lamb, and dairy products—are not necessarily the most heart-healthy foods.

Gamma-linolenic acid. Though primarily used to treat diabetic neuropathy, GLA (typically from evening primrose oil) may help the heart as well. In one five-year study of 102 people who had just been diagnosed with diabetes, those whose diets were enriched with linolenic acid (a precursor to GLA) developed fewer cardiovascular problems and suffered less heart damage compared to a control group.

BUYER BEWARE

Even if studies show that an herb or a natural remedy works, there's no guarantee the one you buy will. No matter what their effects, supplements aren't considered medicines and therefore aren't subject to regulation by the Food and Drug Administration unless they prove blatantly unsafe. That leaves quality control largely at the whim of manufacturers. Among the potential problems:

Shoddy production. With no one looking over their shoulders, there is no guarantee that manufacturers will actually fill bottles with what the label says is inside.

Natural variation. Even if the manufacturer does care about quality, plants of the same species that are raised in different places or under different growing conditions can vary significantly in their chemical makeup.

Lack of knowledge. In many cases, nobody really knows which part of a plant produces the desired therapeutic effect (the root versus the leaves, for example). So the manufacturer may responsibly provide the herb that you want—just not the part that gives results.

Responsible manufacturers understand these problems and do their best to ensure quality. To identify quality products, check the label for:

■ The botanical name if the product is plant-based

■ The recommended dose in milligrams

■ A batch or lot number and expiration date

■ The manufacturer's name and address

■ A statement that the product contains a standardized extract, which ensures a certain dose of the active ingredient

The Nutritional Pharmacy

Certain vitamins and minerals may help control blood sugar and reduce the risk of complications. They're best when they come from foods—but should you get more of them from supplements? Here are three you might consider.

1 **Biotin.** The body needs only about 300 micrograms (a unit measuring one-millionth of a gram) of this B vitamin every day from foods like egg yolks, corn, and cauliflower for normal metabolism (including the breakdown of carbohydrates, fat, and protein from food). But preliminary studies suggest that much larger amounts of 8 to 16 milligrams per day may lower blood sugar. In one study, type 2 diabetes patients who took 9 milligrams of biotin a day for one month lowered their fasting blood-glucose levels by an average of 45 percent. Biotin seems to work by boosting insulin sensitivity and helping the body use glucose. It may also help protect against nerve damage. Biotin is probably safe because the body excretes what it doesn't need.

2 **Chromium.** Your daily requirement for chromium, a still-mysterious trace mineral, is estimated at a meager 50 to 200 micrograms, but most Americans get only about 30 micrograms per day. Some studies find that taking supplements in amounts upwards of 500 micrograms brings down blood sugar (though other studies find no benefit). It's thought that chromium might help cells use insulin. Should you take it? The amounts used in studies are higher than the government's estimated "safe and adequate" limit of 200 micrograms. You can probably go above this amount, although no one knows exactly how much is too much.

3 **Magnesium.** This mineral lends a hand to many chemical processes in the body, and it may help cells use insulin. Deficiencies (common in people with diabetes) may promote eye damage. The official daily value is 400 milligrams, but some research finds that taking as much as 2 grams a day helps people with type 2 diabetes use insulin more effectively. Drawback: Doses that high often produce diarrhea. Avoid high doses if you have kidney disease or are pregnant.

Exploring Other Therapies

Taking a supplement feels like taking a conventional drug because they both come in pill and capsule form. But other types of alternative therapies seem like a different animal altogether. For instance, there are mind-body approaches, techniques linked with Eastern ideas about energy flow, and other unconventional or scientifically unproven ideas.

Do these therapies work? Each needs to be judged on its own merit, but it seems clear from research that more is involved with achieving healing and health than causing chemical changes with drugs or fixing the body with surgery. Even conventional medicine—by controlling for a placebo effect, in which thinking you'll get better can seem to make it happen—tacitly acknowledges that the mind and body are closely entwined. Theories holding that stress and other mental states can affect the immune system, once largely dismissed, are now widely accepted as studies continue to reveal connections between the nervous and the immune systems.

That doesn't mean that every therapy without a plausible explanation is valid and waiting for science to catch up. But some therapies do seem to offer promise. Although they may require an investment in time or money, they probably pose few risks. Here are three worth trying.

Biofeedback: The Mind-Body Loop

Doctors long assumed that automatic functions like breathing, heartbeat, and body-temperature regulation were beyond our control. In fact, that's one reason the nervous system was classified as having two distinct parts—the voluntary one, in which conscious thoughts, say, make your fingers wiggle, and the autonomic one, in which the body, on its own, for instance, makes your heart pump faster when you're in danger or stressed. The two systems were thought to be independent of each other and, in fact, not even on speaking terms. Biofeedback, however, has shown that these systems, like the superpowers during the Cold

War, have hidden communication links that allow the two to influence each other. With biofeedback, you're hooked up to a computerized machine that monitors body functions, such as sweating or brain activity. With training, you can learn to recognize your body's responses to stress and other states and exert conscious control over them.

Research at the National Institutes of Health has found biofeedback to be helpful for more than 100 different conditions, and numerous studies suggest that it may help fight diabetes and its complications. For example, one study published in *Diabetes Care* found that people using biofeedback were able to boost skin temperature in their toes by increasing blood flow by 22 percent. Other studies in people with diabetes have shown that biofeedback can help reduce stress and lower blood pressure, and (perhaps as a result) may be able to help stabilize blood sugar.

To take advantage of biofeedback, you'll need to learn control techniques from a trained practitioner (ask your doctor for a referral), but once you've mastered them, you can practice biofeedback at home.

Acupuncture: Therapy with a Point

According to traditional Chinese medicine, the real reason you develop diseases like diabetes is that you suffer imbalances in the flow of life energy, or chi, through your body. Chi is thought

to run through an invisible system of meridians, or energy pathways, that can be influenced by the insertion of extremely thin needles at specific sites known as acupoints.

In the West, such needle treatments, called acupuncture, have been dismissed as quackery, at least in part because the meridian system doesn't correspond to any known part of the anatomy. But acupuncture has gained a certain amount of credence in Western medicine—it's not unusual to find practitioners who have medical degrees—because studies suggest that it may actually ease certain conditions, particularly nausea and pain. (The treatment itself can feel irritating but generally doesn't hurt.)

Much of the research into acupuncture's effects on diabetes comes from China, where it is more accepted, which some doctors view as cause for skepticism. Still, in one review of several Chinese studies published by a researcher at a university in Beijing, acupuncture appeared to cut blood-sugar levels by about half, on average. It was also seen to improve symptoms of such complications as neuropathy and heart disease. In the West, an English study found that 67 percent of type 2 patients with chronic pain from neuropathy were able to get significant relief through acupuncture.

If you're considering trying acupuncture, find a licensed practitioner and expect to need as many as 25 treatments over the course of two to three months to see an effect.

Magnets: An Attractive Option?

The idea that magnets can influence health isn't new: It was popular in the early 20th century, but magnet therapies were discredited because of a lack of evidence that they worked. Recently, though, the idea has again begun gathering adherents. Treatments range from holding magnets next to afflicted areas of the body to lying on magnetic mattresses.

In the case of diabetes, magnets aren't thought to stabilize blood sugar, but there's some evidence that they may be useful in relieving pain from neuropathy, especially in extremities like the feet. In one pilot study in which 14 people with peripheral neuropathy wore magnetic insoles in their shoes for four months, 75 percent of those with diabetes (and 64 percent of the group as a whole) improved—and some said their pain disappeared altogether. Other studies have produced similar results, though these findings are still preliminary.

Theories that magnets might help promote health aren't as wacky as they might seem. Tiny amounts of magnetic energy are involved in a vast range of biochemical processes in the body, from cell division and energy exchange right down to the subtle forces that hold the body's atoms together. It's thought that magnets may have therapeutic effects by drawing blood (which contains iron-rich hemoglobin) into areas that need more oxygen and nutrients, affecting the flow of ions that help blood-vessel walls relax, or stimulating the nervous system.

IS THE FORCE WITH YOU?

According to traditional Chinese medicine, good health depends on a balance of yin and yang—the positive and negative aspects of the universal life force known as chi, which flows through 14 meridians in the body. Is there anything to it? Some research suggests that traditional acupoints along the meridians differ slightly from the surrounding skin in electrical and magnetic properties while also containing dense concentrations of blood vessels and nerves. Lab tests on animals suggest that acupuncture releases endorphins and other chemical messengers that may help relieve pain.

9

Living Well with Diabetes

Diabetes isn't just a physical disorder; like any chronic condition, it's also an ongoing emotional challenge. At various points, you're likely to face anger, frustration, and possibly feelings of depression and just plain being burned out from dealing with the disease. Learning how to cope is a must. You'll also need some know-how for handling diabetes when you're sick or when you're traveling. The bottom line: Diabetes doesn't need to get you down—or slow you down.

Diabetes is a chronic condition—something you have to live with for the rest of your life. It even requires daily attention, which can seem burdensome. But a key fact to remember is this: While you shouldn't deny the challenges of diabetes, there's no reason that every aspect of an enjoyable life can't be just as rewarding for you as for anybody else.

Quality of life is an important element in diabetes care. In fact, you could argue that it's the point of everything you do to manage your condition—from counting carbohydrates and walking regularly to checking your feet at night and taking daily doses of aspirin. The better you take care of yourself, the less likely you are to experience the complications that account for most of the suffering that goes with diabetes. When it comes to blood sugar, better control equals a better life.

This isn't mere cheerleading. In an attempt to shed light on how to live well with diabetes, researchers have studied quality-of-life issues in people with the disease. One study, published in the *Journal of the American Medical Association*, compared quality of life in people with diabetes who had good blood-sugar control with peers who didn't. Those with good control had milder symptoms, felt better, and were more likely to feel mentally sharp than the other group. As a result, they tended to be more productive and less restricted in every aspect of life.

But living well with diabetes goes beyond the glucose game. It also means managing your emotions (a significant part of dealing with diabetes) and contending with a raft of practical issues from day to day.

The Feelings Factor

"How are you feeling?" There are two ways to interpret that question. One is how you're feeling physically, which people tend to think of first. The other—equally as important—is how you're feeling emotionally. Indeed, a growing body of research shows that mental and physical health are tightly entwined. If you're out of whack emotionally, your health may follow.

Studies find, for example, that people who suffer such negative emotions as anger, depression, and anxiety tend to have higher rates of heart disease and weaker immune-system response than people with a more positive outlook—important considerations for people with diabetes. That doesn't mean you should worry about ruining your health if you're already feeling bad. But paying attention to your emotional well-being can help you get a handle on improving it.

Why Diabetes Can Be a Downer

Anybody with diabetes will probably agree: There's truth to the notion that having a chronic disease makes your life more difficult than that of someone who's disease-free (or, at least, difficult in different ways). Still, it's interesting to note that, according to one recent study of people with chronic conditions (including diabetes, liver infection, and gastrointestinal disease), those with diabetes tended to do better on the quality-of-life front. This study found that the daily grind of dealing with diabetes—including tasks like testing and taking drugs or insulin—doesn't faze people as much as might be expected. The real battle, it turns out, is with emotional, psychological, and social issues. It's easy to see why this potentially life-threatening disease can take a toll:

It never goes away. Diabetes is for life. Even though it's possible to delay or ward off the most debilitating consequences, the knowledge that you're engaged in a never-ending battle can make you feel weary and defeated.

It's often hidden. Diabetes is considered a silent, invisible disease in two different respects. First, even while it's progressing you may not feel any symptoms, which can foster a deceptive sense that you don't really have a disease. As a result, you may find it tempting to stray from your diet, exercise, or treatment plans. (Or you may have the unnerving impression that no matter what you do, diabetes is secretly eating away at your health.) The other hidden aspect of diabetes is that it's not obvious to others. On the surface, everything about you may seem "normal," while underneath, you realize that you're different from those around you in a fundamental way. This can make you feel socially awkward, especially in settings where food is being served.

It's inconsistent. It would be easier if diabetes followed a predictable course that was the same for everyone, but it

DID YOU KNOW

A connection between diabetes and emotions was noticed at least as far back as the 17th century, when British physician Thomas Willis theorized that an emotional state he called "profound sorrow" *caused* diabetes. For more than two centuries, the idea persisted that diabetes might have psychological origins. Today's view is that while negative emotions may make diabetes more difficult to deal with or accelerate the disease process, they're more likely to be a consequence of the illness than a cause.

doesn't. For one thing, your diabetes is different from the next person's (based on your diabetes type, blood-sugar levels, pancreatic function, insulin resistance, and other factors). But your own case of diabetes may also be subject to seemingly erratic changes. For example, blood sugar can move up and down in response to a wide variety of influences, from illness to physical activity (not to mention drug and insulin treatments), and it can be difficult to predict when glucose might drop to the gutter and cause a hypoglycemic episode.

Coping with Your Emotions

Life's already an emotional roller coaster without the added burden of diabetes, so you don't always need to hold your disease responsible for your ups and downs. In fact, doing so may make you feel more helpless and out of control (and prevent you from solving problems not related to diabetes). But it's useful to recognize when diabetes does fan the flames of feeling—and address the emotions head-on.

The first step is to recognize that mood swings are a natural phenomenon with diabetes—even apart from the emotional challenges of managing the disease. Variations in your blood-sugar levels can affect mood directly. Low glucose levels can make you nervous, irritable, and anxious, while high blood sugar can make you feel fatigued and down in the dumps. That means the steps you take to control your blood sugar can have an emotional payoff as well. Still, you can expect to contend with negative feelings that have nothing to do with blood sugar but everything to do with having diabetes.

Defeating Depression

Everybody feels low at least some of the time, and common sense suggests that having a chronic disease is ample reason to be depressed. In fact, people with diabetes may be as much as four times more likely than the rest of the population to bandy with the blues, and they may also suffer from depression longer.

All of which suggests that depression is normal if you have diabetes. But you don't have to—and shouldn't—accept low moods as inevitable or beyond your control.

🔵 **Be alert to symptoms.** Read over the criteria for clinical depression (see "Diagnosing Depression," below) and see a doctor if you qualify. Your problem may have a physiological cause that can be remedied by, say, adjusting your diabetes medication or taking you off drugs that can have depressant side effects (including some blood-pressure medications and antihistamines). Otherwise, your doctor or psychiatrist can prescribe antidepressant medications that fine-tune levels of certain chemicals in the brain. SSRIs—short for selective serotonin reuptake inhibitors—are likely candidates because they're effective and generally have fewer side effects than other antidepressants, though in some people they can cause such side effects as nervousness, insomnia, lack of appetite, and dulled sexual response. Drugs in this class include fluoxetine (Prozac), paroxetine (Paxil), and sertraline (Zoloft).

🔵 **Talk it out.** Sharing your feelings is one of the most effective ways of taking an emotional burden off your shoulders—which is why counseling is a mainstay of treatment for depression. Start by asking a friend or loved one if you can talk about what you're going through. Assure him that he doesn't have to try to solve your problems but that an open ear might do you some good.

🔵 **Socialize more.** Just being with other people in a social setting or a group like a community club, volunteer organiza-

CAUTION

Depression doesn't just affect you emotionally. People who feel chronically blue also tend to have higher blood pressure and are more prone to heart disease than other people predisposed to it. Just as important, feeling low can make you less motivated to take good care of yourself, which puts your blood-sugar control—and your overall health—at risk.

DIAGNOSING DEPRESSION

Doctors distinguish between run-of-the-mill lows that come and go in response to events in your life and the clinging cloudiness of clinical depression, which can hang around for weeks without letting up. If you're clinically depressed, medications may help. You may be clinically depressed if five or more of the following are true for at least two weeks straight:

■ You feel sad, empty, anxious, or irritable just about all the time.

■ You take little interest or pleasure in most, if not all, of your daily activities.

■ You lack energy.

■ Your normal appetite changes or you've lost or gained a significant amount of weight.

■ You feel agitated or sluggish in your responses.

■ You feel worthless or guilty.

■ You have trouble sleeping—or you sleep more than usual.

■ You have difficulty concentrating or making simple decisions.

■ You often find yourself thinking about dying or suicide.

tion, or religious congregation can take your mind off your troubles, brighten your mood, and make you feel less alone.

⮕ **Stick with the program.** Don't let your low mood derail your self-care program, especially when it comes to regular exercise. In fact, physical activity has been shown to lift mild or moderate depression.

⮕ **Don't drink.** Because it's a depressant, alcohol won't drown your sorrows, it will only aggravate them. Drinking in excess, of course, will also add empty calories to your diet and possibly erode your self-discipline.

Attacking Anger

Most people go through a predictable cycle of emotions after they're first diagnosed with diabetes, typically starting with a this-can't-be-true sense of denial that eventually gives way to anger when you realize you're in it for the long haul. You may feel that your body (or nature or God) has betrayed you, that your life has been turned upside down in ways you can't control, or that you don't deserve something like this and it just isn't fair.

These are normal responses that may make you irritable for weeks and even months at the outset. As you gradually accept your diabetes and settle into a self-care routine, your anger may cool down. But it's also possible that anger will persist, especially if you find yourself frustrated by your disease. For example, your best efforts at glucose control may not be producing the results you want. You may resent the intrusion diabetes has made on your daily routine or feel irritated by having to change your eating or activity patterns.

Frustration is a part of dealing with diabetes, but unchecked anger isn't healthy for your relationships, your mental health, or your body. As with depression, anger is linked with higher rates of heart disease. It can seem a difficult emotion to control, but if you're alert to it and prepared to contend with flare-ups, you can get the upper hand. Here's how.

⮕ **Take responsibility.** Making progress toward peace means working toward an attitude of acceptance—not only of the diabetes itself but of the emotional toll it takes as well. Diabetes can be frustrating, and it can make you mad. Those are realities, and it's okay to recognize them as such. This allows you to take a step back and see a bigger picture in which your emotions aren't overwhelming and out of control but rather predictable responses for which you can begin to take responsibility. Part of this responsibility involves understanding where your anger is coming from, and not unfairly blaming other people or circumstances. If you stay calmer, those around you will as well, and you'll likely find less fuel to fire your outbursts.

➲ **Look for patterns.** Try to predict when you're most likely to experience feelings of annoyance, frustration, or rage. Is it waiting in long checkout lines with slow cashiers? Does a particular person tend to get under your skin? Do certain topics of conversation raise your ire? If you don't have a handle on when you tend to get angry, try writing down what's happening every time you get mad to see if patterns start to reveal themselves. In some cases, simply knowing your triggers can give you a greater sense of control. And, of course, it can help you avoid them.

➲ **Ignore the bait.** One exercise some experts suggest is to think of yourself as a fish being baited by a hook. On the hook is a trigger for your anger. Do you take the bait or recognize it for what it is and simply pass it by? Consciously choosing not to bite lets you take control of your anger by refusing to let another person or situation determine your feelings.

➲ **Change your mental channel.** Sometimes, even when you approach anger rationally, you still feel peeved. In those cases, try shifting your thoughts. If you're steaming while stuck in traffic, turn on a radio program or listen to a book on tape. Mentally replay last night's basketball game or crime drama. Repeat a quiet phrase like "Calm down" or a favorite prayer.

Seeking an Anxiety Antidote

If you're feeling depressed, it's likely that you're experiencing anxiety as well—the two emotions often occur in tandem. But even if you're not battling the blues, having diabetes can give you plenty of cause for worry. For starters, there's the fear that progressing complications may impair your quality of life in the

---

STOP ANGER IN ITS TRACKS

According to behavioral-medicine experts at Duke University, you can soothe your seething by asking yourself four pointed questions about what's provoking you:

- Is this important?
- Is my reaction appropriate?
- Can I change the situation?
- If I can, is it worth taking action?

If you answer "no" to any of these questions, the only rational choice is to cool down. While anger isn't always rational, forcing yourself into an objective frame of mind can often be calming in itself.

future. Even if you're doing a good job of monitoring and managing your diabetes, the unseen and unfelt nature of the disease can foster a nagging sense of dread.

Worrying about your diabetes is normal and, to some extent, even healthy because it helps motivate you to follow your treatment plan. But anxiety can sometimes acquire a life of its own and can become counterproductive and unhealthy. If your fears are more intense than they need to be, crop up frequently, or persist even when circumstances no longer justify them, they can distract you from the better things in life, undermine your ability to manage your disease and paralyze more positive thinking. To release yourself from the grip of fear:

➲ **Check in with your doctor.** Remember that nervousness and such symptoms as rapid heartbeat are signs of hypoglycemia as well as anxiety, so your first step is to have your doctor evaluate your recent blood-sugar history. In some cases, a bout of anxiety might simply require an adjustment in your insulin or medication. If that's not the problem, your primary-care physician can refer you to a mental-health professional who may be able to treat your anxiety with drugs.

➲ **Talk back to yourself.** Anxiety can blind you to positive emotions and cause you to focus only on negatives and potential catastrophes. You might fear that a slight slip from your blood-sugar goals is the first step down the road to vision loss or that if you take time to exercise, you'll never get all your work done and you'll be fired. Pay attention to what therapists call automatic thoughts, which set the tone for your mental state. If they tend to be negative ("This will never work" or "I can't handle it"), try to be as objective as possible and ask yourself if evidence supports your thinking or whether you might be wrong. Look back to challenges you successfully met in the past for proof that things can also work out for the better.

➲ **Keep a mattress pad.** Worries have a way of intruding on your thoughts in the middle of the night. If anxiety keeps you up, keep a pad and pen by your bed so you can jot down what's bothering you. Try writing concrete steps you can take to resolve your concerns; this provides a reassuring sense that you've tackled the problem. Getting better sleep will make you more refreshed and energetic in the morning, and this can help you keep your anxieties in perspective.

Putting Stress in Its Place

Too much stress isn't good for anyone, but it may be especially bad for people with diabetes. It can prevent you from effectively managing your condition by thwarting your intentions to eat a good diet, keep up with your exercise program, and remember to do regular finger-prick checks. Worse still, there's considerable evidence that stress makes blood sugar rise.

One way to explain this effect: Hormones released when you're tense or under the gun—particularly cortisol and epinephrine—pump glucose into blood from storage sites in the liver so the body has more energy available to meet a challenge. So-called stress hormones can have other harmful effects as well. One recent study finds that stress inhibits the ability of blood vessels to expand, which might make it a factor in heart attacks.

The best way to deal with stress is to avoid whatever's making you tense. But since that's not always possible, you can benefit from taking other steps:

⟳ **Invest in relationships.** Numerous studies find that surrounding yourself with family and friends buffers the strain of stress better than just about anything else. So-called social support leaves you feeling less isolated while bolstering your sense of control, which alone can make life seem less daunting. When speaking with loved ones (especially a spouse), avoid put-downs and negative language; studies have found that sniping can produce a marked increase in stress hormones.

⟳ **Get with a program.** Ask your primary-care physician to recommend a good stress-management program, perhaps through your health-insurance plan. One study published in 2002 found that people with diabetes who participated in such programs could significantly improve their hemoglobin

DOES STRESS CAUSE DIABETES?

Fact: Stress makes the body release hormones like cortisol.

Fact: Stress hormones make blood sugar go up.

Fact: Stress may encourage fat to accumulate in the belly.

Fact: High blood sugar and belly fat contribute to insulin resistance and, eventually, to diabetes. Conclusion: Stress causes diabetes.

Is it true? It's a controversial notion, and the answer is not yet clear. In a recent Dutch study published in *Diabetes Care*, researchers who surveyed more than 2,200 people with no history of diabetes found that those who reported the most major life stresses were more likely to have undiagnosed diabetes. Yet stress from some significant sources (notably work) didn't seem to affect diabetes rates, calling the stress effect into question.

A1c results—enough to hit blood-sugar targets shown to reduce the risk of various diabetes complications.

⤷ **Follow your faith.** Religious belief can help put the trials and tribulations of life in a reassuringly larger perspective or—if faith doesn't come easily to you—provide an opportunity to receive social support through communal worship, along with a sanctuary from life's storms.

⤷ **Express yourself.** People who write down their thoughts in a journal tend to feel less stress and may even be better able to

FOUR TOP STRESS-RELIEF STRATEGIES

To tame tension, it helps to tackle both its physical and its psychological dimensions. Here are some of the most important steps you can take, according to Mark Abramson, D.D.S., who teaches two stress-management courses at the Stanford University Center for Integrative Medicine and the Health Improvement Program at Stanford University Medical School:

❶ FILL THE BALLOON

Deep breathing has been shown to rapidly calm the body's physical response to stress. "Done properly, three breaths will lower your heart rate and blood pressure," says Dr. Abramson. "It's a very powerful tool, but people generally don't understand how to do it right." Most people breathe in a shallow way that makes the chest expand, with the diaphragm pushing upward. Deeper, stress-relieving breaths, however, should make the diaphragm move downward, expanding your belly. "Picture a balloon under your belly button that you need to fill," says Dr. Abramson. "As you draw air in, imagine the balloon expanding, then slowly let the air out."

❷ PUT PERIODS IN YOUR THOUGHTS

Most stress comes from worrying about the past or the future. "You'll feel less stress if you can stay focused on the present, where there's a finite number of things you have to deal with emotionally," says Dr. Abramson. Start by simply acknowledging—and accepting—what you're feeling right now, without thinking about why or what to do

about it. "Be with what is," Dr. Abramson explains. "We tend to think in run-on sentences. Just think, 'I'm frustrated' and end the sentence there." If your mind strays to the future, consciously bring it back to the moment at hand. Deep breathing can help you stay centered on the here and now.

❸ PRACTICE THANKSGIVING

Before a meal—or whenever else it seems appropriate—make a point of giving thanks. Such habits encourage an awareness of what's good about the present moment—and how things we take for granted (regular meals, a place to live, the luxury of a shower every morning) are true blessings.

❹ BE KIND TO YOURSELF

Most of us judge ourselves harshly, straining for perfection and beating ourselves up for mistakes. "Consciously say to yourself, 'I don't have to be perfect,'" says Dr. Abramson. "Feeling more forgiving of yourself will not only relieve tension in the moment, it'll also improve the way you treat others, which leads to better relationships and further stress reduction over the long term."

resist illness. Just be sure to write down honest feelings about what's bothering you: In one recent study, those who let loose on the page had measurable improvements in immune function while those who repressed their thoughts actually saw declines.

Battling "Diabetes Burnout"

Though dealing with diabetes 24-7 can seem overwhelming at first, many people willingly adjust to a new lifestyle of dedicated self-care. But over time, a creeping sense of fatigue and frustration can set in—what some experts call "diabetes burnout." When you're burned out, you may not feel outright depressed, just sick and tired of the never-ending diabetes grind. As a result, you may find that your all-important motivation begins to wane.

Even though burnout won't directly cause physical changes in the body, feeling frustrated—often because you may sense that you're not making progress against your disease—can have an impact on your health. You may start to slack off your diet, exercise, drug regimen, or self-monitoring programs.

Talking with your doctor or a counselor is your first step if diabetes care is wearing you down. Your doctor may be able to make adjustments in your treatment—fewer shots using different combinations of insulin, for example—to ease your burden. A counselor may be able to suggest new ways of thinking that can boost your sense of purpose. But then you'll need to take steps on your own to fortify your resolve.

➲ **Check your goals.** At some point earlier in your treatment, you and your medical team established objectives for your self-care—blood-sugar targets, meal plan, exercise goals. These were based on what you thought was possible then, but it may be time to review your list of objectives with a fresh eye. Pretend you're starting over. Knowing now what you didn't know then, do you feel your goals are reasonable? Feeling successful in meeting your objectives is a key to staying motivated.

➲ **Evaluate your progress.** Maybe you haven't made as much progress as you would like. But be objective about what you have accomplished. How has your blood-sugar control improved? How about your weight or your overall fitness? Have you managed to be disciplined about testing and taking medication? You may find that you've done better than you give yourself credit for. On the other hand, your frustration may be a good sign: It means you actually are motivated to do better.

➲ **Identify problem areas.** If you're like most people, you've probably been more effective with some elements of your self-care than with others. But don't let your weakness or lack of progress in one area color the entire picture. Instead, try to isolate the aspects of your care with which you have the most trouble. Is it a challenge to control your appetite? Are you forgetting to take your medication or insulin? Is finding time for exercise a constant battle?

➲ **Seek solutions.** Once you've identified problem areas, you can start zeroing in on solutions. Why do you feel a particular challenge is such a struggle? What could change to make it more manageable? For example, if your eating is the issue, ask your dietitian to suggest changes in your meal plan that will make it more appropriate for you and your personal preferences. If you find you hate your workouts, try to find forms of exercise that blend fitness and fun—such as a dance class.

➲ **Enlist support.** Remember, you're not in this battle alone. Talk to other people with diabetes for perspective, ideas, and encouragement. Think about joining a diabetes support group (ask your doctor or diabetes educator for a recommendation), or try to find an Internet chat group that you're comfortable with. The renowned Joslin Diabetes Center, in Boston, runs online diabetes support groups from its website at www.joslin.org. Enlist friends to join you for exercise sessions or to keep posted on your progress: Knowing that someone else is following your case can help spur you on. Many malls have walking clubs that encourage people to step out in their climate-controlled, security-patrolled, bathroom-equipped corridors. Call your local mall to see if it has a club or check the Internet at www.walksport.com to learn about a program, sponsored by New Balance, that awards walkers prizes for their efforts.

Keep your eyes on the prize. Try to stay focused on the quality of life you gain by controlling your diabetes rather than on the negatives—namely, the complications—that you avoid. It's a subtle distinction, but cringing in fear of consequences is generally a less effective motivator than striving for more joy, freedom, and flexibility in your life.

How to Think About Diabetes

When you have diabetes, your attitudes are tugged in two seemingly opposite directions. On the one hand, you need to make good blood-sugar control a top priority, to the extent that your time and daily activities are organized around your self-care routine. On the other hand, you want to live as normal a life as possible. Should diabetes always be in the top of your mind, or should you try not to dwell on it?

These questions represent a spectrum with two unhealthy extremes on either end. One is denial (especially common in the early days of a diagnosis), in which you fail to realize or accept all the changes necessary to take charge of diabetes and ensure a high quality of life over the long haul. The other is obsession, in which you desperately strive for perfection in every aspect of your treatment to the extent that you think about little else.

You need to incorporate a little of both extremes into your attitude about diabetes. A bit of denial allows you to set aside gloomy thoughts of complications so that you can concentrate on enjoying your life today. And a certain amount of obsession encourages you to be diligent about your care. But taken too far, both outlooks can threaten your health—denial because it leads to poor glucose control and obsession because your inevitable failure to achieve perfect control leads to disappointment and discouragement. Finding the right balance depends in part on the way you approach life as a whole.

Seek serenity. The familiar adage that we should have the courage to change the things we can, the serenity to accept the things we can't, and the wisdom to know the difference applies

particularly well to diabetes. It's important to take responsibility for your disease and do everything in your power to manage it, but also to let go of the idea that you'll ever exert total control over diabetes—or any other aspect of your life.

➲ **Embrace ambiguity.** If you wrestle with questions of whether you should consider yourself sick versus well, or in control versus at the mercy of your disease, step back and ask why it's necessary to have all the answers. As with much of life, the path of wisdom may be to simply accept the situation's inherent ambiguities.

➲ **Know yourself.** The real issue in how you think about diabetes may be how you think about yourself. Do you see yourself as a person with a disease or someone who's loving, creative, resourceful, and appreciated by family, friends, and community? The less you define yourself by your condition, the easier it will be to see the measures you take to control your diabetes as stepping stones to fulfilling your truly important roles in life.

Sex and Diabetes

When you think about enjoying life and all its pleasures, great sex may be one of the first things to pop into your mind. The good news is that there's no reason you can't have a full and satisfying sex life if you have diabetes. But you need to understand how your disease can affect different aspects of your sexuality and sexual function.

First, bear in mind that sexual intimacy can be physically vigorous, burning calories. That means that, like exercise, it may put you at risk of hypoglycemia—inconvenient when making love, to say the least. To keep blood sugar stable, it's wise to take glucose readings before and after sex to get an idea of how your body responds. Try having a sugary drink or a small snack beforehand or, with your doctor's approval, adjusting your insulin if you know that sexual intimacy is in the offing.

For Women Only

Sexuality is complex in women even without interference from a chronic disease, so it's no surprise that they generally experience more sexual side effects related to diabetes than men. But the problems are not insurmountable. Among them:

Blood-sugar fluxes. Though it's not a universal experience, many women notice their blood sugar rises a few days before their monthly period begins. Researchers suspect (though not all agree) that fluxes in female sex hormones, such as estrogen and progesterone, temporarily make cells more resistant to insulin. If you suspect this is a problem for you:

▶ For several months, keep a log of when your period begins, then compare it to your daily blood-sugar records. If you find a distinct correlation between your glucose levels and your menstrual cycle, talk to your doctor about adjusting your insulin or doses of medication.

▶ Consider an alternative cause. Some doctors think the real reason blood sugar rises before your period is that the cravings and irritability of premenstrual syndrome make you eat more—or more erratically—thereby causing unusual peaks and valleys in blood-sugar levels. Try eating at regular intervals to keep blood sugar stable, and avoid alcohol and caffeine, which can affect mood.

▶ If you take oral contraceptives, ask your doctor which pill is best for you. Monophasic oral contraceptives (such as Alesse, Loestrin, and Ortho-Cept), which contain fixed amounts of estrogen and progestin, appear to keep blood-sugar levels more stable than triphasic (such as Triphasil and OrthoTricyclen) and progesterone-only contraceptives (such as Micronor and injected Depo-Provera).

Vaginal dryness. Women with diabetes sometimes find they lack natural lubrication during sexual arousal, though this problem isn't limited to people with high blood sugar. To deal with it, try using water-based lubricants, available at any pharmacy. If the problem continues, check with your doctor; you may have low estrogen levels that can be boosted with topical estrogen cream or hormone replacement therapy (HRT). Weigh the HRT option carefully, however. Although it may solve the lubrication problem, it may also raise the risk of other health problems.

Infections. Excess sugar in the blood encourages the growth of fungal organisms and bacteria, making women with diabetes more prone to yeast infections and vaginitis. If you experience vaginal discharge or itching, see your doctor for an antifungal cream or antibiotics.

For Men Only

Sex can sometimes seem more straightforward for men, but the male sexual response is also a complex melding of mind and body that involves numerous systems that can be affected by diabetes.

The major difficulty men may face is erectile dysfunction (also called impotence), the inability to achieve or maintain an erection—a problem that often occurs with age and is hardly limited to men with diabetes. In many cases, the cause is purely physical. When you have diabetes, poor circulation can prevent blood from properly engorging chambers in the penis, and nerve damage can interfere with signals involved with sexual response. (Fortunately, the nerves that enable orgasm are seldom impaired.) But depression and anxiety can cause erectile dysfunction as well, and sexual difficulties may involve a combination of factors. Here are some steps you can take:

➲ **Narrow it down.** Talk to your doctor about possible causes so you know how to treat the problem. It may be a simple matter of adjusting one of your medications. Many drugs, including some for high blood pressure, can interfere with sexual function. If that's not the issue, pay attention to patterns: If erectile dysfunction seems to happen on and off, strikes suddenly, or occurs in some circumstances but not others, the problem may have a psychological component. If you gradually and consistently lose function over time, there's more likely a physical cause.

IF YOU'RE PREGNANT AND HAVE DIABETES

Having a baby when you have diabetes poses risks both for your child and for you, but plenty of diabetic women get through pregnancy without a hitch.

Before conceiving, get a thorough evaluation for complications of diabetes, such as retinopathy, kidney damage, nerve damage, and high blood pressure—all of which can be made worse by pregnancy. To guard against complications and protect the health of the baby, you should be prepared to control your blood sugar even more tightly than before. Women with diabetes have babies with birth defects in only 2 to 3 percent of cases, but those numbers more than triple if your glucose control is only so-so.

Tight control not only reduces the risk of birth defects but keeps the baby from growing too large, which raises the risk of delivery problems. If you have type 1 diabetes, you'll probably need more insulin injections and may want to switch to a pump. If you have type 2, drugs are not advised, so you'll need to start or modify an insulin program. Check with your dietitian to ensure that both you and your baby get proper nutrition, and be sure to stay physically active throughout your pregnancy, both to control blood sugar and to condition your body for labor.

⊃ **Ask about Viagra.** The drug sildenafil citrate (Viagra) induces erections lasting at least an hour in about 80 percent of patients who take it. If side effects like headache, low blood pressure, and diarrhea bother you, other medications are available, though they tend to be less effective. If you have heart trouble, you may not be able to take Viagra.

⊃ **Go to extremes.** If oral drugs don't work, try alprostadil (Caverject). Like Viagra, it relaxes smooth-muscle tissue in the penis to boost blood flow, but it's injected with a needle. Other injectable drugs (papaverine, phentolamine) are available as well. Non-drug approaches include vacuum devices (which use a hand-pumped tube that fits over the penis to draw blood into the organ) and surgically implanted rods that can be bent or inflated by a man (or his partner) when he wants an erection.

Planning for Sick Days

Being sick is no fun for anyone, but it takes a special toll if you have diabetes because it can throw off your blood sugar and put you at risk for significant short-term complications. The best way to deal with sick days is to plan for them before you're laid up. Speak with your primary-care physician, endocrinologist, and dietitian to work out the details of a strategy you can quickly put into action the next time a cold, the flu, or something else strikes.

Illness is a form of stress that—like emotional stress—rouses the body's defenses. One effect is that the liver steps up glucose production to provide more energy. At the same time, stress hormones are released that make cells more insulin resistant. The net result is that blood sugar can rise dramatically when you're ill. Among the serious problems that can result are:

▶ **Ketoacidosis.** If available insulin isn't enough to move glucose into cells (mostly a problem with type 1 diabetes), the body will start tapping its fat stores, releasing toxic ketones and putting you at risk of a coma.

▶ **Hyperosmolar nonketotic coma.** When blood sugar in type 2 patients gets too high, the body tries to get rid of glucose through the urine, which can produce severe dehydration that can also lead to coma.

To keep your blood sugar in check when you're ill and help yourself feel better faster, follow these steps:

Step up your monitoring. It's more important than ever to keep careful track of your blood-sugar levels, so you'll probably need to test yourself more often than you usually do—at least every three to four hours. If your blood sugar goes higher than 240 mg/dl, do a urine ketone test as well. If ketone results are positive—or if your blood sugar consistently hovers above 240—call your doctor.

Noodle with your nourishment. Illness can ruin your appetite (especially if you have trouble keeping food down), but you need to eat enough to provide your body with the energy it needs. Work with your dietitian to develop a sick-day menu that fits in with your eating plan—perhaps one that features foods like oatmeal, toast, and steamy soup, which offer good nutrition but are easy on the stomach. If you find meals unappetizing, try eating small amounts frequently throughout the day.

Get plenty of fluids. This familiar advice is doubly critical when you have diabetes because water is drawn into excess glucose and excreted in the urine, which can cause dehydration. Aim to drink a cup of fluid (which includes soup broth) every half hour or so. If lack of appetite is making it difficult for you to consume enough food to meet your energy needs, sip sugared drinks like non-diet soda, fruit juices, or sports beverages instead of plain water to make sure you're getting at least some calories into your body.

Stay the drug course. Unless your doctor instructs you otherwise, it's important to keep taking your medications or giving yourself insulin even if you're not up to eating. In fact, your doctor may want you to take more insulin when you're feeling under the weather, with the exact amounts depending on your blood-sugar readings and how sick you are. Even if you have type 2 diabetes and don't normally take insulin, it's wise to keep a vial of short-acting insulin on hand in case your doctor feels it's necessary when illness strikes.

⊃ **Watch the OTC remedies.** Some common over-the-counter medicines, such as decongestants with pseudoephedrine, can raise blood sugar. Check with your doctor before taking any drug, herbal remedy, or dietary supplement when you're ill.

⊃ **Keep alert to danger.** Know the signs of ketoacidosis (which include stomach pain, vomiting, chest pain, difficulty breathing, feelings of weakness, sleepiness, fruity-smelling breath, blurry vision) and of dehydration (extreme thirst, dry mouth, cracked lips, sunken eyes, mental confusion, dry skin). Call your doctor right away if you experience symptoms of either of these conditions.

Traveling with Diabetes

Americans have always considered it almost a birthright to pack their bags and hit the trail (or road, rails, or air) whenever the fancy strikes. Fortunately, there's no reason diabetes should hold you back from traveling, as long as you take some reasonable precautions to make sure that while you're getting away, your blood sugar isn't.

Your mantra is "Plan ahead." Let your doctor know your itinerary. Depending on how long you'll be gone, he may want to give you a thorough examination before you depart. And to ensure smooth sailing, heed the following advice.

⊃ **Keep glucose goods close at hand.** If you are traveling by plane, pack your medications, insulin, syringes, test strips, lancets, ketone strips, and other supplies in your carry-on bag so there's no chance of losing them. Consider bringing extra supplies in your checked luggage. Make sure all medications bear the original pharmacy prescription labels.

⊃ **Pack a snack.** Wherever you go, take a totable snack like an apple, an energy bar, a banana, raisins, or cheese and crackers in case your blood sugar starts to dip when you don't have immediate access to other food. If you sample your snacks en route, replenish your supplies as soon as you can.

◯ Anticipate airport security. With the increased security at airports these days, expect your supplies to get a thorough once-over. But the Federal Aviation Administration (as of press time) allows you to board a plane with syringes and insulin-delivery systems as long as you can document that you have a legitimate medical need for them. The letter from your doctor will help, but it won't be sufficient on its own. Make sure you carry your insulin vials in their boxes, which bear preprinted pharmaceutical labels, and once you use the insulin, keep the box. (Don't open your glucagon kit unless you need it.) It's okay to carry lancets on board as well, as long as they're capped and you also carry a glucose meter with a manufacturer's name printed on it. These guidelines are subject to change, and individual airlines may have more stringent rules, so be sure to call ahead for current policies before you leave.

◯ Mind your meals. If you're flying or taking an extended trip by rail, call the carrier a few days before you depart and ask what special meals they have available for people with diabetes or heart disease (there may be more than one option to choose from). When you're en route, wait for meal service to actually begin before you take your pre-meal insulin to make sure you don't experience low blood sugar in the event that service is

TAKE-CHARGE TIPS

Packing is always a challenge, but it's an even bigger challenge when you have diabetes. Follow this advice before you hit the open road.

◯ When it comes to supplies, such as drugs, insulin, test strips, and lancets, the rule of thumb is: Pack twice as much as you think you'll need. It's easier to carry extra than to get more on the road.

◯ In case you do need to restock while you're away, have your doctor give you prescriptions for refills. It's also a good idea to have him provide a printout of all your medications and a letter outlining the details of

your condition so you'll have all the information you need to explain your history in case you need to see a doctor while on the road.

◯ Also ask your doctor to prescribe a glucagon kit, which contains an emergency dose of a hormone that someone with you can inject to make your liver pump out glucose if you have a hypoglycemic emergency that leaves you unable to swallow or makes you lose consciousness.

◯ If you don't already have one, get a medical ID bracelet or necklace that alerts people that you have diabetes and provides a number to call in an emergency.

unexpectedly slowed or canceled. When traveling by car, try to stick to your regular mealtime schedule to keep your blood sugar stable. If that's not possible, carry snacks along with you and be alert to symptoms of low blood sugar, such as nervousness, sweating, and crankiness. If you feel a hypoglycemic episode coming on, pull over immediately and take a sugar pill or have something to eat. Wait at least 10 to 15 minutes for the feeling to pass before continuing on.

➲ **Get in the zone.** Traveling across different time zones can throw your normal insulin and meal schedule completely out of kilter, but you can compensate for the disruption if you're careful. When adding hours to your day by traveling west, you may need to take more insulin. When losing hours by traveling east, you may need less. Check with your doctor for specific recommendations. As for timing your injections and meals, keep your watch set to your home time as you travel to your destination, then switch your watch—and your schedule—to the local time the morning after you arrive.

➲ **Organize for overseas.** If you're traveling outside the country, be aware that insulin you find abroad may be sold in weaker strengths than the insulin available in the United States, which has standardized its insulin in a dose known as U-100. Each insulin strength (such as U-40 and U-80) requires specially matched syringes. Filling a different type of syringe with your U.S. insulin will make your dose inaccurate. Best bet: Stick to your own supplies. If you must buy insulin that's a different strength, also buy syringes to match.

EXERCISING ON THE ROAD

It's tough to stay physically active when traveling—but not impossible. Try to keep your body in gear by planning ahead and snatching opportunities as they arise:

■ If your hotel doesn't have an on-site gym, ask if it provides access to a local health club. If the answer is no, ask which gyms are in the area and see if you can make arrangements on your own—or book a hotel that's more accommodating.

■ Pack comfortable clothes for impromptu walks or workouts, including T-shirts, shorts, socks, and athletic shoes. Don't forget your swimsuit in case the hotel has a pool.

■ Bring lightweight exercise gear that you can use in your hotel room, such as a jump rope, elastic resistance bands (sold in sporting-goods stores), or an aerobics video.

■ If you're away on business, wear dressy walking shoes rather than more formal dress shoes to encourage walking during breaks or before your first meeting.

■ Use airport delays as found time for around-the-terminal walking workouts. When making connections, steer clear of the moving sidewalks and walk the distance under your own power.

10

Breakthroughs
of the Future

A cure for diabetes is still out of reach—but not by much if progress continues at its current pace. Research is yielding fresh insights into the disease and what causes it, and new drugs and surgeries are in the works to treat it. An insulin inhaler is close at hand, as is a mechanical system that amounts to an artificial pancreas. There's even a tantalizing new twist on islet-cell transplants that would virtually eliminate the disease at the root level.

Imagine not having any treatments for diabetes: no insulin, no drugs to control blood sugar, no high-tech surgeries for complications in the eyes or kidneys—and little hope for a long or healthy life. That was the situation into which the World War II generation was born, but this book has shown how diabetes care has made great strides in a relatively short time. And today the pace of innovation is gathering speed.

As the incidence of diabetes has grown, understanding how the disease works and finding effective new treatments has taken on even greater urgency. As a result, researchers are continually making advances that make the future of diabetes care look brighter than ever before. While much about managing diabetes will remain in the hands of patients (particularly when it comes to diet and exercise), you can look forward to an arsenal of new tools in years to come. To some extent, the future is already here. Consider some of the important advances that have taken place within just the past five years or so:

▶ New drugs, such as the alpha-glucosidase inhibitors Precose and Glyset, the combination drug Glucovance, and fast-acting Prandin and Starlix, have been added to the lineup of blood-sugar medications.

▶ New types of insulin provide even more options for keeping blood sugar stable throughout the day and after meals. These include the new insulin glargine (Lantus), which stays evenly active for 24 hours, and rapid-acting lispro and insulin aspart, which start to work within five minutes of taking them.

▶ New glucose-monitoring methods like the laser lancet allow you to test your blood sugar without pricking your finger. Particularly interesting is the GlucoWatch, a device you wear on your wrist that draws blood sugar through the skin using an electric current. The GlucoWatch analyzes the sample, then calculates your blood-sugar level.

Building on the Present

Few medical advances come out of the blue. Instead, they're built on previous groundbreaking work. That means researchers aren't resting on their laurels when it comes to improvements they've made but are forging ahead with new insights and developments. Some of what we can look forward to seeing in coming years:

New insulins. "For decades we didn't have a good basal insulin [like insulin glargine]," says Richard Hellman, M.D., clinical professor of medicine at the University of Missouri, Kansas City, School of Medicine and a board member of the American Association of Clinical Endocrinologists. "Now we do. We will certainly see more of these insulins become available, if for no other reason than that pharmaceutical companies will seek to expand their share of this market." That means more options for patients, along with competitive pressures that may help keep rising medication costs down.

More ouchless monitoring. Companies are working on a number of different ways to get blood-sugar readings without pricking your finger with a lancet—many by analyzing interstitial fluid, a relatively clear liquid that surrounds cells and lies just below the surface of the skin. (Blood-sugar readings from interstitial fluid don't compare head-to-head with readings from actual blood, but meters can translate the difference.) One system now undergoing clinical trials uses lasers to create microscopic holes in the skin that allow interstitial fluid to be siphoned out and drawn through a tube into a wearable meter. Another method, called the SonoPrep Continuous Glucose Monitoring System, uses a low-frequency ultrasound device to disrupt the outer layer of the skin so that fluid can be taken up by a second device that's pressed to the skin. The real goal, however, is a blood-sugar test that's completely noninvasive. One promising approach (but not one that's close to market yet) is to shine a beam of light through the thin tissue of, say, an earlobe or a finger web and analyze the blood by measuring the light spectrum.

New standards for care. Whatever advances in drugs or treatments for complications may be in the works, the most important way to deal with diabetes will still be to control blood sugar as tightly as possible. As studies continue to shed light on how high blood sugar poses risks for diabetes, heart disease, and complications, the medical community is moving to make standards of care more stringent. The American Diabetes Association (ADA) recently lowered the cutoff for a diagnosis of diabetes from a fasting plasma glucose level of 140 mg/dl to 126 mg/dl. Now the American Association of Clinical Endocrinologists is recommending that hemoglobin A1c goals be set at 6.5 percent rather than the ADA's current standard of 7 percent. It's not just a matter of semantics: "Lowering your A1c a small amount with diet and exercise can potentially make even the most exciting new drugs and therapies unnecessary," says Dr. Hellman.

The Future of Insulin Delivery

If you take insulin, finding any way besides injection to get it into your body is probably tops on your wish list—and scientists are working hard to make it happen. That may sound like a tall order, considering that injections have been the only delivery system available in the more than 80 years that insulin has been used. Still, while challenges remain, novel alternatives may be just around the corner.

Numerous methods (including eyedrops, rectal suppositories, and wax pellets placed under the skin) have been tried unsuccessfully throughout the years, but researchers haven't yet run out of ideas. In fact, at least one promising no-needle system is in late-stage clinical trials and appears to be headed for FDA approval. Here's what to watch for.

Breathing a sigh of relief. Closest to market is a powdered form of insulin that you breathe into the permeable tissues of the lungs with the help of an inhaler similar to an asthma inhaler. It's considered the single most viable alternative to injections because it's effective and has already been extensively studied in humans. In people with type 1 diabetes, studies find, inhaled insulin controls blood sugar just as well as short-acting injections do, and it improved glucose control in type 2 patients who previously only took oral medication. One concern is that some people using the inhaler in trials did more poorly in a test of lung function, and some developed a mild to moderate cough. "The inhaler is very close, but research has been dragging as the Food and Drug Administration [FDA] looks more closely at how it affects the lungs," says Carol J. Levy, M.D., C.D.E., assistant professor of medicine at New York–Presbyterian Hospital. Additional tests are

DID YOU KNOW

The biggest problem with delivering insulin to the lungs via an inhaler is that most of the drug—as much as 90 percent of it—sticks in the throat, never making it to its destination. Larger doses are needed to compensate for the problem.

currently under way. One advantage of inhaled insulin over insulin injections: less weight gain.

Exploring oral insulin. Researchers have been stymied for years in their attempts to develop insulin you can swallow because the hormone is naturally broken down during digestion before it reaches the bloodstream. However, a number of approaches in development may overcome this barrier. One method being explored in both the United States and Europe is to encase pills in a resin or plastic coating that breaks down only after the drug reaches the bloodstream. Another tactic is to avoid the gastrointestinal tract altogether by using a spray or patch that allows insulin to be absorbed through the cheek.

Using molecular messengers. On the distant horizon of the coming decades is the prospect of loading insulin into designer molecules called nanoshells—tiny hollow spheres made of silica and coated with gold. On their injection into the body, a hand-held infrared laser would be used to heat the nanoshells, causing them to release small amounts of insulin. Theoretically, each nanoshell injection could provide needle-free insulin for months.

The Disease Frontier

Researchers still have much to learn about diabetes and how to prevent it. In type 2 diabetes, for example, it isn't clear how the body becomes insulin resistant or why obesity poses such great risks. In type 1 diabetes, which can be only partly attributed to genes, the disease's environmental triggers are still largely mysterious.

Here are some of the ways researchers are trying to get at the roots of diabetes and thus shed light on its prevention and treatment.

Looking AHEAD. During the next decade, researchers at 16 centers funded by the National Institutes of Health will be conducting a study called Look AHEAD (Action for Health in Diabetes). The study will compare a program of intensive lifestyle measures, such as diet and exercise specifically meant to produce weight loss, with a less disciplined approach that provides general support and education, but not a weight-loss program, for adults over age 45 with type 2 diabetes. It will be the largest study ever to look at how weight loss affects death rates from cardiovascular problems in people with type 2.

A DIABETES FORECAST

One encouraging finding from the Diabetes Prevention Trial–Type 1 is that the presence of certain types of antibodies known as human leukocyte antigens, or HLAs, is closely associated with development of type 1 diabetes. While most HLAs protect the body, others seem to target islet cell products in the pancreas, such as insulin. "By looking at specific antigens, we can now tell with greater precision whether someone is likely to get type 1 diabetes within the next three years," says Richard Furlanetto, M.D., Ph.D., of the Juvenile Diabetes Research Foundation.

Boosting insulin power. No matter how closely you control blood sugar with insulin, it's tough to get perfect results. Among the challenges: Blood sugar can still swing too high after meals and too low when you're not eating—and when control is good, you tend to gain weight. Enter amylin, a hormone that's released by beta cells in the pancreas at the same time that insulin is secreted. Amylin works together with insulin to control blood sugar. In people with type 1 diabetes, amylin levels are extremely low. In people with type 2 diabetes, amylin levels fail to rise after meals. These abnormalities have led researchers to try to stabilize blood sugar with a synthetic amylin replacement called pramlintide. It appears to work by suppressing secretion of another hormone (glucagon) that raises blood sugar and brakes digestion by slowing the movement of food from the stomach to the small intestine. Clinical trials have been encouraging: In a yearlong study of 538 people with type 2 diabetes, those who got pramlintide injections with meals dropped their hemoglobin A1c scores without changing their insulin dosage or experiencing hypoglycemia—and they lost weight.

Making preemptive strikes. Animal studies have suggested that taking insulin pills twice a day might prevent type 1 diabetes in people at risk of developing it, and a major trial called the Diabetes Prevention Trial–Type 1 recently put the idea to the test in about 400 people. Result: It doesn't work. While disappointed, researchers haven't given up on the idea that exposing the body to supplemental insulin can train the immune system not to attack the pancreas. (Taking insulin pills in these experiments is not meant to lower blood sugar.) Researchers are also looking into similar trials using modified insulin. "Essentially, we're searching for a diabetes vaccine," says Richard Furlanetto, M.D., Ph.D., scientific director of the Juvenile Diabetes Research Foundation, "and there are lots of ideas about how this might be done."

Unlocking secrets with drugs. Many drugs are developed in "backward" fashion—that is, scientists don't always understand why they work, just that they do. But a drug's effectiveness may provide clues about the mechanisms of the disease itself. In the case of type 2 diabetes, scientists are particularly scrutinizing thiazolidinediones, also called glitazones—drugs that help lower blood sugar by making cells more sensitive to insulin. "Insulin resistance is a key trait of type 2 diabetes," says Dr. Furlanetto. "Glitazones are interesting because they don't just have beneficial effects in one type of cell but work across the board in fat, liver, and muscle cells—all places affected by diabetes." Through studies that aim to understand how the glitazones achieve their effects, researchers may be able to develop even better drugs in the future.

Searching for triggers. If the origins of type 1 diabetes are only about half genetic, environmental factors must play a role, too. But which factors? One theory is that exposure to cow's milk early in life may make children more susceptible to diabetes, possibly because of protein similarities between milk and pancreatic beta cells. An international study based in Europe called TRIGR (Trial to Reduce Diabetes in the Genetically At-Risk) is testing this idea by following diabetes rates in children who are breastfed for the first six months of life versus those who are exposed earlier to cow's milk. Preliminary results suggest risks are significantly lower for those who drink less cow's milk. Similar studies are looking into whether exposure to viruses like coxsackievirus (the cause of hand, foot, and mouth disease, a common childhood illness) might also increase the risk of type 1 diabetes.

Fingering faulty genes. Research is moving forward to find the genes responsible for causing diabetes, regulating functions like insulin production, or contributing to complications. For example, an international team of researchers called the Type 1 Diabetes Genetics Consortium is collecting genetic data on families around the world and analyzing it for clues about which genes might contribute to type 1. Similar work on type 2 diabetes is taking place at the National Institutes of Health. Meanwhile, a study called GoKinD (Genetics of Kidneys in Diabetes) is looking to find genes that play a role in diabetic nephropathy, or kidney damage, which appears to run in families.

Understanding the genetics of diabetes could have almost limitless practical payoffs in new drugs and therapies. For instance, researchers at the Joslin Diabetes Center, in Boston, recently announced that they had isolated and cloned the third of three genes thought to be responsible for regulating insulin production by beta cells in the pancreas. The researchers now believe they can use these genes to make cells other than beta cells manufacture insulin. It's possible that such genetically modified cells could then be implanted in people as beta-cell substitutes.

Pursuing peptides. Protein fragments called peptides help regulate a number of processes in the body that may contribute to type 1 diabetes, and scientists are working to develop peptide-based therapies to treat the disease. One drug, called DiaPep277, seeks to fend off assaults on the pancreas by triggering the release of cytokines, hormones that regulate immune-system cells and appear to stop the progression of newly diagnosed type 1. In animal studies and preliminary trials in people, DiaPep277 appeared to preserve insulin function without affecting the immune system's ability to protect the body from infection.

Stopping the destruction. T-cells are crack soldiers in the body's defense against invaders and diseases, but when they turn against insulin-making beta cells in the pancreas (for reasons no one understands), they cause type 1 diabetes. To fend them off, researchers treated 12 recently diagnosed type 1 patients with an antibody thought to quell T-cell uprisings. The results, reported in *The New England Journal of Medicine* in May 2002: After only 14 days of treatment, nine of those receiving the antibody maintained or improved their insulin production after one year, compared with only two patients in a control group that didn't get the antibody. Most type 1 patients have already lost 80 percent of their beta cells at diagnosis. Scientists hope that tackling traitor T-cells will help preserve the remaining 20 percent of insulin-producing capacity in newly diagnosed type 1 patients—providing a significant edge in their ability to control blood sugar.

Working on Weight Loss

Keeping your weight down is a critical factor in controlling type 2 diabetes, but much about how the body regulates appetite, metabolism, fat accumulation, and other factors isn't well understood. As rates of obesity in the United States continue to climb along with rates of diabetes, the government has launched public-education campaigns to bring attention to the dangers of obesity. In the meantime, researchers are working to create new tools for managing your midsection.

The main principles of weight loss remain the same: To lose pounds, you need to burn more calories than you take in. But many people find this difficult because the body seems programmed to keep weight consistent. Much of the research into obesity seeks to understand just how the body's internal controls work. Here are some recent insights.

Finding "fat" genes. What you do (or don't do) has a lot to do with how much you weigh, but it's also clear that fatness runs in families. By some estimates, as much as 40 to 70 percent of such traits as body mass and fat formation in the gut are determined by your genes. Now that the human genome has been mapped, scientists are trying to zero in on the genes—and there are likely to be many—that contribute to weight control. One exciting development was the discovery of a genetic defect that curbed production of a newly identified appetite-regulating hormone called leptin. Now researchers are looking at clusters of genes on two different chromosomes that may predispose people to abdominal fat and insulin resistance. The hope is to determine how the relevant genes interact with each other and eventually be able to custom-design drugs that can fix fat-affecting flaws in an individual's genetic makeup.

Leveraging leptin. Genetic defects may not be the most important influence on leptin. In fact, most obese people have ample amounts of the hormone but don't seem to benefit from its ability to signal when appetite is satisfied. Researchers aren't sure why, but they may now have another piece of the puzzle. In an exciting development at Harvard's Beth Israel Deaconess Medical Center, scientists have identified a protein that appears to help regulate signals that allow leptin to work. The protein has two important effects: It makes lab mice stay slim, even when they are fed a high-fat diet, and it boosts insulin sensitivity. This makes the protein, called PTP1B (protein tyrosine phosphatase 1B), a potentially powerful agent against both obesity and type 2 diabetes. This research, funded by both the National Institutes of Health and the American Diabetes Association, has not yet gone beyond animal testing, but it provides an intriguing basis for further study.

Suppressing the appetite. Everyone dreams of a safe pill that would act as a switch to turn off appetite. But it's unlikely that a single chemical agent will do the trick because the urge to eat is regulated by a complex bio-chemical process with many players. Still, researchers are working to identify the players in hopes of tackling a few of them to give dieters an edge.

One candidate described recently in the British science journal *Nature* is a molecule called OEA (oleyleth-anolamide). Levels of OEA in the intestine increase when you eat. Scientists believe the compound helps trigger feelings of fullness that make you stop eating. In studies at the University of California, rats that were given OEA reduced their food intake and their weight. A chemically similar drug developed by a French company is now being tested in people.

Another prospect is a compound called C75, which appears to curb appetite by affecting several brain chemicals at once. Obese lab rats injected with C75 ate less even after fasting, according to a study at Johns Hopkins University School of Medicine. What's more, the compound seems to increase metab-olism to make animals burn more energy—meaning it may boost weight loss by both cutting and burning calories. Drug tests in people are likely within three years.

Obesity and the brain. If you remember the high-fashion emaciated look known as "heroin chic," then you have a picture of what narcotics do besides blow your mind: They curb the appetite and make you lose weight. Wasting your mind and body is hardly a path to good health, but the link between weight loss and pleasure-producing chemicals in the brain hasn't been lost on scientists. Of particular interest is dopamine, a neurotransmitter produced when you satisfy urges like sex and eating. Brain researchers at Brookhaven National Laboratory have found that obese people have fewer sites, or receptors, on cells for dopamine to dock with than normal-weight people. The scientists speculate that overeating may be caused by a greater need for stimulation to produce satisfaction. Implication: Other activities that boost dopamine in the brain—such as exercise—can take the edge off cravings.

Other studies by the same researchers indicate another difference in obese people: Areas of the brain that process sensual signals about food from the mouth, lips, and tongue are more active than they are in normal-weight people. This raises the possibility that drugs that make food less palatable may help people lose weight despite sensory hot spots in the brain.

Controlling Complications

If you follow all the advice you find in this book, your prospects for avoiding future complications may be bright even without any more medical advances. In fact, the most important developments in preventing damage from diabetes continue to focus on understanding how tight control of blood sugar can reduce your risks. But researchers are also looking into ways to minimize the impact of diabetes on your health even if blood sugar does get out of hand.

Such advances are potentially significant because many people with diabetes—especially type 2, which usually develops without symptoms over a long period of time—already have complications by the time they're diagnosed.

Eye Protection

Vision loss leading to eventual blindness is one of the complications of diabetes that people fear the most. Good blood-sugar control will significantly reduce your risk of eye problems—by as

much as 76 percent. And medical advances should improve those odds even further. Among the possibilities being explored to put a damper on diabetic eye damage:

Genes to battle blindness. In addition to surgery and laser treatment for diabetic retinopathy (in which fragile blood vessels sprout in the eye and burst, causing damage to the retina) scientists may soon add gene therapy. Already, in experiments with mice, researchers at Johns Hopkins Wilmer Eye Institute have used gene therapy to reduce blood-vessel growth from a retinopathy-like condition by as much as 90 percent. One of the genes the scientists used prompts the body to manufacture endostatin, a substance that may inhibit abnormal blood-vessel growth in tumors. A second gene codes for PEDF (pigment epithelium-derived factor), a protein found naturally in the eye that promotes the survival of retinal cells. The safety of using these genes in humans hasn't yet been established.

Help from ACE inhibitors. Already used to bring down high blood pressure, ACE (angiotensin-converting enzyme) inhibitors have shown potential for improving insulin sensitivity and preserving kidney function. Now research suggests that ACE inhibitors may improve circulation to the eyes. If taken before blood vessels proliferate from retinopathy, the drugs may help reduce the risk of proliferation and hemorrhaging in the future.

A nervy proposition. One of the ways high glucose levels can lead to complications is that blood sugar converts to a substance called sorbitol, a modified form of glucose that's especially prone to building up in tissue. In the eyes, sorbitol contributes to clouding of vision, while in the nerves it traps water in cells, which can impair function by making nerves swell. Scientists have found that an enzyme called aldose reductase speeds the conversion of blood sugar to sorbitol, and pharmaceutical companies are working to develop drugs that block the enzyme's effects. So far, aldose reductase inhibitors have not impressed clinicians, according to Dr. Hellman, but research continues in the belief that more effective drugs are still to be found.

Head-to-toe Help

From the heart to the kidneys to the feet, here are the most promising advances currently in the works for treating or preventing other complications of diabetes.

Double-duty drugs. Like ACE inhibitors, another class of drugs that may have unforeseen benefits are thiazolidinediones, also called glitazones. In addition to making cells more sensitive to insulin and preventing damage to the kidneys and eyes due to high blood pressure, some studies have indicated that glitazones may help relax the endothelium, a layer of cells lining the blood vessels and cavities of the heart. If the effect is demonstrated in further studies, glitazones may prove to be useful in fighting cardiovascular complications while they lower blood sugar.

Grappling with growth hormone. Studies suggest that naturally occurring growth hormone may help trigger the onset of kidney damage from diabetes. In one study, for example, lab mice with diabetes whose cells were genetically programmed not to respond to growth hormone didn't develop kidney disease, while other diabetic mice did. Now researchers are working to develop a class of drugs that—when the likelihood of serious disease warrants it—can block growth hormone's action by claiming a "parking space" on cells normally reserved for the hormone. There's also evidence that so-called growth hormone antagonists may help prevent diabetic eye disease.

Stopping the stiffening. Another process that contributes to damage from complications is a stiffening of tissues due to advanced glycosylation end products, or AGEs—structures that form when sugars bind with the amino acids of proteins in a process sometimes likened to the toughening of browned meat. AGEs appear to contribute to virtually every major complication of diabetes, including retinopathy, nerve damage, high blood pressure, foot ulcers, and cardiovascular disease. Impeding their action has long been a research priority. While some chemical agents have shown promise, few have been found to be both effective and safe. But work on AGE inhibitors continues. Scientists are also looking at drugs that may be able to break up the links between proteins created by AGEs after they have formed.

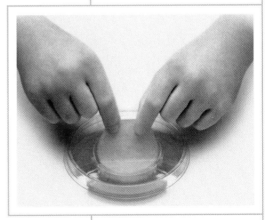

Biological skin substitutes. Though other complications might sound more dire, poorly healing foot ulcers are the most common reason people with diabetes enter hospitals. One way to treat them has been skin-graft operations, which require anesthesia and can be hampered by infection and scarring. But an emerging type of therapy can circumvent these concerns by using what's known as biological skin substitutes, or living skin equivalents. Sometimes called "living bandages," they're biotechnology products that contain the ingredients of skin (such as collagen and other proteins) and fuse with your own tissue to significantly speed healing. Some of these products—for example, Regranex, made from yeast, and Dermagraft, cultured in labs from neonatal skin cells—are already FDA-approved.

Patching Up the Pancreas

Whether you have type 1 or type 2 diabetes, at least part of your problem is that you have a bum pancreas. Either it has conked out altogether (type 1) or it's on the ropes, a shadow of its former self (type 2). As type 2 progresses, the condition of your pancreas—particularly the beta cells that make insulin—may even get worse. Which begs the question: Why not chuck the old, broken parts and get new ones?

Pancreas transplants are nothing new, but they're not a widely prescribed treatment, either. One problem is that the body rejects foreign tissues, which means patients must take drugs that suppress the immune system, potentially making the body sick in other ways. A second problem is that for the million or so candidates for pancreas transplants with type 1 diabetes alone each year, there are only between 1,000 and 3,000 donor pancreases (obtained from cadavers) available. Fortunately, there may soon be alternatives.

Islet Cell Transplants

There may be no reason to get rid of the entire pancreas—which produces digestive enzymes and hormones besides insulin—if it's only the beleaguered beta cells that are in trouble. That's the idea behind islet cell transplants, in which doctors replace clumps, or islets, of cells—including beta cells—that are clustered throughout the pancreas.

The procedure was pioneered in animals as far back as the 1970s and has since been made possible in people. In fact, hundreds of people have received islet cell transplants around the world. Unfortunately, long-term success rates have been dismal, with the procedure working only about 8 percent of the time.

One reason success rates have been so low is that immunosuppressant drugs, such as steroids, appear to be toxic to beta cells. There's new hope, however, that this obstacle might be overcome with an islet cell transplant procedure pioneered in Canada at the University of Alberta, in Edmonton. The technique uses a combination of three new steroid-free drugs that appear to prevent rejection of transplanted islet cells and also halt immune-system attacks that cause type 1 diabetes in the first place.

Early results of what's now called the Edmonton Protocol were electrifying: Researchers reported that some type 1 patients in a small trial were able to stop using insulin for up to 14 months. The protocol has now been used successfully in more than 30 patients, with 85 percent of them free of insulin treatment for more than a year—and many of those have reversed

THE SUPPLY-SIDE CHALLENGE

Even if techniques for islet cell transplants are refined, a significant barrier to making the procedure a mainstream treatment is the lack of donor pancreases from which cells can be extracted.

To resolve this dilemma, researchers are looking for ways to produce islet cells without having to rely on donor supplies. Studies are now looking at how islet cells multiply, in the hope that ways can be found to make them grow faster—work already being pioneered in animals. Researchers are also looking into the possibility of using cells from such animals as pigs in humans.

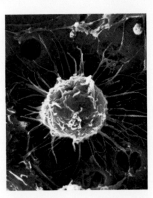

Perhaps the most significant (and controversial) area of research involves the use of embryonic stem cells—cells that have the capacity to become virtually any type of cell in the body. Lab studies have already shown that stem cells can be genetically manipulated to produce insulin, suggesting that they might make a viable source for transplants. Other options might be to use adult stem cells extracted from bone marrow or blood, which may hold promise for producing insulin, or to convert liver cells into insulin-making cells. Animal research has also suggested that stem cells can be developed from unfertilized eggs instead of embryos; if it can be done in humans, this would skirt the ethical issues surrounding the use of embryonic tissue.

their diabetes for two or more years, says Dr. Furlanetto of the Juvenile Diabetes Research Foundation. "This research has really spurred interest in this whole field," he says. New studies of the treatment are now being done at medical centers across the United States and in Europe.

Islet cell transplants are still far from perfected. Some of the transplants have been found to fail with time, and the long-term side effects of the new immunosuppressant drugs are not well understood. But as studies continue, researchers are hopeful that powerful new approaches to restoring pancreatic function will eventually be more widely available.

An Artificial Pancreas

Even with all the progress being made on the transplant front, some researchers believe a different approach is even closer to becoming a reality—developing a mechanical system that mimics the insulin-controlling functions of the pancreas. Such a system requires two basic parts: an internal monitor to keep track of blood-sugar levels and a dispensing device to automatically respond to glucose changes by releasing just the right amount of insulin to keep blood sugar stable.

The basic elements of such a system have already been invented. For example, Medtronic MiniMed has developed an implantable sensor, which will continuously monitor blood-glucose levels, and an implantable insulin pump. Both devices are currently being tested in clinical trials. When commercially available, the pump will communicate with the implantable sensor (or with an external sensor) using radio-frequency electromagnetic waves to provide the patient the exact amount of insulin needed at any given time.

Researchers are now working on ways to keep the devices functioning inside the body for long periods and communicating reliably with one another so that glucose levels and the system's insulin response are always closely matched. "This technology is already feasible," says Dr. Furlanetto, "and with more work, it could revolutionize the treatment of diabetes." Some researchers believe a combined implantable meter and pump system could be available within three to five years.

FROM ISLET CELLS TO ICE CREAM

Ever since she was diagnosed with type 1 diabetes at age 11, Merry Brunson of Greeley, Colorado, resigned herself to daily insulin injections and blood-sugar tests for the rest of her life. By her late 30s, that view hadn't changed, but her condition had.

"As I got older, I had less awareness of when my blood sugar was getting too low," she says. "My family could sense it more than I could. My children would say, 'Mom, are you okay? You need something to eat.' My kids and my husband would follow me around making sure I was all right." There were times her husband would find her convulsing in her sleep from low blood sugar, but the final straw was when she had two seizures while alone with her kids.

She sat down to watch TV, fell unconscious, and went into convulsions. The children had to call 911 and watch their mother be taken away in an ambulance while firemen stayed with them at the house until her husband, Ed, came home. "I have no recollection of what happened," says Brunson, "but it was really upsetting for the kids. It scared me, too: What if the kids were with me and I lost control behind the wheel?" Something had to change. On the advice of her diabetes educator, she tried an insulin pump, which helped. But her blood sugar could still drop to dangerous levels, and she never felt truly in control.

Then her father heard a news report about the Edmonton Protocol—a new way to transplant insulin-producing islet cells without the body rejecting them. Searching online, she found that researchers at the University of Miami seemed most experienced with the procedure in this country, and signed on. Brunson traveled several times between Colorado and Florida for tests and two procedures in which islet cells were infused into her liver through a catheter. "I was awake the whole time," she says.

Shortly after leaving the hospital for the last time, she and Ed went out for her first good meal. No longer taking insulin and nervous about her blood sugar, Merry checked it two hours after the meal and again at bedtime. Both readings were normal. "That was when I realized these things were really working," she says. "It was incredible."

Today, her diabetes is so well controlled, she wonders if she even has the disease anymore. She suffers from mouth sores (a side effect of the treatment) and still checks her blood sugar regularly out of habit. But Brunson now feels safe to live her life and eats what she wants, within healthful limits. "Sometimes, I even indulge in ice cream, with toppings no less, which I never used to do!" Brunson says.

RECIPES

Carrot-Pecan Muffins

These moist whole-grain muffins are sweetened with cider, raisins, carrots, and just a touch of brown sugar. Low-fat yogurt is a healthy substitute for the oil or butter found in other muffins.

Makes 12 muffins

      Nonstick cooking spray
  1/3 cup golden raisins or currants
  1/4 cup apple cider or orange juice
  3/4 cup rye flour
  3/4 cup whole-wheat flour
  3/4 cup cornmeal
   2 teaspoons baking powder
   1 teaspoon baking soda
  1/2 teaspoon salt
   1 cup plain low-fat yogurt
   2 tablespoons dark brown sugar
   1 large egg
   1 large egg white
   2 medium-size carrots, peeled and shredded
      (1 1/2 cups)
   2 tablespoons coarsely chopped pecans or walnuts

1. Preheat the oven to 400°F. Lightly coat twelve 2 1/2-inch muffin cups with nonstick cooking spray or insert cupcake liners. In a small bowl, soak the raisins in the cider for 15 minutes. Meanwhile, in a large bowl, stir together the rye flour, whole-wheat flour, cornmeal, baking powder, baking soda, and salt. Make a well in the center.

2. In a small bowl, stir together the yogurt, sugar, egg, and egg white until blended. Stir in the carrots, raisins, and cider just until combined. Pour the mixture into the dry ingredients and stir just until combined. Do not overmix.

3. Spoon 1/4 cup batter into each muffin cup and sprinkle with the nuts. Bake for 18 to 20 minutes or until golden and a toothpick inserted in the center comes out clean.

NUTRITION PER SERVING:
calories 137; saturated fat 0.5 g; total fat 2 g; protein 5 g; carbohydrate 26 g; fiber 2 g; sodium 242 mg; cholesterol 19 mg

Granola with Toasted Walnuts and Cranberries

A nutritious mix with a touch of sweetness for guaranteed good mornings.

Makes 5 cups

   3 cups old-fashioned or quick-cooking oats
  1/2 cup coarsely chopped walnuts
   2 tablespoons wheat germ
   2 tablespoons sesame seeds
  1/4 teaspoon salt
  1/3 cup honey
   1 tablespoon light brown sugar
   1 tablespoon extra-light olive oil
   1 teaspoon vanilla
   1 cup dried cranberries

1. Preheat oven to 300°F. Combine oats, walnuts, wheat germ, sesame seeds, and salt in a 13 x 9-inch baking pan. Bake until oats and nuts are toasted and fragrant, about 30 minutes. Remove pan from oven. Increase oven temperature to 350°F.

2. Meanwhile, combine honey, brown sugar, and oil in a small skillet over medium heat. Cook until the sugar has melted, about 1 minute. Remove from heat and stir in vanilla.

3. Drizzle honey mixture over oat mixture and stir to coat. Return to oven and bake, stirring occasionally, until oats are crispy, about 10 minutes.

4. With a spoon, break up any clumps. Stir in cranberries. Store in airtight container.

NUTRITION PER SERVING:
calories 154; saturated fat 0.5 g; total fat 5 g; protein 4 g; carbohydrate 25 g; fiber 3 g; sodium 41 mg; cholesterol 0 mg

Egg-White Omelet with Vegetable-Cheddar Filling

From mixing bowl to table in 10 minutes! A low-fat, low-carbohydrate, low-cholesterol start to the day.

Makes 1 serving

- 3 egg whites
- 2 teaspoons chopped fresh dill (optional)
- 1/8 teaspoon salt
- 1/8 teaspoon freshly ground black pepper
- 1/2 cup loosely packed, thinly sliced fresh spinach
- 1 plum tomato, chopped
- 2 tablespoons shredded nonfat cheddar cheese
  Non-stick cooking spray

1. Whisk egg whites, 1 teaspoon water, dill (if using), salt, and pepper in medium bowl until soft peaks form. Toss spinach, tomato, and cheddar in small bowl.

2. Lightly coat omelet pan or small skillet with non-stick cooking spray and set over medium heat 1 minute. Pour egg mixture into pan and cook until eggs begin to set on bottom.

3. Spread filling over half of omelet, leaving 1/2-inch border and reserving 1 tablespoon mixture for garnish. Lift up omelet at edge nearest handle and fold in half, slightly off-center, so filling peeks out. Cook 2 minutes. Slide omelet onto plate and garnish with reserved filling.

NUTRITION PER SERVING:
calories 109; saturated fat 0 g; total fat 0.5 g; protein 18 g; carbohydrate 8 g; fiber 1 g; sodium 906 mg; cholesterol 3 mg

Multigrain Waffles with Apple-Raspberry Sauce

Hot, crisp waffles hit the spot for breakfast or brunch. Sweetened mainly with fruit and apple cider, these are low-fat, thanks to the buttermilk.

Makes 8 waffles

- 1 cup apple cider
- 2 red or green apples, cut into 1/2-inch chunks
- 1/2 teaspoon vanilla
- 1 cup fresh raspberries
- 1/4 cup flaxseeds
- 1/4 cup whole-wheat flour
- 1/4 cup buckwheat flour
- 1/4 cup all-purpose flour
- 2 teaspoons brown sugar
- 2 teaspoons baking powder
- 1/4 teaspoon salt
- 1 large egg, separated, plus 2 large egg whites
- 1 cup buttermilk
  Nonstick cooking spray

1. Bring apple cider to a boil in medium skillet over high heat and cook 1 minute. Add apples and simmer until firm-tender, about 4 minutes. Remove from heat and let cool to room temperature. Stir in vanilla and raspberries.

2. Place flaxseeds in a spice grinder or mini–food processor and grind to the consistency of coarse flour. Transfer to a large bowl and add whole-wheat flour, buckwheat flour, all-purpose flour, brown sugar, baking powder, and salt. Stir to mix well.

3. Combine egg yolk and buttermilk in small bowl. Beat 3 egg whites in large bowl until stiff peaks form. Make a well in center of dry ingredients and stir in egg-yolk mixture. Gently fold in egg whites.

4. Spray a waffle iron (with two 4- to 4 1/2-inch squares) with nonstick cooking spray. Preheat iron. Spoon batter into iron, 1/2 cup per waffle. Cook until golden brown and crisp, about 2 minutes. Repeat with remaining batter. Serve warm with apple-raspberry sauce.

NUTRITION PER WAFFLE:
calories 130; saturated fat 0.5 g; total fat 3 g; protein 5 g; carbohydrate 22 g; fiber 4 g; sodium 187 mg; cholesterol 28 mg

Eggplant Caviar

This mildly spicy and smoky dish is a great make-ahead for company. It will keep for a week in the refrigerator.

Makes about 1 cup (6 servings)

4 cloves garlic, unpeeled
1 eggplant (1 pound)
3 tablespoons finely chopped walnuts
2 teaspoons lemon juice
1 teaspoon olive oil
½ teaspoon each ground coriander and cumin
¼ teaspoon paprika
⅛ teaspoon each ground cinnamon and salt

1. Preheat the oven to 400°F. Wrap the garlic cloves in aluminum foil. Prick the skin of the eggplant a few times with a fork and place it on a baking sheet along with the garlic. Bake for 30 minutes or until the garlic packet feels soft. Bake the eggplant an additional 20 minutes or until soft. Let cool.

2. Unwrap the garlic, squeeze the cloves into a medium-size bowl, and mash them. Halve the eggplant and scrape the flesh into the bowl, discarding most of the seeds. With a fork, mix in the walnuts, lemon juice, oil, coriander, cumin, paprika, cinnamon, and salt. Spoon into a small serving bowl and serve at room temperature or chilled with whole-wheat crackers.

NUTRITION PER SERVING:
calories 20; saturated fat 0 g; total fat 1 g; protein 1 g; carbohydrate 2 g; fiber 0 g; sodium 18 mg; cholesterol 0 mg

Gulf Coast Hot Crab Dip

Lumps of crab in a spicy sauce make a wonderful and festive appetizer. But savor this treat only in small amounts—limit yourself to two or three crackers with dip.

Makes 24 Servings

12 ounces fresh lump crabmeat or 2 cans (6 ounces each) crabmeat, drained
8 ounces fat-free cream cheese, softened

1 cup nonfat sour cream
1 small onion, finely chopped
1 tablespoon prepared horseradish
2 teaspoons Worcestershire sauce
¼ teaspoon hot red-pepper sauce
3 tablespoons plain dry bread crumbs
½ teaspoon paprika
4½ ounces baked low-sodium thin wheat crackers (about 72)

1. Preheat oven to 350°F. Coat gratin dish or deep-dish pie plate with nonstick cooking spray. Pick through crabmeat; discard any shells and cartilage. Rinse crabmeat and drain.

2. Stir cream cheese in medium bowl until smooth. Blend in sour cream, onion, horseradish, Worcestershire sauce, and hot-pepper sauce. Gently fold in crabmeat. Spoon into baking dish; smooth top.

3. Combine bread crumbs and paprika and sprinkle evenly over crabmeat mixture. Bake until bubbly, about 20 minutes. Serve piping hot with crackers.

NUTRITION PER SERVING:
calories 57; saturated fat 0.5 g; total fat 1 g; carbohydrate 6 g; protein 5 g; fiber 0 g; sodium 129 mg; cholesterol 12 mg

Parmesan Breadsticks

Crisp, scented twists—perfect for healthy nibbling—also make a meal with soup or a salad.

Makes 40 breadsticks

- 3 ¼ cups all-purpose flour
- 1 cup Parmesan cheese
- 2 teaspoons chopped fresh rosemary or ½ teaspoon dried
- 2 teaspoons salt
- 1 teaspoon pepper
- 1 teaspoon rapid-rise dry yeast
- 1 ¼ cups very warm water (120° to 130°F)
- ¼ cup semolina flour or cornmeal
- 1 teaspoon olive oil

1. Mix 1 ½ cups all-purpose flour, Parmesan, rosemary, salt, pepper, and yeast in a large bowl. Blend in water. Add 1½ cups more flour to form a soft dough. Dust work surface with flour. Turn dough onto floured surface and knead until smooth and elastic, about 10 minutes, working in remaining flour to keep dough from sticking. Divide dough into two equal pieces. Cover with a damp kitchen towel and let rest 10 minutes.

2. Sprinkle two 16 x 12-inch sheets of waxed paper with 1 tablespoon semolina each and pat dough pieces into 10 x 6-inch rectangles. Brush with oil and cover with a kitchen towel. Let rise in a warm place until doubled, about 30 minutes. Refrigerate 1 piece of dough.

3. Preheat oven to 400°F. Line two baking sheets with parchment paper and sprinkle with half of remaining semolina. Cut unrefrigerated dough crosswise into 20 equal strips, each about 8 inches long. Hold dough strips by the ends, twisting and stretching until about 12 inches long. Place twists 1 inch apart on baking sheets. Let rise, uncovered, 10 minutes.

4. Lightly coat breadsticks with nonstick cooking spray. Bake 10 minutes. Remove breadsticks from oven and lightly coat again with cooking spray. Bake until golden and crisp, about 8 minutes longer. Transfer to a wire rack and cool completely. Repeat with the remaining dough.

NUTRITION PER BREADSTICK:
calories 56; saturated fat 0.5 g; total fat 1 g; protein 2 g; carbohydrate 9 g; fiber 0 g; sodium 163 mg; cholesterol 2 mg

Pat-in-the-Pan Pizza

Homemade and healthy—you'll flip over this pie! It will make a satisfying meal if you add a salad and a fresh-fruit dessert, but stick to one serving of pizza.

Makes 6 servings

- ½ cup plus 2 tablespoons lukewarm water (105°–115°F)
- 1 packet (¼ ounce) active dry yeast
- ⅛ teaspoon sugar
- 2 cups all-purpose flour
- ½ teaspoon salt
- 1 tablespoon olive oil
- 8 ounces turkey sausage
- I cup pizza sauce
- 1 cup shredded part-skim mozzarella cheese
- 1 small green bell pepper, thinly sliced
- 1 small red bell pepper, thinly sliced
- 1 small yellow bell pepper, thinly sliced
  Nonstick cooking spray

1. Lightly coat a jelly-roll pan or sheet pan (about 18 x 12 inches) and large skillet with nonstick cooking spray.

2. Stir water, yeast, and sugar in small bowl and let stand until foamy, about 5 minutes. Combine flour and salt in large bowl. Pour in yeast mixture, drizzle in oil, and beat with wooden spoon until dough pulls away from side of bowl. Dust work surface lightly with flour. Turn out dough and knead 3 minutes. Cover with damp towel and let rest 5 minutes.

3. Preheat oven to 425°F. Meanwhile, remove sausage meat from casings, put into skillet, and set over medium heat. Cook sausage just until it begins to brown, about 5 minutes, breaking up meat with a spoon. Drain on paper towels.

4. Shape dough into 16 x 12-inch rectangle on pan. Forma high standing edge (about ½ inch), gently pinching edge. Spread pizza sauce evenly over the dough. Top pizza with mozzarella; green, red, and yellow peppers; and sausage. Bake until cheese melts and crust is golden, about 10 minutes.

NUTRITION PER SERVING:
calories 326; saturated fat 3 g; total fat 10 g; protein 21 g; carbohydrate 38 g; fiber 2 g; sodium 708 mg; cholesterol 41 mg

Chili Popcorn

This low-calorie snack is made with corn popped in a hot-air popper. If prepared ahead, it can be recrisped on a baking sheet in a 350°F oven for 6 to 8 minutes just before serving.

Makes 10 1-cup servings

- 1 teaspoon paprika
- ½ teaspoon chili powder
- ¼ teaspoon salt
- ⅛ teaspoon garlic powder
  Pinch ground red pepper (cayenne), or to taste
- 1 tablespoon grated Parmesan cheese
- 10 cups popped corn, without salt or oil
  Butter-flavored nonstick cooking spray or water

1. Preheat the oven to 350°F. In a small bowl, combine the paprika, chili powder, salt, garlic powder, red pepper, and Parmesan cheese. Spread the popcorn in an even layer on two large baking sheets and coat lightly with the nonstick cooking spray or water from a spray bottle. With a fork sprinkle the seasonings over the popcorn and toss the popcorn to coat.

2. Bake for 5 to 10 minutes or until crisp. Serve immediately or store in an airtight container.

NUTRITION PER SERVING:
calories 29; saturated fat 0 g; total fat 0 g; protein 1 g; carbohydrate 5 g; fiber 0 g; sodium 66 mg; cholesterol 0 mg

Cabbage-and-Apple Slaw with Blue-Cheese Dressing

It's almost too good to be true—a velvety, low-fat blue-cheese dressing!

Makes 8 servings

- ²/₃ **cup fat-free sour cream**
- ²/₃ **cup plain fat-free yogurt**
- ¼ **cup cider vinegar**
- 1 **tablespoon low-fat mayonnaise**
- 4 **teaspoons sugar**
- 1 **teaspoon hot red-pepper sauce**
- 1 **teaspoon salt**
- ⅓ **cup crumbled blue cheese (2 ounces)**
- 8 **cups finely shredded red and/or green cabbage**
- 4 **Granny Smith apples, cut into thin wedges**
- 2 **red bell peppers, slivered**

1. Whisk together the sour cream, yogurt, vinegar, mayonnaise, sugar, hot-pepper sauce, and salt in a large bowl. Stir in blue cheese.

2. Add cabbage, apples, and red peppers to bowl and toss to combine. Serve at room temperature or chilled.

NUTRITION PER SERVING:
calories 150; saturated fat 1 g; total fat 3 g; protein 5 g; carbohydrate 30 g; fiber 5 g; sodium 441 mg; cholesterol 5 mg

Oriental Green Salad

The protein in this vegetable salad comes from the tofu in the luscious creamy dressing. To make ginger juice, put a ½-inch piece of fresh ginger through a garlic press or grate the ginger and press out the juice with a spoon; discard the pulp.

Makes 4 servings

For the dressing:
- 4 **ounces soft tofu (soybean curd)**
- ¼ **cup water**
- 1 **tablespoon reduced-sodium soy sauce**
- 1 **garlic clove, crushed**
- 2 **teaspoons rice vinegar**
- ½ **teaspoon ginger juice**
- ¼ **teaspoon sugar**

For the salad:
- 1 **small head romaine lettuce or 6 ounces spinach leaves, cut into 1-inch-wide ribbons (6 cups)**
- 2 **medium-size carrots, peeled and shredded (1 ½ cups)**
- 4 **radishes, thinly sliced (⅓ cup)**

1. To prepare the dressing: In a food processor or blender, whirl the tofu, water, soy sauce, garlic, vinegar, ginger juice, and sugar for 1 minute or until smooth.

2. To prepare the salad: In a large salad bowl, place the lettuce, carrots, and radishes. Pour the dressing over the vegetables and toss until coated.

NUTRITION PER SERVING:
calories 55; saturated fat 0 g; total fat 1 g; protein 4 g; carbohydrate 8 g; fiber 3 g; sodium 143 mg; cholesterol 0 mg

3. Stir in rice, lemon zest, lemon juice, and salt, and return to a simmer. Remove ½ cup hot liquid and whisk into whole egg and egg whites in medium bowl. Whisking constantly, pour warm egg mixture into simmering soup.

NUTRITION PER SERVING:
calories 114; saturated fat 0.5 g; total fat 2 g; protein 8 g; carbohydrate 17 g; fiber 3 g; sodium 728 mg; cholesterol 53 mg

Cream of Leek and Potato Soup

A satisfying low-fat soup to start a meal or—in larger portions— to be the main dish.

Makes 7 ½ cups

- 1 tablespoon olive or canola oil
- 8 ounces leeks, white part only, thickly sliced
- 1 large onion, coarsely chopped
- 6 cups chicken or vegetable stock
- 1 pound all-purpose potatoes, peeled and diced
- ⅛ teaspoon each salt and ground white pepper
- ⅓ cup low-fat sour cream
  Chopped chives, for garnish (optional)

1. In a 4-quart saucepan, heat the oil over moderate heat. Stir in leeks and onion, then ¾ cup of the stock. Cover and cook, stirring frequently, about 10 minutes, until soft but not browned.

2. Add the potatoes to the saucepan and stir to coat with the leek-and-onion mixture.

3. Pour in half of the remaining stock and bring to a boil. Simmer, partially covered, 15 to 20 minutes, until potatoes are very soft.

4. Remove from the heat. Using a ladle, transfer the contents of the pan to a blender or food processor and purée until very smooth.

5. Pour the remaining stock into the pan. Add the vegetable purée and bring the soup to a simmer, stirring constantly, 2 to 3 minutes. Season with the salt and pepper.

6. Remove from the heat and stir in the sour cream. Ladle into soup bowls and garnish with the chives (if using).

NUTRITION PER CUP:
calories 111; saturated fat 1g; total fat 3 g; protein 4 g; carbohydrate 17g; fiber 2g; sodium 105 mg; cholesterol 2 mg

Greek Spinach, Egg, and Lemon Soup

This Greek-style "cream of spinach" soup has no cream—and hardly any fat.

Makes 4 Servings

- 3 cups reduced-sodium, fat-free chicken broth
- 3 scallions, thinly sliced
- 3 cloves garlic, minced
- 1 package (10 ounces) frozen chopped spinach
- ½ teaspoon oregano
- 1 cup cooked brown rice
- 1 teaspoon grated lemon zest
- 3 tablespoons fresh lemon juice
- ½ teaspoon salt
- 1 large egg plus 2 egg whites

1. Combine ¼ cup broth, scallions, and garlic in medium saucepan. Cook over medium heat until scallions are tender, about 2 minutes.

2. Add remaining 2 ¾ cups broth, spinach, and oregano, and bring to a boil. Reduce to a simmer, cover, and cook until spinach is tender, about 5 minutes.

Red Gazpacho

Marinate finely chopped vegetables in oil and spices and serve chilled. You'll enjoy the vitamin benefit of raw vegetables plus great fresh taste.

Makes 6½ cups

- 3 ounces French or Italian bread
- 1 large sweet red or green pepper, coarsely chopped
- 1 red onion, coarsely chopped
- 1 small cucumber, peeled, seeded, and sliced
- 8 ounces plum tomatoes, cored and quartered
- ¼ cup packed basil or parsley
- 1 clove garlic, finely chopped
- 2 tablespoons olive oil
- 2 tablespoons red or white wine vinegar
- 3 cups reduced-sodium tomato juice
- ⅛ teaspoon freshly ground black pepper

1. Remove the crusts from the bread and tear the bread into pieces. Place in a bowl and cover with water. Allow to stand at least 5 minutes.

2. Drain some of the water from the bowl and, with your hands, squeeze out most of the remaining water from the bread. Reserve the soaked bread.

3. Place the sweet pepper, red onion, and cucumber in a food processor and process until very finely chopped. Pour the mixture into a large bowl.

4. Place the tomatoes and basil in the food processor and process until very finely chopped but not totally puréed. Add to the pepper mixture in the bowl.

5. Place garlic, oil, wine vinegar, soaked bread, and tomato juice in the food processor and process until blended. Stir into the soup until combined.

6. Add black pepper. Cover the bowl and refrigerate the soup for at least 1 hour before serving.

NUTRITION PER SERVING:
calories 129; saturated fat 1 g; total fat 5 g; protein 3 g; carbohydrate 19 g; fiber 3 g; sodium 167 mg; cholesterol 0 mg

MEATS

Herb-Roasted Beef

A change in proportions makes this recipe healthy. Roast a generous serving of vegetables with a small piece of meat to get a nutritionally balanced meal.

Makes 6 servings

- 2 pounds lean boneless beef rib roast
- ⅛ teaspoon each salt and pepper
- 1 cup fresh herbs, such as parsley, basil, sage, rosemary, thyme, and chives, or 1½ tablespoons dried of each
- 2 tablespoons Dijon mustard
- 1 tablespoon olive or canola oil
- 3 large onions, cut into eighths
- 6 small zucchini, cut into thirds
- 1 cauliflower, cut into florets

1. Preheat the oven to 350°F. With a sharp knife, trim all the fat and cartilage from the beef roast. Season the meat with salt and pepper.

2. Place the fresh herbs and mustard in a food processor and process to chop herbs fine and combine mixture. Scraping down the sides of the bowl, transfer mixture to a small bowl. (Mix dry herbs and mustard in bowl.)

3. Spoon the herb mixture onto the roast, spreading it evenly to cover all sides. Coat the bottom of a large roasting pan with the oil. Place the meat in the pan and roast, uncovered, for 30 minutes.

4. Arrange the onions, zucchini, and cauliflower

around the meat in the roasting pan and toss the vegetables to coat them thoroughly in the oil.

5. Roast the meat and vegetables about 1 hour or until a thermometer inserted in the center of the meat reads 160°F (for medium). Turn the vegetables occasionally so that they cook evenly.

6. Remove pan from the oven. With a slotted spoon, transfer the vegetables to a serving dish and keep them warm. Transfer the roast to a carving platter, cover, and let stand for 5 minutes. Slice beef and serve with vegetables.

NUTRITION PER SERVING:
calories 317; saturated fat 3 g; total fat 10 g; protein 39 g; carbohydrate 20 g; fiber 7 g; sodium 278 mg; cholesterol 82 mg

Flank Steak with Red Onions

If flank steak is unavailable, substitute top round London broil steak. You can also cook this dish on an outdoor grill. Just poke holes in the foil holding the onions.

Makes 4 servings

- 2 medium-size red onions, sliced ½ inch thick
- 2 cloves garlic, crushed
- ⅔ cup balsamic or malt vinegar
- 1 tablespoon olive oil
- 2 tablespoons black currant or seedless raspberry jam
- ½ teaspoon salt
- ½ teaspoon ground red pepper (cayenne)
- 1 pound flank steak

1. Place the onions, garlic, vinegar, oil, jam, salt, and red pepper in a self-sealing plastic food storage bag. Push out all the air and seal the bag, then knead the marinade through the bag until it is combined. Using a sharp knife and cutting a scant ⅛ inch deep, score the steak on both sides in a diamond pattern. Add the steak to the marinade, coat the steak well, and reseal the bag. Place the bag on a plate and marinate the steak in the refrigerator for at least 30 minutes or up to 3 hours.

2. Preheat the broiler, setting the rack 5 inches from the heat. Place an 8-inch square of aluminum foil on one end of the broiler pan. Using a slotted spoon, remove the onions from the marinade and arrange them on the foil. Place the steak directly on the pan next to the onions. Broil the onions for 5 minutes on each side, and the steak for 5 to 6 minutes on each side for medium-rare, 7 to 8 minutes for medium. Remove onions when they are done and keep them warm.

3. Transfer the cooked steak to a cutting board and let stand for 10 minutes; then thinly slice it against the grain, holding the knife at a slight angle. Place the slices on individual plates and spoon any juices over them. Serve with the broiled onions.

NUTRITION PER SERVING:
calories 264; saturated fat 6 g; total fat 14 g; protein 24 g; carbohydrate 16 g; fiber 1 g; sodium 352 mg; cholesterol 57 mg

Lamb Chops Teriyaki

Tempt your taste buds with the flavors of the Orient.

Makes 4 Servings

- 6 scallions
- 2 tablespoons sesame seeds
- ¼ cup low-sodium soy sauce
- 2 tablespoons cider vinegar
- 2 tablespoons honey
- 1 small garlic clove, minced
- ¾ teaspoon ground ginger
- 8 bone-in loin lamb chops (4 ounces each), well trimmed
- 8 ounces cellophane noodles
- 4 medium carrots
- 1 red bell pepper
- 1 cup drained whole baby corn
- 1½ teaspoons cornstarch

1. Cut 2 scallions into thin slices and cut remaining scallions into 2-inch pieces. Toast sesame seeds in a small nonstick skillet over medium-high heat, stirring constantly, about 3 minutes. Remove from heat. Stir in soy sauce, vinegar, honey, garlic, ginger, and thinly sliced scallions.

2. Roll narrow tail end of lamb chops into medallions and secure with toothpicks. Put chops in baking dish and pour in soy mixture. Cover and refrigerate 1 to 2 hours, turning occasionally.

3. Cook noodles according to package directions. Drain. Cut carrots and pepper into matchsticks. Blanch carrots and pepper in water to cover, 3 minutes. Add remaining scallions and corn. Blanch until vegetables are crisp-tender, about 2 minutes longer. Drain and toss with noodles.

4. Preheat broiler. Remove chops from marinade; pour marinade into small saucepan. Broil chops 6 inches from heat until done to taste, 4 minutes on each side for medium. Transfer to platter, remove toothpicks, and keep warm.

5. Bring marinade to a boil over medium-high heat. Cook, stirring, about 2 minutes. Dissolve cornstarch in ⅓ cup cold water and whisk into marinade. Boil over medium-high heat, whisking, until sauce thickens, about 2 minutes. Toss half of sauce with noodle mixture and drizzle remaining half over chops.

NUTRITION PER SERVING:
calories 390; saturated fat 3 g; total fat 8 g; protein 27 g; carbohydrate 52 g; fiber 6 g; sodium 615 mg; cholesterol 90 mg

Pork Stir-Fry with Noodles

This delectable stir-fry calls for a Chinese cooking technique known as velveting, in which meat, fish, or chicken pieces are coated with cornstarch, cooked briefly, then rinsed under cold water. Velveting seals in the juices, tenderizes the meat, and gives it a pleasing texture.

Makes 4 servings

- 1 large egg white
- 2 tablespoons cornstarch
- 1 tablespoon cold water
- 12 ounces boneless pork loin, cut into 2 x ¼ x ¼-inch strips
- 1 tablespoon vegetable oil
- 1 medium-size yellow onion, cut into ½-inch cubes (1 cup)
- 1 medium-size carrot, peeled and thinly sliced (½ cup)
- 4 ounces mushrooms, thinly sliced (1 ¼ cups)
- 3 ounces green beans, trimmed and halved lengthwise (1 cup)
- ½ teaspoon ground ginger
- 1 ¾ cups chicken stock or low-sodium chicken broth
- 1 tablespoon reduced-sodium soy sauce
- 6 ounces spaghetti, fettuccine, or egg noodles, cooked and drained
- 2 green onions, including tops, thinly sliced (¼ cup)

1. In a medium-size bowl, stir together the egg white, 1 tablespoon of the cornstarch, and the water. Add the pork and toss to coat. Cover with plastic food wrap and refrigerate for at least 30 minutes or as long as overnight.

2. In a large saucepan of boiling water, cook the coated pork strips for 45 seconds. Drain, then rinse quickly with cold water and pat dry with paper toweling.

3. In a 12-inch nonstick skillet, heat 2 teaspoons of the oil over high heat. Add the onion and carrot and stir-fry for 2 minutes. Add the mushrooms, green beans, and ginger, reduce the heat to low, and cook, covered, for 3 minutes. Meanwhile, in a small bowl, mix together the stock, soy sauce, and remaining 1 tablespoon of cornstarch and set aside. With a slotted spoon, transfer the vegetables to a plate.

4. Raise the heat to high and add the remaining 1 teaspoon of oil to the skillet. Add the pork and spaghetti and stir-fry for 1 minute. Stir in the stock mixture, then add the vegetables and cook, stirring occasionally, for 2 minutes or until the sauce has thickened. Stir in the green onions and serve.

NUTRITION PER SERVING:
calories 394; saturated fat 3 g; total fat 11 g; protein 28 g; carbohydrate 45 g; fiber 2 g; sodium 260 mg; cholesterol 54 mg

Spinach-Stuffed Meat Loaf

Extend lean ground beef with ground turkey and a spinach stuffing to make a healthy family favorite.

Makes 6 Servings

- 1 pound lean ground beef
- 8 ounces lean ground turkey
- 1 small onion, finely chopped
- ½ cup fresh bread crumbs
- ⅛ teaspoon garlic salt
- 1 tablespoon tomato paste
- 1 egg white
- ½ cup part-skim ricotta cheese
- 1 package (10 ounces) frozen chopped spinach, thawed and drained
- ⅛ teaspoon each salt and pepper
- 2 large onions, thinly sliced
- 2 carrots, coarsely chopped
- 1 can (28 ounces) crushed tomatoes

1. In a bowl, mix beef, turkey, chopped onion, bread crumbs, garlic salt, and tomato paste. In another bowl, mix egg white, ricotta, spinach, salt, and pepper.

2. Preheat oven to 350°F. Turn out the beef mixture onto a large sheet of wax paper, and form into a 9- x 10-inch rectangle with your hands.

3. Spoon the spinach stuffing lengthwise down the center of the meat, leaving about 1 inch uncovered at each short end.

4. With the help of the wax paper, lift the long edges of the meat. Fold the meat over the stuffing to enclose it.

5. Using your fingers, pinch the edges of the meat together. Place loaf seam side down in a nonstick roasting pan. Add onions, carrots, and tomatoes to pan.

6. Bake about 1 ½ hours or until meat and vegetables are cooked. Transfer meat to a platter. Purée vegetables in a blender and serve sauce with the meat loaf.

NUTRITION PER SERVING:
calories 294; saturated fat 2 g; total fat 6 g; protein 32 g; carbohydrate 28 g; fiber 2 g; sodium 405 mg; cholesterol 71 mg

Veal Cutlets with Lemon-Garlic Sauce

The garlic's flavor is muted, while the lemon sings out loud and clear.

Makes 4 Servings

- 1 large clove garlic
- 4 veal cutlets (4 ounces each)
- ½ teaspoon salt
- 1 tablespoon Dijon mustard
- 1 lemon, very thinly sliced
- ⅔ cup reduced-sodium, fat-free chicken broth
- ¼ cup fresh lemon juice
- 2 teaspoons cornstarch

1. Preheat oven to 375°F. Wrap garlic in foil and bake until tender (package will feel soft when pressed), about 45 minutes. When cool enough to handle, cut off top of clove, squeeze out garlic pulp into small bowl, and mash until smooth.

2. Preheat broiler. Sprinkle cutlets with ¼ teaspoon

salt and brush with mustard. Top each cutlet with 3 lemon slices. Broil cutlets 4 inches from heat until cooked through, about 2 minutes. Transfer cutlets to a platter and cover loosely with foil to keep warm.

3. In a small saucepan, whisk broth and lemon juice into cornstarch. Whisk in remaining ¼ teaspoon salt and roasted garlic. Bring to a boil over medium heat and boil until sauce is slightly thickened, about 1 minute. Spoon sauce over veal on platter.

NUTRITION PER SERVING:
calories 169; saturated fat 1 g; total fat 3 g; protein 28 g; carbohydrate 6 g; fiber 0 g; sodium 384 mg; cholesterol 96 mg

POULTRY

Grilled Chicken with Herbs

Grilling allows fat to drip off the chicken into the fire, so less winds up on your plate. You can also make this recipe in the broiler.

Makes 4 Servings

- 1 chicken (about 3 ½ pounds), cut into serving pieces, wings reserved for another use
- 3 cloves garlic, finely chopped

3 tablespoons chopped parsley
2 tablespoons chopped basil
2 tablespoons chopped mint
⅓ cup olive or canola oil
½ teaspoon pepper
⅛ teaspoon salt

1. Remove the skin from the chicken pieces by loosening it with the tip of a sharp knife. Then use your fingers to pull off the skin. With the knife, cut off any fat and make 2 to 3 slashes in each piece of chicken.

2. Make the marinade: In a small bowl, combine the garlic with the parsley, basil, mint, oil, pepper, and salt.

3. Place the chicken pieces in a large dish, add the marinade, and turn the chicken in the mixture so that it is well coated. Cover the dish and marinate in the refrigerator at least 4 hours, turning the chicken occasionally.

4. Prepare the grill or preheat the broiler, setting the rack 4 inches from the heat. Arrange the chicken pieces bone side down on the grill or broiler rack, reserving the marinade. Grill the chicken about 20 minutes or until browned on one side, brushing once with the reserved marinade. Turn the pieces over, brush with the remaining marinade, and grill 10 minutes longer or until cooked through and the juices run clear.

NUTRITION PER SERVING:
calories 306; saturated fat 3 g; total fat 15 g; protein 40 g; carbohydrate 2 g; fiber 0 g; sodium 208 mg; cholesterol 126 mg

Lemon-Garlic Cornish Game Hens

This recipe calls for 6 cloves of garlic. However, they mellow as they cook, leaving a rich, almost sweet flavor. You can cook the hens on the barbecue if you prefer.

Makes 4 servings

6 cloves garlic, minced
¼ cup plus 2 tablespoons lemon juice
2 Cornish game hens (1 ¼ pounds each), split and skinned
½ teaspoon black pepper
1 teaspoon sugar

1. In a small bowl, mix the garlic with ¼ cup of the lemon juice, then rub the mixture over the hens. Cover the hens with plastic food wrap and let them marinate in the refrigerator for 2 hours.

2. Preheat the broiler, setting the rack 8 inches from the heat. Sprinkle the hens with the pepper, then arrange them on a broiler pan. Broil for 8 minutes, turn the hens over, and broil 7 to 8 minutes longer or until the juices run clear when a thigh is pricked with a fork. If the hens start to overbrown, tent them with aluminum foil.

3. Meanwhile, in a small bowl, combine the remaining 2 tablespoons of lemon juice and the sugar. When the hens have finished cooking, remove them from the oven and brush them with the lemon-sugar mixture. Serve with steamed asparagus and wild rice.

NUTRITION PER SERVING:
calories 247; saturated fat 2 g; total fat 7 g; protein 41 g; carbohydrate 5 g; fiber 0 g; sodium 114 mg; cholesterol 119 mg

Moroccan Chicken with Almonds

For a Moroccan-style presentation, spoon couscous onto a large round platter and place the chicken pieces and sauce on top. Garnish with sprigs of cilantro. Serve with tall glasses of iced mint tea.

Makes 8 servings

3 tablespoons olive oil
1 1/2 teaspoons ground cumin
1 teaspoon paprika
1 teaspoon turmeric
1/4 teaspoon ground allspice
8 whole chicken legs (about 4 pounds), split into drumsticks and thighs, skin removed
1 large onion, finely chopped
4 cloves garlic, finely chopped
1 cup dried apricots
1/2 cup chopped cilantro
1 teaspoon salt
1/2 cup slivered almonds

1. In a large skillet, heat oil over medium heat. Add cumin, paprika, turmeric, and allspice, and cook 1 minute. Working in batches, add chicken and cook 4 minutes per side or until golden brown. As chicken browns, transfer to 7- to 8-quart casserole.

2. Add onion and garlic to skillet, and cook 10 minutes or until golden brown and tender. Transfer to casserole with chicken.

3. Add 1 1/2 cups of water to skillet and bring to a boil. Add apricots, 1/4 cup of cilantro, and the salt to the skillet, and return to a boil. Pour apricot mixture into casserole with chicken. Bring to a boil, reduce to a simmer, cover, and cook 30 minutes or until chicken is tender. Stir in almonds and remaining 1/4 cup cilantro.

NUTRITION PER SERVING:
calories 305; saturated fat 2.5 g; total fat 15 g; protein 29 g; carbohydrates 15 g; sodium 407 mg; cholesterol 104 mg

Stir-fried Chicken with Snow Peas and Baby Corn

Here is a quick and delicious stir-fry recipe for busy nights that is good enough for company.

Makes 4 servings

4 teaspoons reduced-sodium soy sauce
4 teaspoons dark sesame oil
1 tablespoon rice wine, dry sherry, or rice vinegar
1 pound skinned and boned chicken breasts, cut into 1-inch cubes
1/2 cup chicken stock or low-sodium chicken broth

mixed with 2 teaspoons cornstarch
1 tablespoon vegetable oil
1 tablespoon minced fresh ginger
1 tablespoon minced garlic
4 green onions, white part only, sliced (1/3 cup)
4 ounces snow peas, trimmed (1 cup)
1 can (14 ounces) baby corn, drained and rinsed

1. In a medium-size bowl, mix 2 teaspoons each of the soy sauce and sesame oil with the wine. Add the chicken and let marinate for 30 minutes. In a small bowl, combine the stock-cornstarch mixture with the remaining 2 teaspoons each of soy sauce and sesame oil.

2. In a 12-inch nonstick skillet, heat the vegetable oil over moderately high heat. Add the ginger, garlic, and green onions and stir-fry for 30 seconds. Add the chicken and stir-fry for about 2 minutes or until no longer pink on the outside. Add the snow peas and corn and stir-fry 2 minutes more.

3. Add the cornstarch-stock mixture to the skillet, lower the heat, and simmer, stirring, for 2 to 3 minutes or until the sauce is slightly thickened and the juices run clear, not pink, when the chicken is pricked with a fork.

NUTRITION PER SERVING:
calories 302; saturated fat 2 g; total fat 11 g; protein 31 g; carbohydrate 23 g; fiber 2 g; sodium 536 mg; cholesterol 66 mg

Turkey and Black Bean Enchiladas

Mexican-style fast food to savor with salsa—and without guilt. The fat count is way down.

Makes 4 servings

2 1/2 cups medium salsa
1/4 cup chopped cilantro
1 teaspoon ground cumin
8 corn tortillas (6 inches)
8 ounces cooked turkey breast, shredded
I cup canned black beans, rinsed and drained
1 small red onion, finely chopped
1 cup shredded reduced-fat Cheddar cheese (about 4 ounces)
Nonstick cooking spray

1. Preheat oven to 350°F. Coat a 7 x 11-inch baking dish with nonstick cooking spray.

2. Combine salsa, cilantro, and cumin in a shallow bowl at least 6 inches in diameter.

3. Working with 1 at a time, dip tortillas in salsa mixture, coating it completely. Place on plate or sheet of wax paper. Top each tortilla with 2 tablespoons salsa mixture. Top with one-eighth of turkey, beans, and red onion. Sprinkle with 1 tablespoon cheese. Roll tortilla up and place seam-side down in baking dish. Repeat filling and rolling with remaining tortillas.

4. Spoon remaining salsa mixture over enchiladas and sprinkle with remaining ½ cup cheese. Bake until bubbling, about 15 minutes.

NUTRITION PER SERVING:
calories 369; saturated fat 3.5 g; total fat 7 g; protein 34 g; carbohydrate 45 g; fiber 9 g; sodium 1,088 mg; cholesterol 62 mg

Turkey Kebabs with Fennel and Red-Pepper Relish

Marinate bites of turkey breast in white wine and fresh herbs. Then skewer with small onions and grill until golden brown.

Makes 4 servings (2 skewers each)

For the turkey kebabs
- 8 stalks fresh rosemary or 8 wooden skewers
- 1 pound boneless, skinless turkey-breast steaks
- ½ teaspoon salt
- ½ teaspoon freshly ground black pepper
- ¼ cup dry white wine
- 3 tablespoons fresh lemon juice
- 2 large garlic cloves, minced
- 1 tablespoon chopped fresh rosemary leaves
- 1 tablespoon chopped fresh sage leaves
- 1 tablespoon fresh thyme leaves
- 1 teaspoon fennel seeds, lightly crushed
- 2 tablespoons extra virgin olive oil
- 16 small white onions, peeled

For the red-pepper relish
- 2 large red bell peppers
- ½ fennel bulb, trimmed
- ⅓ cup pitted black olives (preferably Kalamatas)
- 1 tablespoon fresh lemon juice
- 1 tablespoon extra virgin olive oil
- 1 large garlic clove, minced
- ½ teaspoon freshly ground black pepper

1. If using the rosemary stalks, pull off and reserve the leaves from the bottom end of each stalk, keeping a cluster of about 2½ inches of leaves at

the top. Soak the rosemary stalks (or the wooden skewers if using instead) in water while you marinate the turkey.

2. Cut the turkey into 24 cubes, about 1½ inches each. Sprinkle the turkey with the salt and pepper and spread in a single layer in a shallow baking dish. In a small bowl, whisk the wine, lemon juice, garlic, rosemary, sage, thyme, and fennel seeds; whisk in the oil. Drizzle the marinade over the turkey and toss until all of the pieces are coated. Cover with plastic wrap and marinate in the refrigerator for 30 minutes, turning once.

3. Meanwhile, make the relish. Seed the red peppers and cut into ¼-inch dice. Trim the fennel bulb and cut into ¼-inch dice. Cut the olives into ¼-inch dice. In a medium-size bowl, mix the diced peppers, fennel, and olives with the lemon juice, oil, garlic, and pepper.

4. Preheat the grill or broiler to high. Thread the marinated turkey pieces and the onions onto the soaked rosemary stalks or skewers. In a small saucepan, bring the remaining marinade to a boil over high heat.

5. Grill or broil the kebabs for about 12 minutes, basting often with the marinade, or until the turkey is cooked through and is golden brown. Serve 2 kebabs to each person, with ½ cup of relish and a generous scoop of cooked couscous or wild rice.

NUTRITION PER SERVING:
calories 321; total fat 14g; saturated fat 2g; protein 36g; carbohydrate 12g; fiber 2g; sodium 431mg; cholesterol 95mg

Turkey Piccata

The enticing aroma of this elegant entree sets the stage for a great meal. Turkey is a healthful—and less expensive—substitute for veal in this classic recipe that is high in protein and low in both fat and carbohydrates.

Makes 4 servings

- 1 tablespoon olive oil
- 4 turkey cutlets (4 ounces each)
- 2 tablespoons flour
- 2 cloves garlic, minced
- 1 teaspoon grated lemon zest
- ¼ cup lemon juice
- 1 cup reduced-sodium, fat-free chicken broth
- 1 teaspoon cornstarch blended with 1 tablespoon water
- 1 tablespoon capers, rinsed and drained
- 2 tablespoons chopped parsley

1. Heat oil in a large nonstick skillet over medium heat. Dredge turkey in flour, shaking off excess. Sauté turkey until golden brown and cooked through, about 2 minutes per side. With tongs or a slotted spoon, transfer turkey to a plate; cover loosely with foil to keep warm.

2. Add garlic to pan and cook, stirring, until tender, about 1 minute. Add lemon zest, lemon juice, and chicken broth to pan and bring to a boil. Boil 1 minute.

3. Stir in cornstarch mixture and capers, and cook until slightly thickened, about 1 minute. Stir in parsley. Serve turkey with sauce spooned on top.

NUTRITION PER SERVING:
187 calories; saturated fat 1 g; total fat 4 g; protein 30 g; carbohydrate 6 g; fiber 0.5 g; sodium 178 mg; cholesterol 70 mg

Grilled Tuna Teriyaki

Though broiling is called for in this recipe, you can also cook the tuna steaks on an outdoor grill for an equally high-protein, low-carbohydrate meal.

Makes 4 servings

- 2 tablespoons reduced-sodium soy sauce
- 1 tablespoon rice wine, dry sherry, or rice vinegar
- 1 large clove garlic, minced
- 1 tablespoon minced fresh ginger or 1 teaspoon ground ginger
- 4 tuna steaks, ¾ inch thick (6 ounces each)
- 1 tablespoon vegetable oil

1. In a shallow dish large enough to hold the tuna, combine the soy sauce, rice wine, garlic, and ginger. Place the tuna in the marinade and turn to coat it; cover and refrigerate for at least 30 minutes.

2. Preheat the broiler, setting the rack 6 inches from the heat. Discard the marinade and pat the tuna steaks dry with paper toweling, then brush both sides with the oil. Arrange the tuna on a broiler pain and broil for 3 minutes on each side or until the fish flakes easily when tested with a fork. Serve with sautéed peppers and steamed brown rice.

NUTRITION PER SERVING:
calories 225; saturated fat 1 g; total fat 5 g; protein 40 g; carbohydrate 1 g; fiber 0 g; sodium 304 mg; cholesterol 76 mg

Grilled Shrimp with Mustard Dipping Sauce

A pound of shrimp, six seasonings, and you're in for great healthy, low-fat grilling.

Makes 4 servings

- 2½ tablespoons Dijon mustard
- 1½ tablespoons fresh lemon juice
- 2 teaspoons ground coriander
- 2 teaspoons ground cumin
- ½ teaspoon pepper
- ½ teaspoon salt
- 1 pound (24) large shrimp, peeled and deveined

1. Stir together mustard, lemon juice, ½ teaspoon coriander, ½ teaspoon cumin, and ¼ teaspoon pepper in small bowl. Set mustard dipping sauce aside.

2. Combine salt with remaining 1½ teaspoons coriander, 1½ teaspoons cumin, and ¼ teaspoon pepper in large bowl. Add shrimp, tossing to coat.

3. Preheat grill to medium. Thread shrimp onto four long skewers. Place shrimp on grill and cook until opaque throughout, about 1 minute per side. Serve at room temperature or chilled with mustard dipping sauce.

NUTRITION PER SERVING:
calories 88; saturated fat 0.5 g; total fat 2 g; protein 15 g; carbohydrate 3 g; fiber 1 g; sodium 684 mg; cholesterol 135 mg

Scallop and Cherry-Tomato Sauté

Sizzling scallops and tiny tomatoes go from skillet to table in minutes for a fast and nourishing meal.

Makes 4 servings

- 1 pound sea scallops
- 4 teaspoons cornstarch
- 2 teaspoons olive oil
- 3 cloves garlic, minced
- 1 pint cherry tomatoes
- ⅔ cup dry vermouth, white wine, or chicken broth
- ½ teaspoon salt
- ⅓ cup chopped fresh basil
- 1 tablespoon cold water

1. Dredge scallops in 3 teaspoons cornstarch, shaking off excess. Heat oil in large nonstick skillet over medium heat. Add scallops and sauté until golden brown and cooked through, about 3 minutes. With slotted spoon, transfer scallops to bowl.

2. Add garlic to pan and cook 1 minute. Add tomatoes and cook until they begin to collapse, about 4 minutes. Add vermouth, salt, and basil to pan. Bring to a boil and cook for 1 minute.

3. Meanwhile, stir together remaining 1 teaspoon cornstarch and cold water in small bowl. Add cornstarch mixture to pan and cook, stirring, until sauce is slightly thickened, about 1 minute.

4. Return scallops to pan, reduce to a simmer, and cook just until heated through, about 1 minute.

NUTRITION PER SERVING:
calories 176; saturated fat 0.5 g; total fat 3.5 g; protein 20 g; carbohydrate 10 g; fiber 1 g; sodium 483 mg; cholesterol 37 mg

Sole Baked in Parchment

Baking in parchment or foil packets steams the fish and brings out the natural flavors of the fish and its seasonings. Simply wrap and bake until tender.

Makes 4 servings

 1 **lemon**
 2 **tablespoons olive oil (1 tablespoon if using foil)**
 1 **tablespoon dry white wine (optional)**
 1/2 **teaspoon lemon pepper**
 1/8 **teaspoon salt (optional)**
 1 **pound slender asparagus (or medium, halved), trimmed and cut into 2-inch pieces**
 4 **sole or flounder fillets (4–6 ounces each), fresh or frozen and thawed**

1. Preheat the oven to 450°F. Prepare four 12-inch-square pieces of parchment paper or aluminum foil; fold in half and cut out a half-heart shape on the fold.

2. Using a vegetable peeler, cut 1/2-inch strips of zest from the lemon. Cut each strip into thin matchsticks and place in a bowl with 2 tablespoons of lemon juice.

3. Stir the oil, wine (if using), lemon pepper, and salt (if using) into the lemon zest and juice. Add the asparagus and gently toss until well coated.

4. Place 1 fillet on a half of each parchment paper heart and top each with about a quarter of the asparagus and lemon mixture. Fold the paper over the asparagus.

5. Starting at one end, close the edges by making small pleats. Work around the length of the paper to seal the packet. Fold the end piece under the packet.

6. Bake on a baking sheet 10 to 12 minutes or until paper puffs and fish is cooked. Transfer to individual dishes, carefully open paper, and serve at once.

NUTRITION PER SERVING:
calories 196; saturated fat 1 g; total fat 9 g; protein 24 g; carbohydrate 6 g; fiber 2 g; sodium 105 mg; cholesterol 55 mg

Steamed Fish with Ginger and Sesame

Master the art of steaming and you'll be a whiz at tasty, quick, low-fat meals. Steamed fish, infused with spices and other seasonings, is delicious.

Makes 4 servings

 2 **tablespoons grated fresh ginger**
 3 **cloves garlic, minced**
 1/2 **teaspoon grated lime zest**
 1/2 **cup chopped cilantro**

4 tilapia fillets (5 ounces each)
½ teaspoon salt
2½ teaspoons dark sesame oil
2 tablespoons fresh lime juice
½ cup water
1 teaspoon cornstarch blended with 1 tablespoon water

1. Combine ginger, garlic, lime zest, and ¼ cup of cilantro in small bowl. Lay fillets skinned side up on work surface and sprinkle with salt and cilantro mixture. Fold fillets in half. Drizzle sesame oil over folded fish and place fish on a heatproof plate.

2. Place a cake rack in a skillet large enough to hold plate of fish and add water to just fall short of cake rack. Cover and bring to a simmer.

3. Carefully place plate of fish on rack over simmering water. Cover and steam until cooked through, about 5 minutes. With slotted spatula, transfer fish to a platter and cover loosely to keep warm.

4. Pour cooking liquids on plate used for steaming into a small saucepan. Add lime juice and water and bring to a boil. Stir in cornstarch mixture and cook, stirring, until sauce is slightly thickened, about 1 minute. Stir in remaining ¼ cup cilantro. Pass sauce at the table in a small serving bowl.

NUTRITION PER SERVING:
calories 182; saturated fat 1 g; total fat 6.5 g; protein 27 g; carbohydrate 3 g; fiber 0 g; sodium 107 mg; cholesterol 120 mg

Stuffed Fish with Corn Salsa

Stuff whole fish with a zesty vegetable or fruit salsa in place of the traditional high-fat bread stuffing.

Makes 4 servings

1 tablespoon olive or canola oil
1 onion, finely chopped
1 clove garlic, finely chopped
2 stalks celery, thickly sliced
½ teaspoon chili powder
1 cup fresh or frozen corn kernels, thawed
1 small cucumber, peeled, seeded, and diced
1 fresh or canned jalapeño pepper, chopped
3 tablespoons chopped fresh parsley or 1 tablespoon dried
2 tablespoons lime juice
⅛ teaspoon each salt and pepper
1–2 pan-dressed mild fish, such as snapper, perch, or trout (2 pounds total)

1. Preheat the oven to 450°F. In a nonstick skillet, heat the oil over moderate heat. Sauté the onion

and garlic, stirring, about 5 minutes or until soft but not browned. Add the celery and chili powder; cook 3 to 4 minutes longer.

2. Transfer the onion mixture to a large bowl. Add the corn, cucumber, jalapeño pepper, parsley, lime juice, salt, and pepper, and toss gently to combine.

3. Coat a baking sheet with vegetable oil cooking spray. Using a spoon, stuff the fish cavity with salsa mixture and transfer to the baking sheet.

4. Bake 40 to 55 minutes or until fish flakes easily when tested with a fork.

NUTRITION PER SERVING:
calories 268; saturated fat 1 g; total fat 6 g; protein 37 g; carbohydrate 17 g; fiber 3 g; sodium 202 mg; cholesterol 63 mg

VEGETABLES

Braised Red Cabbage with Apples

Apples and red cabbage, both high in fiber, are appealing even without butter or oil.

Makes 6 servings

- 1 medium-size head red cabbage (about 1 3/4 pounds), cored and thinly sliced
- 2 medium-size Granny Smith apples, peeled, cored, and grated (1 1/2 cups)
- 1 tablespoon brown sugar
- 2 tablespoons all-purpose flour
- 1/4 teaspoon black pepper
- 1 cup dry red wine or unsweetened apple juice

1. In a large enameled or stainless-steel saucepan, mix the cabbage, apples, sugar, flour, and pepper. (Iron or aluminum will react with the cabbage and turn it brown.) Stir in the wine and bring to a boil over high heat.

2. Lower the heat, cover, and simmer, stirring occasionally, for 25 to 30 minutes or until the cabbage is tender. Serve with pork chops or venison.

NUTRITION PER SERVING:
calories 108; saturated fat 0 g; total fat 1 g; protein 2 g; carbohydrate 20 g; fiber 4 g; sodium 40 mg; cholesterol 0 mg

Broiled Tomatoes

This super-quick recipe turns the ordinary tomato into an elegant side dish for poultry, meat, or fish.

Makes 4 servings

- 1/3 cup fresh basil leaves, minced, or 1 1/2 teaspoons dried basil, crumbled
- 1/4 cup parsley leaves, minced
- 1/4 cup plain dry bread crumbs
- 2 cloves garlic, minced
- 1/4 teaspoon salt, or to taste
- 1 tablespoon olive oil
- 4 medium-size tomatoes, halved horizontally

1. Preheat the broiler, setting the rack 6 inches from the heat. Line the broiler pan with a sheet of aluminum foil. In a small bowl, stir together the basil, parsley, bread crumbs, garlic, salt, and oil.

2. Place tomato halves, cut sides up, on the prepared broiler pan and broil for 2 minutes. Top with the basil-crumb mixture and broil 3 minutes longer or until the topping is crisp and the tomatoes are hot clear through.

NUTRITION PER SERVING:
calories 85; saturated fat 1 g; total fat 4 g; protein 2 g; carbohydrate 11 g; fiber 2 g; sodium 194 mg; cholesterol 0 mg

Grilled Summer Vegetables

Reap a harvest of healthy benefits in every delectable serving of these smoky vegetable treats.

Makes 4 servings

- 2 small fennel bulbs (about 8 ounces each), cleaned
- 1 small eggplant (about 1 pound), cut lengthwise into 2 slices 1/2 inch thick
- 4 plum tomatoes, halved
- 3 large bell peppers (preferably 1 green, 1 red, 1 yellow), cut into strips 1/2 inch wide
- 1/2 teaspoon salt
- 1/2 teaspoon pepper
- 2 tablespoons orange juice
- 8 basil leaves, slivered
- 1 garlic clove, minced
- 1 teaspoon grated orange zest
  Nonstick vegetable spray

1. Preheat grill to high. Prepare fennel: Cut off stalks with fronds and set aside. Peel bulbs and cut vertically into ½-inch slices. Coat fennel, eggplant, tomatoes, and bell peppers with nonstick cooking spray (preferably olive-oil–flavored) and sprinkle with salt and pepper.

2. Grill vegetables until tender and evenly browned, about 4 minutes on each side, turning once. Transfer to a serving platter and sprinkle with orange juice.

3. Finely chop 1 tablespoon reserved fennel fronds and mix in small bowl with basil, garlic, and orange zest. Sprinkle over vegetables. Serve vegetables warm or at room temperature.

NUTRITION PER SERVING:
calories 118; saturated fat 0 g; total fat 1 g; protein 4 g; carbohydrate 28 g; fiber 9 g; sodium 364 mg; cholesterol 0 mg

* * * * *

SEASONING VARIATION: In a shallow dish, marinate vegetables in a mixture of ½ cup balsamic vinegar, 1 clove minced garlic, 1 tablespoon minced onion, and 1 tablespoon minced parsley for 30 minutes or more. Drain and coat with nonstick cooking spray before cooking. Grill until tender and evenly browned, about 4 minutes on each side, turning once. Season with salt and pepper and serve.

VEGETABLE VARIATION: There are many summer vegetables that taste wonderful off the grill. Whether you marinate them or not, coat the vegetables with a nonstick spray before putting them on the grill. Slice zucchini or summer squash lengthwise for grilling. Slice sweet onions and separate into rings or put onion quarters on a skewer. You can also skewer mushrooms. Trimmed asparagus spears can go directly on the grill, at right angles to the bars of the grill.

Lemony Sugar Snaps

Catch them while you can—succulent sugar snap peas have a short season in early summer. Their crisp pods and bright flavor make them a delicious low-fat treat.

Makes 4 servings

1 ½	pounds sugar snap peas
2	teaspoons olive oil
3	shallots, thinly sliced
1	clove garlic, minced
1	tablespoon grated lemon zest
1	teaspoon salt

3 whole cloves
8 whole coriander seeds
8 whole black peppercorns
¼ teaspoon ground allspice
1 whole garlic clove
1 teaspoon sugar
1 tablespoon butter or margarine (optional)

1. In a medium-size enameled or stainless-steel saucepan, bring the beets, stock, vinegar, cloves, coriander seeds, peppercorns, allspice, garlic, and sugar to a boil over moderate heat. Lower the heat and simmer, covered, for 35 minutes or until the beets are just tender. With a slotted spoon, transfer the beets to a serving dish.

2. Boil the remaining liquid for 5 minutes or until reduced to ¼ cup. Stir in the butter (if using) and pour the liquid over the beets. Serve with broiled salmon or scrod and steamed new potatoes.

NUTRITION PER SERVING (WITHOUT BUTTER):
calories 62; saturated fat 0 g; total fat 0 g; protein 2 g; carbohydrate 14 g; fiber 4 g; sodium 117 mg; cholesterol 0 mg

PASTA, BEANS & GRAINS

Beefy Pasta Salad

Light enough for a steamy summer night, but filling enough to satisfy anyone.

Makes 4 servings

8 ounces rotelle or other small pasta shape
6 cups broccoli spears
10 ounces well-trimmed sirloin steak
1¼ cups plain fat-free yogurt
3 tablespoons light mayonnaise
1 tablespoon balsamic vinegar
I cup basil leaves
1 teaspoon salt
1 pound plum tomatoes, quartered
1 medium red onion, halved and thinly sliced

1. Cook pasta in a large pot of boiling water according to package directions. Add broccoli spears during last 2 minutes of cooking; drain.

2. Meanwhile, preheat broiler. Broil steak 4 inches from heat for 4 minutes per side for medium, or until done to taste. Transfer steak to cutting board and thinly slice across the grain, on the diagonal.

1. Remove strings from both sides of sugar snap peas.

2. Heat oil in large nonstick skillet over medium heat. Add shallots and garlic and cook, stirring, until shallots are softened, about 3 minutes.

3. Add sugar snaps, lemon zest, and salt to skillet and cook, stirring, until peas are just tender, about 4 minutes.

NUTRITION PER SERVING:
calories 99; saturated fat 0.5 g; total fat 2.5 g; protein 4 g; carbohydrate 15 g; fiber 5 g; sodium 454 mg; cholesterol 0 mg

Spiced Beets

Serve this popular beet dish warm, cold, or at room temperature. If you serve it chilled, do not use the optional butter.

Makes 4 servings

6 medium-size beets (1½ pounds), peeled and quartered
1 cup chicken stock or low-sodium chicken broth
¼ cup cider vinegar

3. Combine yogurt, mayonnaise, vinegar, basil, and salt in a food processor and process until smooth. Transfer dressing to a large serving bowl.

4. Add steak and any juices accumulated on cutting board and toss to coat. Add pasta, broccoli, tomatoes, and onion to bowl and toss again. (Recipe can be made ahead and refrigerated. Bring back to room temperature before serving.)

NUTRITION PER SERVING:
calories 471; saturated fat 4.5 g; total fat 15 g; protein 29 g; carbohydrate 58 g; fiber 7 g; sodium 781 mg; cholesterol 50 mg

Cold Sesame Noodles and Vegetables

A satisfying pasta salad with an exotic Asian accent—and veggies galore. Serve with a grilled turkey burger for a heartier meal.

Makes 6 servings

- 8 ounces whole-wheat linguine
- ⅓ cup cilantro leaves
- 2 tablespoons peanut butter
- 2 tablespoons reduced-sodium soy sauce
- 2½ teaspoons honey
- 1 tablespoon rice vinegar or cider vinegar
- 1 tablespoon dark sesame oil
- 2 cloves garlic, peeled

- ½ teaspoon salt
- ¼ teaspoon cayenne pepper
- 2 carrots, slivered
- 1 red bell pepper, slivered
- 1 large stalk celery, slivered
- 2 scallions, slivered

1. Cook linguine in large pot of boiling water according to package directions. Drain, reserving ½ cup cooking water.

2. Combine cilantro, peanut butter, soy sauce, honey, vinegar, sesame oil, garlic, salt, and cayenne in a food processor. Puree. Transfer to a large bowl.

3. Whisk in reserved pasta cooking water. Add linguine, carrots, bell pepper, celery, and scallions. Toss. Chill at least 1 hour before serving.

NUTRITION PER SERVING:
calories 200; saturated fat 1 g; total fat 5.5 g; protein 7 g; carbohydrate 33 g; fiber 6 g; sodium 422 mg; cholesterol 0 mg

Herbed Polenta

There are two ways to make this Italian peasant dish. You can cook the cornmeal until thick, add vegetables, and serve like a stew. Or you can chill the cornmeal, cut into rounds, and broil.

Makes 6 servings

- 1 cup yellow cornmeal
- 2 cups water
- 2 cups 1% low-fat milk
- ⅛ teaspoon each salt and pepper
- 2 tablespoons chopped parsley, chives, or basil
- 2 tablespoons finely grated Parmesan cheese

1. Combine cornmeal with 1 cup water in a small bowl. Bring milk and remaining water to a boil in a nonstick saucepan. Season with salt and pepper.

2. Reduce heat slightly and slowly stir cornmeal into milk mixture. Cook, stirring constantly, about 5 minutes or until mixture boils and thickens slightly.

3. Reduce the heat to very low and simmer the polenta gently, stirring frequently, about 10 minutes or until the mixture is smooth and thickened.

4. Remove the saucepan from the heat. Add the chopped herbs and cheese and stir well to mix thoroughly.

5. Turn the polenta out onto a nonstick baking pan

and spread to a depth of ¼ inch with a palette knife. Chill for 2 hours to set. Preheat the broiler.

6. With a cookie cutter, cut rounds from polenta. Use trimmings to make more. Or cut into 6 wedges. Broil on a rack about 5 minutes, until golden.

NUTRITION PER SERVING:
calories 128; saturated fat 1 g; total fat 2 g; protein 6 g; carbohydrate 22 g; fiber 2 g; sodium 128 mg; cholesterol 5 mg

Sausage-and-Herb Lasagna

It's hard to imagine that a sausage lasagna can be low in fat and modest in calories, but this one is!

Makes 8 servings

15	lasagna noodles (12 ounces)
1	container (15 ounces) 50%-less-fat ricotta cheese
⅓	cup freshly grated Parmesan cheese
½	cup chopped fresh basil
¼	cup fat-free egg substitute
¼	teaspoon pepper
8	ounces lean sweet Italian turkey sausage, casings removed
3	medium onions, chopped
2	cans (14 ounces each) no-salt-added tomato sauce
½	teaspoon salt
1	package (8 ounces) 50%-less-fat shredded mozzarella cheese

1. Cook noodles according to package directions. Drain, then cool in a shallow pan of cold water for 5 minutes. Transfer noodles to a wire rack set over paper towels. Blend ricotta, 2 tablespoons Parmesan, basil, egg substitute, and pepper in bowl.

2. Cook sausage and onions in a nonstick skillet over medium-high heat until sausage is cooked through, 7–10 minutes, breaking up sausage with a spoon. Stir in 1½ cups tomato sauce and the salt.

3. Preheat oven to 350°F. Spread ½ cup tomato sauce in bottom of 13 x 9-inch baking dish. Layer lasagna: Set 3 noodles, side by side, in dish. Spread one-third ricotta mixture over noodles. Top with one-third sausage mixture and sprinkle with ½ cup mozzarella. Repeat layering twice. Weave remaining 6 noodles in lattice pattern on top, trimming them as necessary. Spread remaining tomato sauce over

noodles, then top with remaining mozzarella and remaining Parmesan.

4. Loosely cover with foil. Bake 40 minutes. Remove foil and bake until mixture is bubbling around edges, about 20 minutes longer. Let stand 15 minutes before cutting.

NUTRITION PER SERVING:
calories 381; saturated fat 5 g; total fat 10 g; protein 29 g; carbohydrate 46 g; fiber 4 g; sodium 722 mg; cholesterol 43 mg

Tabbouleh

This colorful and healthful Middle Eastern dish can be refrigerated for up to 4 days (if you use radishes, add them just before serving).

Makes 4 servings

	Boiling water
¾	cup bulgur
1	medium-size red onion, chopped (1 cup)

1 medium-size tomato, coarsely chopped, with its juice (1 cup)

½ cucumber, seeded and coarsely chopped (½ cup)

4 large radishes, slivered (optional)

1 cup flat-leaf parsley, coarsely chopped

2 tablespoons minced fresh mint or 2 teaspoons mint flakes, crumbled

1 tablespoon olive or canola oil

1 teaspoon grated lemon rind

4 tablespoons lemon juice

¾ teaspoon salt

8–10 drops hot red-pepper sauce

1. In a large heatproof serving bowl, pour 1 cup of boiling water over the bulgur and let stand for 20 minutes or until the water is absorbed. Meanwhile, in a small bowl, pour just enough boiling water over the onion to cover and let stand for 10 minutes. Drain.

2. Add the onion, tomato, cucumber, radishes (if using), parsley, mint, oil, lemon rind, lemon juice, salt, and red-pepper sauce to the bulgur. Toss until well combined. Refrigerate, covered, for 6 hours or until chilled. Serve cold or at room temperature.

NUTRITION PER SERVING:
calories 153; saturated fat 1 g; total fat 4 g; protein 5 g; carbohydrate 28 g; fiber 8 g; sodium 418 mg; cholesterol 0 mg

Tex-Mex Red Beans

Simmer the beans until tender. Add vegetables and serve with rice or corn bread for a meatless main dish; make a hearty casserole with sausage and rice; or use the beans as a filling for enchiladas.

Makes 6 servings

1 cup dried red kidney beans

2 tablespoons olive or canola oil

2 onions, coarsely chopped

2 cloves garlic, finely chopped

2 sweet red or green peppers, chopped

1 can (14 ounces) crushed tomatoes

1 bay leaf

¼ teaspoon dried thyme

⅛ teaspoon each ground cumin, salt, and pepper

1 cup vegetable stock

1. Cover beans with cold water and let stand 8 hours. Drain. In a large pot, boil beans in 2 quarts water for 10 minutes, then turn down the heat and

simmer 45 minutes. Drain.

2. In a Dutch oven, heat oil. Sauté onions and garlic, stirring, 5 minutes. Add sweet peppers and sauté 5 minutes.

3. Add tomatoes, herbs, cumin, salt, and pepper, stir, and bring to a boil. Stir in beans and stock. Simmer, partially covered, for 20 minutes. Discard bay leaf.

NUTRITION PER SERVING:
calories 201; saturated fat 1 g; total fat 5 g; protein 10 g; carbohydrate 32 g; fiber 10 g; sodium 131 mg; cholesterol 9 mg

DESSERTS

Blueberry Bavarian

This creamy "berried treasure" is low in fat, but you may not even notice.

Makes 6 servings

1 cup low-fat (1%) milk

¼ cup fat-free dry milk

2 packages (12 ounces each) frozen blueberries, thawed

½ cup plus 1 tablespoon sugar

¼ teaspoon salt

1 cup fat-free sour cream

1 packet unflavored gelatin

¼ cup cold water

½ cup fresh blueberries

1. Combine milk and dry milk in a small bowl and whisk until well blended. Place in freezer for up to 30 minutes.

2. Combine frozen blueberries, ½ cup sugar, and salt in a medium saucepan over low heat. Bring to a simmer and cook until the sugar has dissolved, berries have broken up, and mixture has reduced to 2¼ cups, about 10 minutes. Let cool to room temperature. Stir in ⅔ cup sour cream.

3. Sprinkle gelatin over cold water in heatproof measuring cup. Let stand 5 minutes to soften. Set measuring cup in small saucepan of simmering water and heat until gelatin has melted, about 2 minutes. Let cool to room temperature.

4. With a hand mixer, beat chilled milk until thick, soft peaks form. Beat in remaining 1 tablespoon sugar until stiff peaks form. Beat in gelatin mixture. Fold milk mixture into blueberry mixture.

5. Spoon into 6 dessert bowls or glasses. Chill until set, about 2 hours. At serving time, top each with a dollop of sour cream and fresh blueberries.

NUTRITION PER SERVING:
calories 202; saturated fat 0.5 g; total fat 1 g; protein 7 g; carbohydrate 43 g; fiber 3 g; sodium 178 mg; cholesterol 2 mg

Chocolate Angel Food Cake

You can dust this heavenly cake with confectioners' sugar or top each serving with a dollop of unsweetened whipped cream.

Makes 12 servings

      1 **cup sifted cake flour**
  1 ¼ **cups granulated sugar**
    ⅓ **cup unsweetened cocoa powder**
    ¾ **teaspoon ground cinnamon**
    ½ **teaspoon salt**
  1 ½ **cup egg whites (about 12 large eggs)**
  1 ½ **teaspoons cream of tartar**
      2 **teaspoons vanilla extract**
      2 **tablespoons sifted confectioners' sugar (optional)**

1. Preheat the oven to 325°F. In a medium-size bowl, sift together the flour, ¾ cup of the granulated sugar, the cocoa, cinnamon, and salt.

2. In a perfectly clean large bowl, beat the egg whites with an electric mixer set on high speed until foamy. Add the cream of tartar and beat until soft peaks form. Gradually add ¼ cup of the remaining sugar in a steady stream and continue beating until the whites are stiff and glossy but not dry. Beat in the vanilla. Sprinkle the remaining ¼ cup of sugar over the top of the whites and fold in gently. Gently fold in the flour mixture.

3. Spoon the batter into an ungreased 10-inch tube pan and bake for 45 minutes or until a toothpick inserted in the center comes out clean. Invert the pan and let cool. Transfer the cake to a serving platter and dust with the confectioners' sugar (if using).

NUTRITION PER SERVING:
calories 133; saturated fat 0 g; total fat 1 g; protein 5 g; carbohydrate 29 g; fiber 0 g; sodium 147 mg; cholesterol 0 mg

Italian Biscotti

These crisp cookies are baked twice. First you make a log and bake until firm. Then slice the log into individual cookies and bake again.

Makes 20 biscuits

         Nonstick cooking spray
  2 ½ **cups all-purpose flour**
  1 ¼ **cups sugar**
      2 **large eggs**
      2 **egg whites**
      1 **tablespoon canola oil**
      2 **teaspoons anise or vanilla extract**

1. Preheat oven to 350°F. Lightly coat a 15½- x 10½-inch jelly-roll pan with nonstick cooking spray and dust with flour.

2. In a medium bowl, combine flour and sugar. In a small bowl, lightly beat the eggs, egg whites, oil, and anise extract. Using a rubber spatula, stir the egg mixture into the dry ingredients until a dough is formed.

3. Using the rubber spatula, transfer the dough onto the pan. Wet the spatula with water and shape the dough into a log about 15 x 3 inches.

4. Bake for 30 to 35 minutes, after which time the log will have flattened considerably. Remove from the oven and cut crosswise into ¾-inch slices. Place the slices on a clean baking sheet and continue to bake for 15 minutes or until lightly crisp. Remove from oven and place biscotti on a wire rack to cool.

NUTRITION PER BISCUIT:
calories 120; saturated fat 0 g; total fat 1 g; protein 3 g; carbohydrate 25 g; fiber 0 g; sodium 12 mg; cholesterol 21 mg

Marble Cheesecake

A dazzling, delectable dessert that can fit within almost any diet plan.

Makes 12 Servings

- 3 ounces low-fat honey graham crackers (6 whole crackers)
- ½ cup toasted wheat germ
- 1 tablespoon plus 1 cup sugar
- 2 tablespoons extra-light olive oil
- 1 container (19 ounces) silken tofu, well drained
- 1 pound fat-free cream cheese
- 3 tablespoons flour
- 1 large egg plus 2 large egg whites
- 1 teaspoon vanilla
- ¼ cup chocolate syrup

1. Preheat oven to 350°F. Combine graham crackers, wheat germ, and 1 tablespoon sugar in food processor and process to fine crumbs. Add oil and process until moistened. Place mixture in a 9-inch springform pan and press into bottom and partway up the sides. Bake until set, about 10 minutes.

2. Add drained tofu, remaining 1 cup sugar, cream cheese, flour, whole egg, egg whites, and vanilla to food processor (no need to clean bowl) and process until smooth and well blended.

3. Measure out 1 cup tofu mixture, place in small bowl, and stir in chocolate syrup. Pour remaining plain tofu mixture into crust in springform pan.

4. Pour chocolate mixture in a ring on top of batter and swirl in with a knife. Bake 45 minutes. Turn off oven and leave in oven 45 minutes undisturbed. Cool to room temperature before chilling overnight.

NUTRITION PER SERVING:
calories 225; saturated fat 1 g; total fat 5 g; protein 11 g; carbohydrate 35 g; fiber 1 g; sodium 245 mg; cholesterol 21 mg

Strawberry Frozen Yogurt

Frozen yogurt, a refreshing light dessert, requires an ice cream maker. Follow the manufacturer's instructions for proper freezing.

Makes 6 servings

- 1 envelope unflavored gelatin
- 1 cup 1% low-fat milk
- ⅓ cup sugar
- 1¼ cups plain nonfat yogurt
- 1 cup strawberries, fresh or frozen and thawed
- 1 tablespoon kirsch (optional)

1. In a saucepan, sprinkle gelatin over milk and let stand for 1 minute. Stir in sugar and set over moderately low heat, stirring, about 2 minutes, until dissolved.

2. Allow to cool until thickened, stirring occasionally. Transfer mixture to a large bowl and whisk in yogurt. Fold in the strawberries and kirsch (if using).

3. Freeze the mixture in an ice cream maker.

NUTRITION PER SERVING:
calories 76; saturated fat 0 g; total fat 0 g; protein 4 g; carbohydrate 14 g; fiber 1 g; sodium 44 mg; cholesterol 2 mg

A

PHOTOS

16 TOP TO BOTTOM PhotoDisc, Siede Preis/Getty Images, PhotoDisc, PhotoDisc, **19** PhotoDisc, **22** PhotoDisc, **24** Romilly Lockyer/Brand X Pictures/PictureQuest, **27** Comstock, **40** PhotoDisc, **44** Photodisc, **47** PhotoDisc, **48** C Squared Studios/PhotoDisc/PictureQuest, **50** PhotoDisc, **56** Open Door Images/PictureQuest, **68** LifeScan, Inc., **73** PhotoDisc/PictureQuest, **75** Abbott Laboratories, MediSense Products, **76** Cygnus, Inc., **80** Photodisc, **91** PhotoDisc, **93** TOP Comstock, BOTTOM DigitalStock, RIGHT PhotoDisc, **96** DigitalStock, **98** LEFT PhotoDisc, RIGHT Reader's Digest Assoc./GID/Mark Ferri, **99** ALL PhotoDisc, **102** TOP TO BOTTOM PhotoDisc, Comstock, PhotoDisc, Comstock, **105** TOP LEFT DigitalStock, MIDDLE LEFT PhotoDisc, BOTTOM LEFT Reader's Digest Assoc./GID/Gus Filgate, TOP RIGHT Reader's Digest Assoc./GID/Lisa Koenig, MIDDLE RIGHT Reader's Digest Assoc./GID/David Murray and Jules Selmes, BOTTOM RIGHT Reader's Digest Assoc./GID/Martin Jacobs, **106** Comstock, **119** PhotoDisc, **128** PhotoDisc, **129** TOP TO BOTTOM PhotoDisc, C Squared Studios/Getty Images, PhotoDisc, Rim Light/PhotoLink/Getty Images, **134-135** ALL Reader's Digest Assoc. Inc., ©Beth Bischoff, **161** BOTH Disetronic, **162** Becton Dickinson, **171** PhotoDisc, **173** Reader's Digest Assoc./GID/Colin Cooke, **183** Getty Images/Eyewire, **189** Corbis/PhotoQuest, **197** Reader's Digest Assoc./GID/Lisa Koenig, **198** Reader's Digest Assoc./GID, **200** Reader's Digest Assoc., **201** Corbis Images, **203** Reader's Digest Assoc., **204** Reader's Digest Assoc./GID/Alan Richardson, **208** Corbis Images, **216** PhotoDisc, **222** Open Door Images/Picturequest, **231** Reader's Digest Assoc./GID/ Steven Mays, **239** Getty Images, **242** PhotoDisc, **245** Novartis, **247** Photo Researchers, **248** BOTH Medtronic **250-277** Reader's Digest Assoc.

ILLUSTRATIONS

Medical illustrations: Duckwall Productions
All other illustrations, including Cover: ©Tracy Walker/www.i2iart.com